HUMAN MEMORY:
Structures and Processes

A Series of Books in Psychology

EDITORS:

Richard C. Atkinson
Jonathan Freedman
Gardner Lindzey
Richard F. Thompson

HUMAN MEMORY:
Structures and Processes

Roberta L. Klatzky

University of California, Santa Barbara

W. H. FREEMAN AND COMPANY

San Francisco

Library of Congress Cataloging in Publication Data

Klatzky, Roberta L
    Human memory.

    Bibliography: p.
    Includes index.
    1. Memory. I. Title. [DNLM: 1. Memory.
BF371 K63h]
BF371.K53   153.1   75–17925
ISBN 0-7167-0729-2
ISBN 0-7167-0728-4 pbk.

Printed in the United States of America

9 8 7 6 5 4 3

To the memory of Arnold Klatzky

CONTENTS

PREFACE

Each of us has a memory. We use it with such ease that it rarely occurs to us to marvel at our capacity for knowledge and the ways in which it is used. But the human memory is a remarkably complex entity, and although psychologists have studied it for many years, they are only beginning to describe and understand its complexities. Still, in the last two decades or so, research on human memory has provided an ever clearer representation of the memory system; it is that emerging representation which this book attempts to describe.

Memory is discussed in this book in an information-processing framework, one in which the memory system is depicted as continuously active in receiving, modifying, storing, and retrieving information. It is a view that includes perception and learning as part of memory, and topics in those areas are discussed. Although no attempt is made to cover every topic of interest to researchers in the field, those that are covered have been selected to provide a fairly broad treatment of the current state of memory research and theory. The discussion begins with perception, continues through topics subsumed under the general label "short-term memory," and concludes with "long-term memory"—including semantic memory, models of encoding and retrieval, and forgetting.

In writing this book, I was greatly aided by my reviewers. I gratefully acknowledge the reviewing assistance of Richard Atkinson, Robert Crowder, Douglas Hintzman, Earl Hunt, James Juola, Thomas Landauer, and Edward E. Smith. Their comments were not always favorable, but they were invariably helpful, and I know that the book benefited from my having their advice. I was aided as well by the support and guidance of Buck Rogers, and I thank him. I am grateful to Jim Geiwitz, who provided understanding, encouragement, and friendship throughout the course of the project.

May 1975   ROBERTA L. KLATZKY

HUMAN MEMORY:
Structures and Processes

1

INTRODUCTION

What does it mean to remember? The famous psychologist William James once said that to remember is to think about something which we previously experienced, and which we were not thinking about immediately before (James, 1890). James' definition has intuitive appeal; still, the concept of memory is not readily captured in a single phrase.

This book is concerned with what it means to remember. It will address such specific questions as how we mentally represent our knowledge about the world, how we get access to that knowledge when we need it, why we may fail to get access to it, and how we integrate new information with our existing body of knowledge. Each of these problems is a part of the study of memory, and this book will discuss some of the ways that psychologists have conducted that study. In doing so, it will present a variety of topics and ideas, each related to the central question— what does it mean to remember?

The approach to human memory taken by this book is often given the labels "cognitive psychology" and "the information-processing approach." These labels become more meaningful if we compare the cognitive approach of this book to an older, and still viable, approach to the study of memory. This older approach is that of stimulus-response (S-R) theory, or associationism. According to the S-R approach, the ability to remember depends on the formation of associations, or bonds, between stimuli and responses—the strength of those bonds (called habit strength) determining the ability to remember. If a particular bond is sufficiently strong (as the bond between "2 + 2 =" and "4" usually is) we can be said to have a memory; the nature of the memory depends on the stimuli and responses involved.

For example, most of us remember to stop our cars at red lights most of the time. This habit can be attributed to our having an association between a stimulus (a red light) and a response (stopping the car). Of course, our example is rather simple—almost any organism can learn to stop at a red light, and in that sense, has a memory. But associationists argue that the S-R theory can also account for more subtle and complex human behaviors. One way in which this is accomplished is by assuming that there are *internal* stimuli and responses. In essence, what this means is that there are stimuli and responses that are not directly observable (and are thus unlike red lights and the pressing down of brake pedals). In fact, many human responses to the environment are probably internal or, if external, too small to be noticed. These hidden responses may serve as stimuli for other responses, and in this manner, unobserved S-R chains could come to exist. By this means, more complex mental events can be brought into the framework of S-R theory.

There are, however, problems with the associationist approach. For one thing, the associationists focus on the contingencies between stimuli and responses and on the principles of conditioning (which describe how associations are formed and how habit strength can be manipulated). They have little to say about the events that intervene between stimulus and response. Furthermore, the associationist approach has seemed inadequate to bring us any closer to understanding many of the most interesting events related to memory—how we form hypotheses and test them, why we wrestle with memories that seem to be just on the tip of our tongue, how we conjure up familiar faces, and so on.

The cognitive approach to memory has a considerably different emphasis from the associationist approach. The word cognitive, which is derived from cognition, meaning *knowledge*, emphasizes mental activities, not just stimuli and responses. It is precisely this shift of emphasis—away from a passive system that accepts stimuli and automatically produces S-R chains, and toward a notion of mental action—that characterizes cognitive theories. According to Neisser, whose book *Cognitive Psychology* (1967) gave real impetus to the approach, the focus of a cognitive theory is knowledge—how it is acquired, modified, manipulated, used, stored; in short, how it is processed by the human organism. Thus, information processing (a term cognitive psychologists have borrowed from computer scientists) broadly refers to the human being's active interaction with information about his world. Of central importance in this processing are the mental activities that occur between a stimulus and a response. Those activities are not viewed simply as links in an S–R chain (although, as we shall see later, the concept of association does have a place in cognitive psychology).

Haber (1969) has pointed out some basic assumptions of the information-processing approach in psychology. Slightly modified, his assumptions can be called (1) the stage assumption and (2) the limited-capacity assumption—and, as a corollary, the continuity assumption.

First, let's examine the stage assumption. We assume that our area of study—the processing of some information—can be broken down into subprocesses, or stages. That is, the time between the S and the R can be divided up into smaller intervals, and each of those corresponds to some subset of the events that intervene between S and R. We shall see that information can be remarkably transformed as it goes from one stage to another. To return to our red-light example, we might break up the total process as follows: First, the light registers in our visual system. Second, we recognize the visual sensation for what it is—a red traffic light. (To do this, we must use information stored in memory; that is, knowledge about what a red traffic light looks like.) Third, we apply a rule that we have in our memory—stop the car when you see a red light. Of course, we could break the process down further if we wished. But note that in the course of the stages we have already described, the original information—a visual event—has undergone successive transformations. From a visual event, it was changed to a recognized category (red lights), then changed again to a condition for applying a rule (stop the car when . . .). This illustrates a general point: isolating a stage of information processing is not done arbitrarily; rather, a stage of processing (sometimes called a *level* of processing) generally corresponds to some representation of the stimulus information. As the information goes from one stage to another, its representation changes accordingly.

The limited-capacity assumption can also be applied to the red-light example. At each stage of processing, we can identify limits on the human capacity to process information. For example, if we add to our red light a traffic policeman, several careless pedestrians, and an ambulance, we might have too many stimuli to register in the visual system at the same time. This results in an overload on capacity, and overloads can lead to all sorts of complications. For one thing, some information may not enter the system (we may never see one of the pedestrians or perhaps even the red light). Alternatively, we might *recode* the stimulus situation—that is, we might transform it to a new stimulus (perhaps with the label "dangerous situation"). Another option might be to process the information more selectively—we might just look at the policeman and ignore the light, the pedestrians, and the ambulance.

The two basic assumptions just described lead to an important corollary. It is that when we take an information-processing approach, we are bound to get into some areas of psychological study that have been traditionally kept separate from the study of memory. Learning, for example, can be viewed as the process of adding to or modifying the human memory system. Perception, or the original registration of the stimulus, is also inseparable from memory and can be considered to be the first stage in the continuous processing of information.

Why is the label "cognitive psychology" applied to the approach we have been describing? The cognitive character of the approach lies, as we have mentioned, in the view of the human organism as an active seeker of knowledge and processor of information. That is, humans are seen as acting on information in various ways. For example, the processor can decide whether or not to recode information from one form to another, to select certain information for further processing, or to eliminate some information from the system. We shall see that this view of the human as an active information processor permeates the newer theories about memory. Cognitive theorists conceive of perceiving and remembering as acts of construction, by means of which people actively build mental representations of the world.

BASIC CONCEPTS AND DEFINITIONS

Before we begin our study of memory, it is important to establish a few basic concepts and definitions. First, we must establish a set of distinctions among three basic terms drawn from the field of information processing and applied to human memory: encoding, storage, and retrieval. *Encoding* refers to putting information into a system. The process of encoding may include modifying the information so that it is in an appropriate form for the system, human or mechanical, it is being put into (for example, information may be encoded for a computer by punching holes into IBM cards). Information in an encoded form is often referred to as a memory "code." *Storage* refers to just that—storing information in a system. Of course, things may happen to stored information. It may be affected by subsequent information, or it may be lost. *Retrieval* refers to the action of getting at the stored information. Any of these three processes may break down for some reason—in human memory, this results in the failure to remember. It follows that all three processes must be intact in order for us to remember: we have to encode the information, store it until it is called for, and then be able to retrieve it.

Another term that will be used frequently in this book is "model," as in "model of memory." As used here, the term refers to a theoretical model. Thus, we might say that in the previous discussion, we built a model of the mental processes that occur when someone stops for a red light. Sometimes, a theoretical model becomes a "mathematical model"— that is, it incorporates mathematics in order to describe processes in more detail. One advantage of having a model of a mental process is that you can use the model to make predictions about behavior. These predictions can then be compared with how people actually behave, and, if the predictions are not supported, we know it is time to build a new model.

List-Learning Procedures

In discussing human memory, we will describe the results of many experiments using common experimental procedures. Our last set of preliminary definitions will cover some of these basic laboratory procedures. These are not the only ones that will be discussed in this book; however, they are to some extent standard and are used in a great number of experiments. These procedures have in common a basic form: in each, a subject (the person in the experiment) learns a *list of items*. The items might be single words, pairs of words, or "nonsense syllables." (Nonsense syllables are also called CVCs, for Consonant-Vowel-Consonant, which is the form they take. Examples are DAX, BUP, and LOC.) The learning of the list takes place over a series of *trials*. Each trial consists of a presentation of the items to the subject and a test to see what has been learned.

These list-learning procedures began with the work of Hermann Ebbinghaus (1885), who was the first person to study learning and forgetting in a systematic way. Ebbinghaus conducted a long series of experiments on a single subject—himself. In his experiments, he learned lists of nonsense syllables. In fact, it was Ebbinghaus who invented the syllables; he did so because he wished to eliminate what he considered an undesirable experimental factor—*meaning*. Ebbinghaus reasoned that if he used actual words in his lists, the meanings of the words would influence the results of his experiments. But Ebbinghaus wanted to study the formation and retention of *new* associations, independent of the existing ones. To avoid this unwanted source of variation, he chose to use nonsense syllables, intending them to be relatively free from meaningful associations.

Ebbinghaus constructed lists of nonsense syllables that he presented to himself at a constant rate. He read the lists until he thought he knew them; in some cases, well after he could recall them perfectly. Later, he tested himself again on the lists. His measure of how much had been retained in memory was a measure of *savings,* that is, how much work was needed to relearn the lists after a given amount of time had elapsed. The amount of savings indicated how much of what was learned had been saved.

Ebbinghaus made many contributions to the study of memory. Not only did he devise experimental techniques in which sources of error were controlled, but he used those techniques to discover a great deal about human memory and learning. One important discovery made by Ebbinghaus was that if a list was short enough—say, seven or less items— he could learn it in just one reading. If the list increased to eight or more items, the learning time increased dramatically. In fact, there was a discontinuity at around seven items—below it, there was immediate learning; above it, learning took several trials—the number of trials increased with the number of items. The seven-item limit is called the *memory span,* and we shall discuss it in more detail in Chapter 2.

A second major discovery made by Ebbinghaus was that the amount of savings was markedly affected by the *retention interval* (the time between initial learning and later testing). He found that savings were great with a short retention interval and decreased regularly as the interval increased; that is, the amount forgotten increased as time passed. The course of forgetting is illustrated in Figure 1.1. There is very rapid forgetting over the first few minutes (that is, the amount of savings decreases rapidly), but gradually the rate of forgetting decreases (the amount of savings decreases more slowly).

Ebbinghaus's original list-learning procedure was similar to what is today called *serial learning.* Serial learning is characterized by the fact that the subject must learn the list of items in a given order. Suppose, for example, that our list, a very short one, is: BOOK, PIPE, CONE, BOARD, SHEET. Those five words would be presented to the subject, and then he would attempt to repeat them in order. If he forgot one of the words, or gave it out of order, he would be said to have made an error.

There are really two ways of testing a subject in serial-learning tasks. One is to give him the entire list, and then test his memory of it. That is called the *study–test procedure,* since the subject studies the list and then is

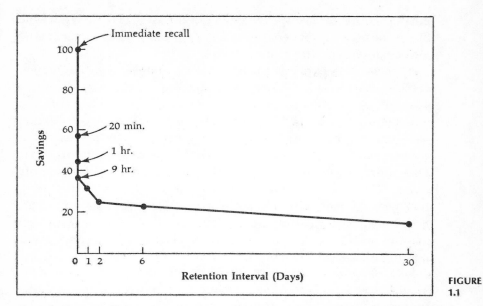

Ebbinghaus's forgetting function. Retention of previously learned lists of nonsense syllables, as measured by savings, is plotted as a function of the retention interval—the time between initial learning and the retention test. [After Ebbinghaus, 1885.]

FIGURE 1.1

tested on all of it. Alternatively, we could use the *anticipation procedure*— instead of studying the entire list and then being tested on all of it, the subject is tested on and studies one item at a time. This is accomplished by having him attempt to anticipate each item before he sees it. The subject starts out by being presented some marker (for example, an asterisk) indicating the beginning of the list. Seeing the marker, the subject tries to state the first item on the list. (That is the test of the first item.) Then, he is given the first item (the study), and he tries to state the second, (the test of the second), and so on throughout the list. The first time through the list, of course, he will almost certainly be unable to state any of the items, but eventually, after several trials, he will be doing well.

Many variables have been found to influence serial learning. One is the rate at which items are presented. (Ebbinghaus, you may recall, used a constant rate of presentation.) In general, slower rates lead to faster learning. Another important finding about serial learning is that the serial position of items affects learning. The serial position of an item is simply its order number in the list, the first item having serial-position one, the second having serial-position two, and so on. The number of errors is greater for items in the middle of the list than for items at either of the ends. This is the serial-position effect, and it holds true for lists of any length beyond the memory span.

A second procedure that has been used very often in memory experiments is *paired-associate learning;* this procedure is characterized by the fact that each item is really a compound; that is, it has two parts. For example, an item might be a word and a number, like BOOK–7. The subject learns to report the second part of the item given the first (so that he can respond "7," given "BOOK"). Usually, the items are not learned in a fixed order in paired-associate learning, unlike the serial-learning procedure. Thus, the order of the items can change from one trial to another, but the pairs themselves do not. For example, the items BOOK–7 and DOG–8 might occur one after another on one trial and be several items apart on another trial; however, BOOK would always be paired with 7; DOG would always be paired with 8.

Like the serial list, the paired-associate list can be learned with either a study–test procedure or an anticipation procedure. If the study-test procedure is used, all the items are presented, and then all are tested. A test usually consists of the presentation of only the first parts of the items. The subject attempts to give the second parts as his response. For example, the experimenter presents BOOK–? and the subject says "7." If the anticipation procedure is used, as in serial learning, each item is tested and then presented before the next is tested and presented, and so on. The test anticipates the study. For example, the subject is given BOOK–? as the test of the BOOK–7 item. Then he is given BOOK–7 (the chance to study). Next, he may be tested on DOG–?; then given DOG–8, and so on.

One supposed advantage of paired-associate learning is that a single item can be considered as a stimulus (the first part) and a response (the second part). Some theorists have assumed that the procedure allows associations between stimuli and responses to be studied directly. We will see, however, that just because an item is learned, it does not mean that what is learned is a simple bond between the stimulus and the response. Subjects often learn the item by a technique of *mediation*, which involves idiosyncratically changing the items in some way. For example, an item JAK–B may be mentally changed to "Jack and the Beanstalk." In this instance, what is learned is quite different from the direct association of "JAK + B."

A third experimental procedure is that of *free recall.* In free recall, unlike serial recall, the subject is free to report the items in any order he chooses. If the same list is used for several trials, its order of presentation changes from one trial to another. (Free recall generally takes the form of study–

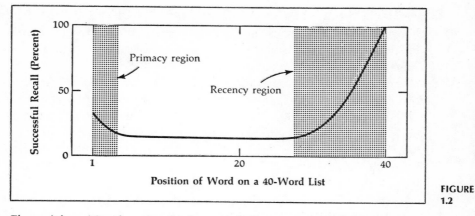

FIGURE
1.2

The serial-position function for free recall. The percent of times that words were recalled, for words in each position in a forty-word list. The function is divided into a primacy region, a recency region, and a flat central region. [Data after Murdock, 1962.]

test, because the anticipation method determines the order in which list items are reported—exactly what is *not* wanted for this procedure.)

Like serial recall, free recall produces a serial-position effect, as shown in Figure 1.2. That is, the percentage of the time that items in a given position are recalled is highest for items in the beginning and end positions and lower for the items in the middle. As indicated in the figure, the various portions of the serial-position curve (obtained when Percent Recall is plotted against Position of Word) are given different names. The first portion of the curve, showing recall of items from early in the list, is given the name *primacy* effect. The last portion of the curve, showing recall of the last few items, is called the *recency* effect.

Another of the list-learning procedures is recognition testing. In recognition tasks, what is distinctive is the form of the test. The subject is given items from a list of words he has studied and is asked to indicate whether or not he recognizes them as having been part of the list. Thus, the recognition paradigm is characterized by the fact that the subject sees the list items when he is tested instead of having to recall them. Of course, if he is given only items from the list, he can just say "Yes, that was on it" to each one and be correct. In order to test his ability to recognize items from the list, we must introduce into the test items called "distractors"—items that were not on the list.

For example, the subject might be given a yes/no test. For the test he would see a series of items, one at a time. Each time an item appeared, he would say "yes" if he thought it had been on his list and "no" if he thought it had not been. Usually, half the items on the test would be from the list and half would be distractors. The yes/no test is analogous to the true/false testing we encounter in school.

Another form of recognition testing is the forced-choice test. In a forced-choice procedure, the subject sees two or more items at a time, not just one. One of those items was on the list; the rest were not. His job is to pick out the item that was on the list. If the subject sees two items at a time, then the test is called a "two-alternative forced choice"; if three, a "three-alternative forced choice," and so on. As you may have noticed, the forced-choice test is a kind of multiple-choice test.

Finally, a recognition test can use a batch-testing procedure, in which everything—all the list words and all the distractors—is presented at once. The subject then tries to indicate which words were on the list. Often, all the test items are printed on a page and the subject circles those he thinks are from the originally presented list.

It is important to note that recognition testing is sometimes used in combination with the other procedures described above. For example, we could combine the recognition procedure with the paired-associates procedure by testing each stimulus term with a set of response alternatives. A subject who had first been presented with DAX-7 might be tested with:

DAX-?   5 8 7 1 *(Pick one)*

Recognition can also be combined with serial learning. In that case, we might ask the subject to recognize which ordering of a set of items corresponded to the order in which they had previously been presented.

These, then, are the definitions related to the basic list-learning procedures. (1) In serial learning, items are learned in a particular order. (2) In paired-associate learning, the list items come in pairs. (3) In free recall, the list items can be reported in any order. (4) In recognition, the subject sees the list items when he is tested. Although we will have little to say about serial learning in this book, we will find the other procedures important to our discussion. For example: paired-associate tasks are important in the study of forgetting (Chapter 9), free-recall testing has been extensively used in experiments on the organization of memory (Chapter 10), and recognition tests will be important in our discussion of retrieval theories (Chapter 11).

2

OVERVIEW
OF THE HUMAN
INFORMATION-
PROCESSING
SYSTEM

In the first chapter, humans were characterized as processors of information, and human memory was called an information-processing system. We noted that two important characteristics of such a system are (1) that it can be broken down into a series of stages, and (2) that processing at each stage is limited. In the present chapter, we shall look at the human information-processing system in more detail. A theoretical model of this system will be proposed and considered. In subsequent chapters, this initial model will be greatly expanded, but it is important at this point for us to get an overview of the system.

THE SYSTEM AND ITS COMPONENTS

A model of the human-information processing system is illustrated in Figure 2.1. What the figure shows, essentially, is what happens to information about a stimulus from the "real world" as it passes through the system.

In the first stage of information processing following stimulus presentation, a certain amount of information about the stimulus (which has just occurred outside the system) is registered, or entered, in the system. "Sensory register" is the name given to the site of that registration. It is called a sensory register because the information enters the system by

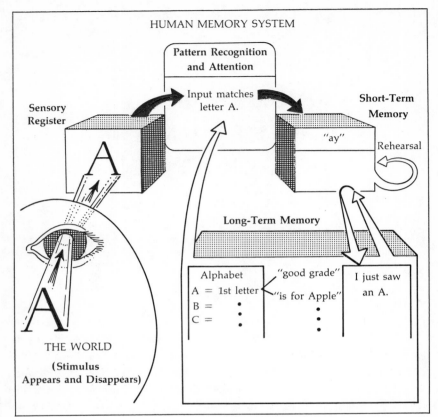

FIGURE
2.1

A model of the human information-processing system.

one or more of the five senses and is held briefly in sensory form (for example, a sound is held in auditory form). (Thus, there is a sensory register for each sense.) The information can stay in a register for a brief time, but the longer it sits there the weaker it gets, until it vanishes completely. This gradual weakening is called *decay,* and it limits the capacity of the system at this particular stage—the register is limited by the length of time a stimulus can stay there without decaying.

While information is in a sensory register, important processes come into play. One of these is *pattern recognition,* a complex process that results in contact between the information in a sensory register and previously acquired knowledge. That is, a pattern is said to be recognized when the sensory aspects of the pattern are in some way equated with meaningful concepts. A more specific sense of the label "pattern recognition" is naming. Clearly, when we assign a name to a stimulus—"the letter ay" for example—we have taken visual information (that the stimulus consists of a triangle with sides extending past two of the vertices) and equated it with a known concept ("the letter ay"). However, pattern recognition does not always mean naming (we can recognize some patterns without being able to name them), so it is better to think of pattern recognition in the more general sense of assigning meaning to a stimulus.

Closely related to pattern recognition is another process called *attention*. The word "attention" has several meanings for cognitive psychologists. It can mean "expect," as when you expect a phone call and listen for the phone to ring. Still another meaning of attention is simply "capacity"—to attend to a stimulus may imply that it requires some of a limited capacity available. Attention can also mean simply "pay attention to" in the sense of tuning in, not tuning out. (You should pay attention to your instructor if you don't want to miss important information from the lecture.) It is the last sense of "attention," often called "selective attention," that will be most important in our discussion.

Inputs to the system that have been recognized and attended to (tuned in) can be passed on to another stage of the system. In this stage, the information is stored briefly in *short-term memory* (STM), much as it was held in one of the sensory registers—except that it is no longer in a raw, sensory form. The letter A, for example, is not held as some unidentified visual stimulus, but as a letter, A. Another difference between the sensory registers and STM is the length of time a piece of information can be retained. An item in the visual register decays rather rapidly, say, in a second, but an item in STM may be held indefinitely by a holding process called "rehearsal." Rehearsal serves to recycle material over and over again through STM, and this keeps renewing it, so that decay is never complete. However, without rehearsal, information in STM is lost, as it is lost from the sensory register, and we have yet another limitation on the capacity of the system. In fact, there are two limitations on STM—the number of stimuli that can be held simultaneously in STM with the help of rehearsal is limited, and the length of time an item can stay in STM without rehearsal is also limited. The loss of an item from STM is one type of "forgetting"—a term which can refer to loss of information from any point of storage in the memory system.

Finally, information may be sent from STM even deeper into the system, into an essentially permanent storehouse called *long-term memory* (LTM). Long-term memory holds an amazing variety and amount of information—including the meanings of words, what happened to us the day before yesterday, the names of people we know, labels for common objects, the rules of English grammar, and so on. In fact, it holds all our knowledge about the world.

With this brief look at the system, it becomes clear that we have been talking about two different types of features. There are memory stores—the sensory registers, STM, and LTM—that are permanent, built-in components of the system. These features are called "structural features" of the system because they are part of its structure. On the other hand, we have mentioned such processes as attending to a stimulus, recognizing a stimulus, and rehearsing information. These aspects of the system are not thought of as part of its structure, but instead as processes that vary from one stimulus to another. Because these processes are used by the information processor to control the flow of information, they are called "control processes" (after Atkinson and Shiffrin, 1968).

Let's go back a bit. We have traced the progress of some information from the real world into the deepest recesses of the human memory system, but in doing so, we have only touched upon a few high points of an extremely complex entity. Before we continue our exploration of that complex entity, let's take a somewhat closer look at each of the features and processes we have mentioned thus far.

The Sensory Registers

First, let's consider the sensory registers. A visual register for a stimulus entering via the sense of sight has been mentioned. We also assume there to be registers for the other four senses: hearing, touch, smell, and taste. The two registers that psychologists have looked at most are the register for vision, called "the icon" by Neisser (1967), and the register for hearing, which we shall refer to as "the echo" (again, Neisser's term).

In general, a sensory register serves the function of briefly holding information about a stimulus in the system in what is called "veridical" form—that is, in much the same form it was initially presented—until it can be put into a new form and sent further on into the system. As mentioned above, the length of time that information is held there is quite brief, under any circumstances, because information held in a register is subject to a process of very rapid decay. However, information can also be removed from a register, or "erased," because new information came in. One can see why such a feature is necessary—for example, if the icon (visual register) had no such erasing feature, we would constantly be seeing sets of overlapping visual images rather than discrete scenes.

Attention and Pattern Recognition

The two important control processes, pattern recognition and attention, which have been depicted as occurring between the register and STM (a somewhat misleading depiction, as we shall see later), are responsible for getting registered information into the system at deeper levels. What is the function of selective attention? The answer to this question lies in our assumption that the processing capacity of the system is limited. At any given time, an incredible amount of information impinges on our sense organs. As you read this, you are receiving visual stimulation; at the same time, your sense of touch tells you that you are sitting on something (or perhaps standing), and that your fingers are touching this book; and you are probably also hearing sounds, unless you are in a sound-proof room. Some of the available information is important, some is not. Selective attention makes it possible for you to focus on, or tune in, the relevant information, filtering out the rest. Thus, attention ensures that it is the important information that is brought into the limited-capacity system, instead of any old information at all (which would mean that important information would be lost).

A commonly cited example of selective attention at work is called the cocktail-party phenomenon. It goes like this: Picture yourself at a cocktail partly, engrossed in conversation. Suddenly you hear your name, coming from another conversational group. You quickly tune in the group that is discussing you, and you may hear some very interesting things. But you have now lost track of the discussion in which you were initially participating. Selective attention makes it possible for you to tune in Group 2, but only at the expense of Group 1.

The other important process we mentioned is pattern recognition: the process of matching incoming sensory information with previously learned information that is stored in LTM. The purpose of pattern recognition is easy to understand. It is to convert raw information (like visual forms or patterns of sound), relatively useless to the system, to something meaningful. This may mean assigning a name to a stimulus, but it need not. The importance of pattern recognition is also easy to see. Just think of what might happen if you failed to categorize incoming visual information as "a bear," and instead categorized it as "a horse." Such a failure of the recognition system could be fatal.

Pattern recognition is not a simple process. Consider a fairly straight-forward example: We see an immense variety of written, printed, and scrawled alphabet letters in our everyday lives. How are we able to recognize them in all of their multitudinous shapes and sizes? This particular problem is sufficiently complex that no one has been able to construct a machine to do the job—to read the addresses on letters for example. If you could construct such a machine, you could make a fortune, for as matters now stand, human beings must serve as pattern recognizers—as bank tellers, mail sorters, and so forth. What makes pattern recognition so difficult is that one category can include a great many patterns. For example, the letter A can also be written as A, a, or a. Also, the very same pattern can appear to the system in many sizes and orientations: A, A, ◁. Even more tricky to account for is the fact that novel patterns, never seen before, can be recognized: A! Indeed, most hand-printed letters are novel, even unique, in that each probably differs from every other. When you consider it this way, it is clear that there is an almost infinite number of different patterns, all of which must be recognized as belonging to the same category, and it is this unlimited variety that makes machine recognition so difficult.

Short-Term Memory

However it is done (a topic to be taken up later), recognition of a pattern means that the resulting information can be sent into STM, a store which has a number of other names—it is also called primary memory, immediate memory, or working memory. Studies of STM have been largely confined to the use of verbal material—letters, words, and so on. Thus, most of our information about this store comes from the verbal domain. It has been suggested, for example, that a verbally coded item (that is, an item in the form of a word or label) will last less than a half-minute in STM if it is not rehearsed, and that about a half-dozen such items can be held in STM at one time. Rehearsal itself is an immensely interesting STM phenomenon. Some theorists have proposed that the process of rehearsing is like subvocally, or silently, repeating the rehearsed item, and that each such repetition serves the same function as putting the item into STM in the first place; that is, the item returns fresh and unforgotten. Although whether rehearsal is really implicit speech is an open question, rehearsal does seem to be used to maintain items in STM. A second function of rehearsal relates to the transfer of information to LTM. It has been suggested (for example, by Atkinson and Shiffrin, 1968) that the more an item is rehearsed in STM, and the longer it stays in STM, the more likely it is to be remembered later. This means, essentially, that the rehearsal process can provide an opportunity for strengthening the representation of the information in LTM, so that later it is more amenable to recall.

Another oft-cited finding concerning STM is that a verbal label held in STM is coded acoustically. What this means is that the word is represented in sound form—not as it appears to the visual sense. This is true even if the word first entered the system via the icon. We know this because when retrieval from STM is inadequate, and a wrong answer is reported (this is called a confusion error, because something *not* in STM is confused with something that was put in there), the confusion is between things that sound alike, rather than things that look alike (Conrad, 1964). For example, b is more likely to be reported when v was visually presented and put into STM than x is, because both b and v sound alike. This is true even though x may look more like v.

Long-Term Memory

Long-term memory, that immensely complex storehouse, has also been most extensively studied with the use of verbal materials, usually presented in the form of long lists. As we shall see, this approach has resulted in some extremely important findings, but it has also been a bit misleading. After all, remembering lists of words is somewhat different from remembering a conversation, a recipe, or the plot of a movie. Recently, LTM has been studied in the context of memory for language—not just isolated words, but meaningful linguistic discourse. Studying memory with stimulus material that is close to natural language leads to a much more extensive knowledge of how LTM works in everyday life.

Some important hypotheses made about LTM are worth mentioning here. One is that unlike STM and the sensory registers, LTM is a *permanent* store. If this hypothesis is true, why is it that we can't remember everything we have ever known? Supporters of the hypothesis contend that forgetting is a retrieval problem—the information is there, but we can't get at it.

Another interesting hypothesis regarding LTM is that information there can be coded in many ways—acoustically, visually, or semantically (in terms of meaning). For example, information about the sound of a train must be in my LTM, because I recognize it when it occurs. The sight of my sister's face must be there, because I know her when she appears. The name of my home town must be there, because I can say it when I am asked what it is.

We begin to get some idea of the complexities of LTM when we realize that stored in LTM is *everything* we know about the world. Washington could not tell a lie; dogs must eat to live; shoes are worn on the feet. Not only is this vast amount of information stored in LTM, each piece of it can be reached by a multitude of pathways. Just as an example, consider the single word SMILE. We can reach that word through its definition: "Tell me a word meaning configuration of the mouth which indicates happiness." We can reach it by filling in the blank in "Let a _____ be your umbrella." And we also can reach it by other routes as well.

In general, information in LTM seems to be arranged in such a way that retrieval is accomplished with relative ease. Given some piece of information (such as the word SMILE), we can easily find the spot in LTM where related information is stored (a capacity called "content address-ability," which means that we can find the location, or address, of infor-mation, given a key portion of the content). Moreover, we can quickly find related information in LTM. The very rapidity with which we can retrieve suggests both that retrieval is not a haphazard, undirected pro-cess, and that LTM must be a highly organized entity.

We have concluded our overview of the human information-processing system, but we cannot simply accept the system, as described, without question. In following chapters, we shall see that many qualifications of this preliminary model are necessary. At this point, however, one quali-fication is particularly appropriate; it concerns the distinction we have drawn between STM and LTM.

THE DUPLEX THEORY—
TWO MEMORIES OR ONE?

According to our model, information can be stored in the memory system in the sensory registers, in STM, and in LTM. Distinctions among these three types of storage are made on both logical and empirical grounds. For example, the hypothesis that there are sensory registers can readily be defended, for clearly there must be sites in the system to store inputs from the senses long enough for them to be initially recog-nized. Experimental evidence for the existence of such registers has also been obtained. (Most of this evidence is rather recent; it will be dis-cussed in Chapter 3.)

On the other hand, the theory that divides nonsensory memory into two stores, STM and LTM—called the "duplex theory"—has been less readily accepted by some memory theorists. Because of this, we will first look at some important evidence supporting the duplex theory, and then discuss its limitations and some alternative theoretical approaches.

One line of evidence used to support the duplex theory is physiological in nature. In 1959, Brenda Milner described a group of behaviors accompanying damage to the hippocampal areas of the brain. These behaviors, taken together, have come to be called "Milner's syndrome." A person with Milner's syndrome appears unable to remember events in the recent past, even though he can remember events that occurred in the remote past—before his brain was damaged. Such a brain-damaged patient has no loss of intelligence or of skills he acquired before the damage. He can also remember information immediately after he is given it; that is, he can repeat back what he is told, and he can even remember information for several minutes if he is permitted to say it over and over without interruption (rehearse). However, he seems unable to retain new information for any longer than he can rehearse it. All this suggests very strongly that the brain-damaged patient has a long-term store (where events of the remote past are held), and also a short-term memory (used for immediate repetition and rehearsal). It is as if he has lost the connection between STM and LTM and with it, the ability to transfer new information to LTM. Thus, Milner's syndrome fits in well with a duplex theory; in fact, such a theory helps to explain how such behavioral defects could occur.

Other evidence for duplexity has come from experimental work on memory. One interesting series of findings has to do with confusion errors made in recalling information. One situation in which confusions occur is that of the "memory span" or "immediate memory" task. (Recall that immediate memory is another name for STM.) In such a task, a person is given a brief list of items and immediately asked to repeat them. In theory, this task draws on information in STM, because the letters have been so recently presented. A confusion error is said to occur if the subject reports a letter that was not in the list instead of a letter that was. As noted previously, such confusions are made more often between pairs like B and v, which sound similar, than between acoustically dissimilar pairs, even if the letters were presented visually.

Now consider the LTM analog of the immediate-memory experiment. We show a subject a list of words, say, and ask him to recall them an hour later. His typical confusions will not be acoustic, but semantic. For example, if the word LABOR was in the list, a subject is much more likely to report WORK than LATHER. Thus, he confuses a word similar in meaning with the list word, but he does not confuse words on the basis of sound. In short, errors in recall from LTM are generally semantic (Baddeley and Dale, 1966), but most recall errors from STM are acoustic, suggesting that items are stored in STM by sound and in LTM by meaning.

The duplex theory has also been supported by the experimental procedure known as free recall. We have noted that when a free-recall task is performed, a serial-position curve can be plotted, and that this curve

19

has a primacy portion, a flat central portion, and a recency portion. (See Figure 2.2a.) The duplex theory explains that curve as follows. The primacy effect is said to be a result of recall from LTM. It occurs because the first words in the list came into an "empty" STM; that is, the subject had nothing else to concentrate on and he could therefore rehearse the first few words many times. But eventually—say after the first six words or so—he had more words to keep track of than he could hold in STM at one time (owing to its limited capacity). Each subsequent word could be rehearsed only a few times before it was lost from STM. Thus, the first words in the list were rehearsed more and therefore stored more effectively in LTM. In contrast, items in the middle of the list all came into a filled STM; all had about the same number of rehearsals, and therefore all are remembered at about the same relatively low rate.

The recency effect is explained this way: items at the end of the list are still present in STM when the recall of the list begins; for this reason, the subject can report them immediately out of STM, and his recall is very good for such items. This explanation is supported by the finding that subjects usually do report words from the end of the list right away when the test begins.

The duplex explanation of the form of the free-recall serial-position curve is supported by experiments showing that the primacy and recency portions of the curve can be separately manipulated. These manipulations supposedly affect LTM and STM respectively. (See Figure 2.2.) For example, suppose we present the list of words and then delay recall for a 30-second period. During that period, we ask the subject to do some arithmetic—presumably preventing him from rehearsing the words in STM. We would expect the recency portion to be affected by this manipulation, because the subject would be unable to bring the last words in the list out of STM when recall begins. This, in fact, occurs: The recency effect disappears in such an experiment (for example, Postman and Phillips, 1965; Figure 2.2b).

On the other hand, suppose we attempt to affect LTM, by varying the rate at which words are presented. At a fast rate—a word per second—the subject has little time to rehearse, and LTM storage should be much less than for words presented at a slower rate of one word every two seconds. (However, STM storage should be unaffected, because the subject can hold the last few words in STM at either presentation rate.) Again, the hypothesis is confirmed. The primacy and middle portions of the free-recall serial-position curve are higher at the slow rate of presentation because more rehearsals could occur at that rate, leading to better LTM storage. At the same time, the recency portion of the curve is essentially unaffected by the rate of presentation (Murdock, 1962; Figure 2.2c).

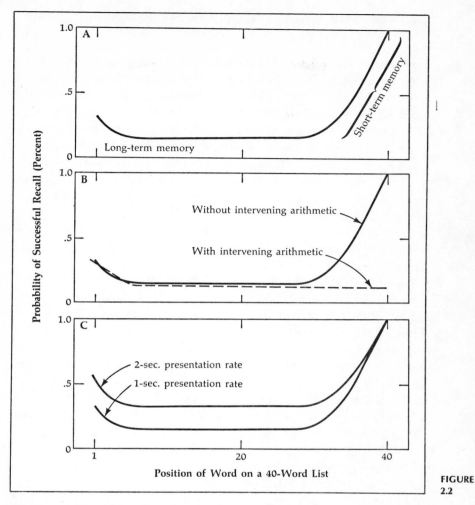

(A) The serial-position function for free recall, showing contributions of long-term memory (primacy region and central region) and short-term memory (recency region) **(B)** The effects of an arithmetic task interpolated between presentation of the list and free recall: with arithmetic, the serial-position function is flattened in the recency area. **(C)** The effects of presentation rate on the serial-position function for free recall: At faster rates, the primacy region and central region are lowered, but the recency portion is minimally affected by presentation rate. [Curves are idealized data, after experiments of Murdock, 1962; Postman and Phillips, 1965.]

FIGURE
2.2

The duplex theory has been widely accepted by memory theorists in the last decade or so, but it is not as problem-free as it might appear to be. For one thing, much of the evidence for duplexity can be interpreted without postulating an STM that is separate from LTM. Wickelgren (1973) examined nine major lines of evidence favoring the duplex theory and rejected six of them on that basis. For example, consider the different effects that using an interpolated task (that is, a task that occurs between presentation of the list and free recall) has on the primacy and recency portions of the serial-position curve. We know that such a task "wipes out" the recency portion of the curve but has relatively small effects on the primacy portion; these different effects of interpolated material are used as evidence for duplexity. However, the evidence weakens when we recognize that items in the primacy portion of the list are always subjected to the effects of interpolated material. That is because the earliest items in the list are followed by all the subsequent items before those early items are recalled. Thus, the latter part of the list, that which intervenes between the presentation of the first items and their recall, actually serves as interpolated material. Moreover, as we shall see in Chapter 9, an interpolated task may greatly affect the recall of information that immediately preceded it, but as more interpolated material is added, the effect of each additional piece of material is less than the effect of the piece before. It is not surprising, then, that a post-list task has little effect on recall of items from the first portion of the list, since that portion has already been subjected to the effects of the latter part of the list by the time a post-list task is performed. That is, the effects of the post-list task on the recency portion of the list are comparable to the effects of the middle and recency parts of the list on the primacy portion. It can thus be seen that interpolated tasks do not necessarily have different effects on different areas of the serial-position curve, and that consequently, evidence for duplexity based on the effects of a post-list task cannot be considered conclusive.

Other experimental findings also cast doubt on the validity of the duplex theory. We shall look at several discrepant results as we discuss STM and LTM in more detail in later chapters; however, a few such results will be mentioned here.

One line of evidence for duplex theory deals with the difference between the representational format of information, or the memory code, of STM and that of LTM. STM, we have noted, represents information acoustically, whereas in LTM information is coded semantically. However, we will soon discuss experimental evidence for nonacoustic—visual and semantic—codes in STM, and we have already noted that LTM must contain acoustic and visual information (as well as information about smells, tastes, and touches). Otherwise, how would we recognize faces or sounds that we had not seen or heard for some time? Thus, the acoustic–semantic distinction between the two memories is not as clear as some experiments have made it appear to be.

We have also said that items are stored in STM without rehearsal for only a few seconds, but that items can be stored in LTM indefinitely. This might be a means of distinguishing between the stores, but estimates of the duration of STM vary widely. The same can be said about STM capacity; that is, the number of items that can be maintained there at any one time. Again, estimates vary. One source of this confusion is that STM and LTM—if they are actually separate entities—are highly interdependent. Not only is there a connection between the two, so that rehearsals in STM lead to building memories in LTM, but LTM contributes greatly to STM encoding. Consider the case where we put a visually presented letter in STM—how would we know it was indeed a letter without going to LTM for its visual appearance and its name? Because recognizing patterns involves LTM, STM encoding also involves LTM. In addition, the representation of items in STM can be affected by LTM after they are recognized. For example, the nonsense syllable wis could be stored in STM as a word, "Wisconsin." The process of mediation, which is what occurs when wis is stored as "Wisconsin," uses LTM information to convert the syllable to a more meaningful unit.

In trying to make these complex operations and memory codes fit a duplex framework, some psychologists have sometimes pulled, stretched, and distorted STM and LTM beyond recognition. This has led others to ask, "Why bother with duplex theory at all?"

One alternative to the duplex theory is what has been called a "levels-of-processing" theory (Craik and Lockhart, 1972; Posner, 1969). It is a variant of the information-processing theory, because it divides up the course of processing into stages (here called levels). However, in this approach there are no structural component stages like STM or LTM. Instead, what were structural components are now seen as processes, much like pattern recognition and attention.

As an example, suppose we treat STM storage as a process. Instead of viewing an item stored for a short time as sitting in a particular memory store, we see it as passing through a certain process—in this case, the process of being acoustically represented shortly after its presentation. One advantage of this approach is that if we now discover that a particular item may be represented visually in what we think of as STM, we don't have to think of that visual representation as violating some important principle (the principle being that STM codes are acoustic). We just think of the matter as another process that can operate; the process of visually coding an item shortly after its presentation.

In all of this speculation, it's a good thing to keep in mind that no matter what theory you may accept—and this statement goes beyond arguments about STM and LTM—it is a *theory*. The evidence favoring the duplex theory that we have mentioned—such as changes in the recency portion of the free-recall curve, differences in confusion errors over short and long retention intervals, or physiological observations—indicates that it is at least *useful* to divide memory into short-term and long-term processing. This division may lead us to postulate two memory stores, like STM and LTM, but it could also lead us to postulate two levels of processing, two memory codes, or still other duplex processes or mechanisms. Just which of these distinctions we adopt is not crucial. What is important is to remember that a theory can be a useful tool for describing and explaining events without being an exact, literal account.

3

THE SENSORY REGISTERS

The model of human memory presented in Chapter 2 included as one type of component *sensory registers*, in which incoming information could be held for a brief period in veridical form—that is, as a faithful reproduction of the original stimulus—before it was recognized and passed on through the system. It was suggested that such a register existed for each sense. Sensory registers have been given a variety of names by psychologists: sensory-information stores, iconic stores, and precategorical stores. (The last label, "precategorical," is used to indicate that the incoming information has not yet been recognized, or matched with an appropriate category.)

THE VISUAL REGISTER

The most extensively studied sensory registers are the two that correspond to our visual and auditory senses. They have been called the icon and echo, respectively (Neisser, 1967). Much of what we know about iconic storage (that is, storage in the icon) comes from the work of George Sperling (1960; Averbach and Sperling, 1961). Sperling's research began with his observations of results of experiments with immediate-memory tasks. In such experiments, subjects are asked to report back a series of letters that they have just viewed briefly. Sperling's results were quite consistent: how well the subjects performed depended on how many letters they viewed. If a list contained about four or fewer letters, the subjects could report them perfectly. But when the number of letters was increased to about five or more, performance broke down—the subjects could no longer report all of the letters in the list; in fact, they could report only an average of about four or five. The upper limit that we have just called "about four or five" (in other words, the point at which performance on an immediate-memory task falls below 100% accuracy) is called the memory span. For example, we could say on the basis of the experiments just described that the memory span, or span of immediate memory, is about five for letters. (The "for letters" is important, because the memory span varies somewhat with the nature of the material that is to be remembered.)

In experiments such as those just described, it matters little how the letters that the subject sees are arranged. For example, six letters might be arranged in a single row, or in two rows of three each, and performance would not vary. Let us consider a specific experiment drawn from Sperling's work. Suppose the subject is presented with nine letters in the form of a 3 by 3 matrix. (That is, there are three rows of three letters each.) The letters are exposed for a very brief time, 50 milliseconds (msec). A millisecond is one 1/1000 second, so that would be .05 second, which is less time than a subject requires to move his eyes. After the exposure, the subject reports what he can, with some (by now) predictable results: on the average, he can report back only four or five letters.

You might suspect that the subject could not report all nine letters because he didn't see them all; after all, .05 second is not much time. But, briefness of exposure is not the reason for the subject's failure; if the exposure time is increased up to a half-second (plenty of time to see the letters), the results do not change. This really isn't surprising: the experiment we have just described is a memory-span task, not unlike the one studied by Ebbinghaus, and the results are similar to those we previously noted for such tasks. That is, in a variety of presentation conditions, subjects can immediately recall brief lists perfectly, but as the lists increase in length, recall fails.

The procedure just described, in which a subject sees a list of letters and then attempts to recall as many as he can, is called the whole-report procedure. It is known by this name because the subject is requested to recall the whole list, or as much of it as he can. Sperling not only studied performance with whole reports, but he also developed a new procedure for immediate memory, called the partial-report procedure. In the partial-report experiment, the subject briefly views a set of letters, arranged in three rows. Immediately after the letters vanish, the subject hears a tone of high, medium, or low frequency. The tone is an instruction that tells the subject which row of the matrix he is to report. Hearing a high tone, he is to report the top row; a middle tone, the middle row; a low tone, the bottom row. Then, immediately after the tone, the subject attempts to report the requested row of letters. The sequence of events (presentation of letters, then tone, then report) is called a trial, and the experiment itself comprises a series of such trials.

Another way to conduct a partial-report task is to ask the subject to report a specific letter from the matrix. In this case (Averbach and Coriell, 1961), the signal of what to report is not a tone, but a visual display that follows the matrix of letters: a white field containing a black bar. The bar occupies a position just *above* the previous position of one of the letters, and it indicates that the subject should report that letter. In general, the crucial feature of partial-report situations is that some kind of signal follows presentation of the letters and points out what part of the entire set of letters is to be recalled.

We know the results of the whole-report experiment: no matter how many letters are in the list, the subject can report no more than about five of them. The results of the partial-report procedure are quite different, as can be seen in the data of Sperling's experiment (shown in Figure 3.1). Consider what happens when nine letters are shown. In the partial report situation, subjects are nearly 100% accurate, no matter which row they were asked to report. But this means that the subject must have had all nine of the letters available in his memory at the time the tone sounded; otherwise, he would surely have made an error on some row at some time. That is, immediately after the letters were presented, at the time the tone sounded, the subject must have had information in memory about all nine letters.

In general, we can use the rate of accuracy to estimate how many letters the subject had available in memory at the time of the tone. We simply multiply the accuracy rate (percent correct) by the number of letters presented. For example, subjects performed with about 76% accuracy for displays of twelve letters (three rows of four each), indicating that about nine of the letters were available in memory at the time of report, which agrees almost perfectly with the results of the experiment with nine letters.

The results of Sperling's experiment, shown in Figure 3.1, indicate that what is available in memory immediately after the stimulus is presented is much more than what can be reported in a whole-report situation. This conclusion leads to a question: why is there such a discrepancy between partial report and whole report? Why does the subject have a memory span of only five letters, when he can actually remember nine?

Before answering that question, we should consider a variation on the partial-report procedure. As we described the procedure, the report signal followed immediately after the set of letters. It is possible, however,

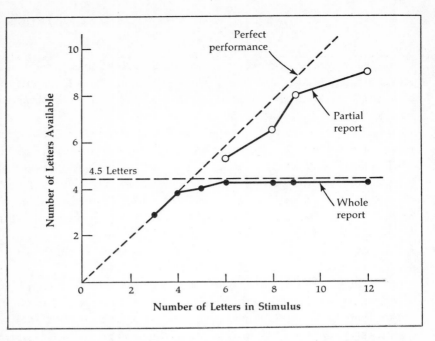

FIGURE
3.1

Performance in Sperling's experiments with whole- and partial-report procedures. The partial-report results show letters available, calculated as the
percentage of letters called for that are reported by observers, multiplied by
the number of letters in the display. The whole-report results show letters
available, calculated as the number of letters observers could correctly
report. The diagonal line shows where performance would fall if subjects
could report perfectly. [After Sperling, 1960. Copyright 1960 by the American
Psychological Association.]

to delay the signal. The results of varying the delay of the signal are
shown in Figure 3.2 (for a matrix of twelve letters). At no delay, performance indicates that about nine of the letters are available, as we have
seen. But as the delay increases to 1.0 second, subjects make more and
more errors, until finally their performance is about the same as it would
be with the whole-report procedure; that is, about five letters.

Now, to return to our question. What Sperling's experiments show is
that what is available in memory immediately after the visual presentation of a stimulus is more than what remains a second later. The results
of the partial-report studies, with no delay of the signal to report, measure
what is available immediately after the stimulus has been presented. The
whole-report experiments, on the other hand, measure what is available
in memory some time after the stimulus has terminated—much less than
was there at first. And the results obtained when the partial-report

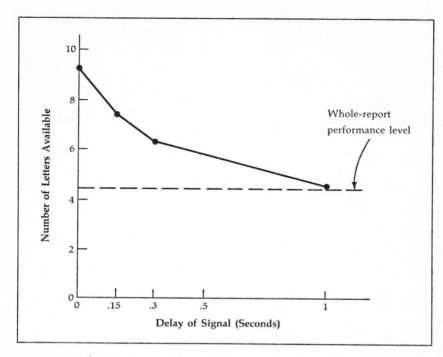

**FIGURE
3.2**

Letters available in the partial-report situation (calculated as for Figure 3.1) for various delays of the signal to report. Also shown is performance with a whole-report task for comparable material. [After Sperling, 1960. Copyright 1960 by the American Psychological Association.]

signal is delayed show what happens in between those two points. What seems to happen is that the original, veridical representation of the stimulus gradually decays, so that less and less of the stimulus information is retained as time passes. In short, Sperling's results demonstrate the existence of a form of immediate visual storage that is highly accurate but that decays very rapidly.

The immediate storage that Sperling's experiments demonstrate empirically (that is, in a way that can be observed) corresponds to what we have been calling in our model the sensory register. His experiments deal with the register for vision, the icon. In our model (Chapter 2), the purpose of the icon is to hold visual information briefly in its original form, so that further information about the stimulus can be sent on in the system. Because iconic storage is a rather primitive kind of memory, in which things are represented in much the same form as they actually occurred, it is strongly affected by the conditions of occurrence. In this

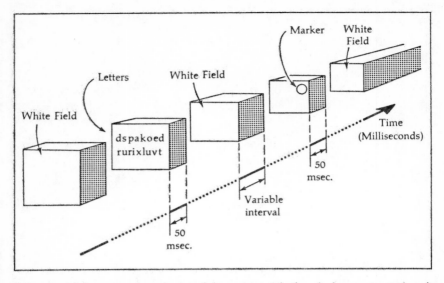

FIGURE
3.3

Diagram of the procedure for partial reports with the circle as report signal. [After Averbach and Coriell, 1961. Copyright 1961, The American Telephone and Telegraph Co.]

respect it is unlike later stages of memory. Among the important variables affecting iconic storage are the illumination preceding and following the visual stimulus (in Sperling's experiments, the letters), the visual stimulation that follows the stimulus, and the exposure time.

We can investigate the effects of illumination by comparing two conditions: one in which a dark field precedes and follows the letters, the other in which a light field precedes and follows the letters. It appears that when the field is dark, the icon lasts longer. We infer this from the finding that the period of iconic decay (experimentally defined as the longest delay of the partial-report signal at which subjects still do better than with whole reports) is greater with dark fields. This suggests that the light fields may make it harder for the system to "see" the information in the icon; that the visual stimulation produced by the light fields somehow interferes with it. After all, a light field is a visual event in its own right.

This suggestion becomes even more plausible if we examine what happens when we follow the letters with something other than a tone or bar (Averbach and Coriell, 1961). Suppose we follow the letter matrix with a single circle that would encircle one of the letters if the letter were still there. (This is illustrated in Figure 3.3.) The "circled" letter is then to be reported. The effects of this manipulation are somewhat surprising, as

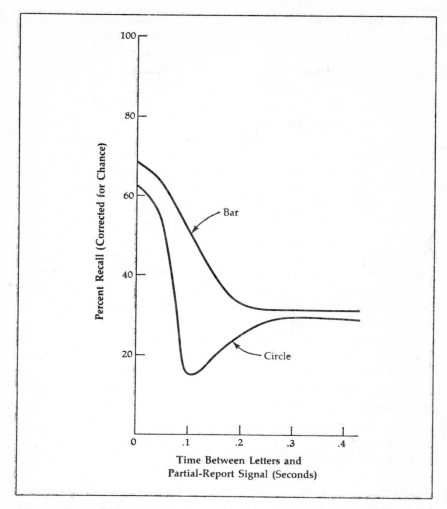

FIGURE
3.4

Effects of two different partial-report signals: a circle and a bar. They yield similar results when the delay of the signal is either small or large, but performance with the circle is markedly inferior for intermediate delays. [After Averbach and Coriell, 1961. Copyright 1961, The American Telephone and Telegraph Co.]

shown in Figure 3.4. The figure shows that, when the signal marker is delayed either for a relatively long period (a half-second or so) or not at all, performance with the circle as a marker does not differ much from performance with a bar marker. However, in between the no-delay condition and the long-delay condition, the circle leads to much poorer performance than the bar does.

The data in Figure 3.4 have been interpreted as follows. When the circle follows immediately after the letters, it is effectively superimposed on a letter; what the subject "sees" is that one letter has a circle *around* it; he reports that letter. (This is similar to what happens with the bar marker—at short delays, the subject sees the letter with a bar *over* it.) At very long delays, both the circle and the bar appear after the icon has decayed. In between, however, what happens is different. The circle actually erases and replaces the letter it was supposed to mark. Instead of seeing a letter and a circle, the subject sees only a circle. This phenomenon is known as backward masking, because the circle acts backward in time to mask, or erase, the letter that preceded it. (The bar, which is more offset from the letter's position, does not produce erasure.)

The erasure phenomenon is related to the different effects of light and dark fields noted above. We suggested that a light field interfered with the icon because it was itself a visual stimulus. Now we find that a stimulus that immediately follows the letter array and is in the same position as a letter can do much the same thing. When we relate the phenomenon of erasure to our concept of the sensory register, we can see that erasure serves an important function. It prevents iconic representations from staying too long in the sensory register. If there were no erasure, then each iconic representation could fall on top of those which preceded it, leading to a piling up and scrambling of visual information. Preventing such a scramble is the function served by erasure. It clears away the debris of preceding iconic storage as new information is registered.

THE AUDITORY REGISTER

Without an icon, we would be able to "see" visual stimuli only while they were before our eyes. That could make it impossible to recognize briefly occurring stimuli, for recognition takes time, perhaps more time than the stimuli are exposed to view. Consider next what would happen if the sensory register for audition, the echo, did not exist. By the same reasoning, we would be able to "hear" sounds only when they were physically present. But that limitation would have a striking effect: we would have great difficulties with the comprehension of speech! To illustrate the point, Neisser (1967, p. 201) gives an example of a foreigner who is told, "No, not zeal, *seal!*" He notes that the foreigner could not benefit from this advice unless he could retain the "z" in zeal long enough to compare it to the "s" in seal. Other examples of the usefulness of the echo can readily be seen. We could not recognize the rising intonation of a question such as "You came?" if the first part of the rising-intonation pattern were not available for comparison when the second occurred. In general, because sounds occur over some period of time, there must be a place to store their components for a time. That place is the sensory register for hearing.

The echo has been experimentally demonstrated in an experiment analogous to Sperling's demonstrations of the icon. Subjects in the echoic experiment (Moray, Bates, and Barnett, 1965) served as "four-eared men." That means they listened to as many as four messages simultaneously. The messages came via separate channels. To digress a bit, a *channel* means a source of information—in this case, sound. The concept may be familiar if you have a stereo system. There usually are two speakers, each reproducing its own distinct version of the music that is played. In the same vein, it is possible to construct a four-channel system for such an experiment. One way to do so is to set up four loudspeakers and to put a listener in the middle of the four. Another method is to use headphones, splitting each phone so that it carries two sources of sound. Moray and his colleagues found that both systems—four loudspeakers or split headphones—worked about equally well. For our purposes, the main point about channels is that subjects are able to discriminate among them. That is, when directed to listen to one specific channel, they can do so. They do not hear a jumble of sound, but they can recognize the fact that there are different messages coming from different sources.

Now, to the four-eared men. In the Moray-et-al. experiment, the subject took part in a series of trials. On each trial, he listened to messages played simultaneously on two, three, or four channels (loudspeakers). Each message consisted of one to four letters of the alphabet. The subject's task was to recall the letters after he had heard them. In one condition of the experiment, he tried to recall all the letters; that was the whole-report case. In another condition, a partial-report procedure analogous to Sperling's was used. The signal to report was not a tone, but a light. On a board held by the subject as he listened were two, three, or four lights, in positions corresponding to the positions of the loudspeakers being used. One second after the messages were over, one of the lights would flash, signaling the subject to recall the letters spoken on that particular channel—in other words, to give a partial report. Moray and his colleagues found that subjects could recall a greater percentage of letters when a partial report was requested than when the whole report was requested, regardless of the number of channels or letters per channel. We can infer, as we did from Sperling experiments, that immediately (1 second) after the letters had been presented, there was more information in memory about them than there was later. Presumably, that information was available in the auditory analogue of the icon: the echo.

Knowing, or at least presuming, that the echo exists, we can ask how long the representation of sound remains in it. The answer is not clear—estimates of the duration of echoic storage vary considerably. One estimate of its duration comes from a study by Darwin, Turvey, and Crowder (1972), which used a partial-report technique like that of Moray et al. Darwin and his colleagues had subjects listen to simultaneously presented lists composed of three items each (the items were letters or digits), one such list on each of three channels. The subject reported either all the items he could remember (the whole-report condition) or he was signaled with a visual indicator to report the items on just one channel (the partial-report condition). The indicator was presented either zero, 1, 2, or 4 seconds after the messages ended. The results of this experiment are shown in Figure 3.5, which shows that at short delays, up to 2 seconds, performance in the partial-report condition was superior to that of whole report. But as the signal for partial report was delayed up to 4 seconds, partial report lost its superiority. This result indicates that echoic memory, which we assume gives rise to the superiority of partial reports (just as in the analogous visual situation), lasts for about 2 seconds.

Other experiments that have attempted to estimate the duration of the echo have presented subjects with sounds that could not be identified without a subsequent clue. The underlying assumption of these experiments is that a clue can help the subject identify a sound only if there is a sound to apply it to—that is, only if there is a sound still remaining in the echo when the clue is given. By delaying the clue for various intervals and determining the longest delay at which the clue still facilitates identification of the sound, an estimate of the duration of echoic storage is obtained. When the clue helps, there is still information in the echo; when the clue no longer helps, the echoic information must be gone (or at least enough of the sound is gone so that the clue does not help). As we would suspect, the clue is usually found to be less and less effective as more time elapses between the initial sound and the clue. It seems that sound gradually decays in echoic storage, and that is why the clue becomes gradually less useful.

Consider, for example, the experience of a subject listening to a word in a noisy background that obscures it, much as static obscures the sound of a radio broadcast (Pollack, 1959). The subject cannot immediately identify the word because of the noise. Some time after the word is presented, the subject is given a two-alternative, forced-choice recognition test. That is, he is shown two words, the one that he heard and a distractor, and asked to identify the one he heard. One of the words on the

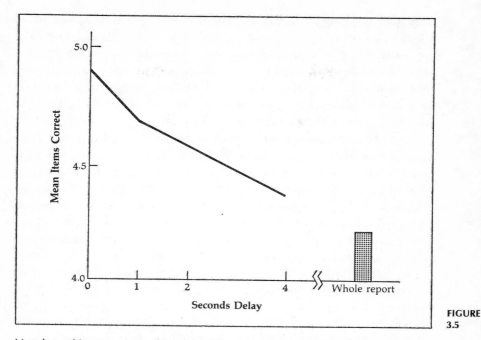

FIGURE
3.5

Number of items reported in a partial-report task with auditory stimuli, as a function of the delay of the signal to report. Also shown is the performance in the whole-report task for the same material. [From Darwin, Turvey and Crowder, 1972.]

recognition test serves as the clue discussed above. It should assist in identification of the initial word to the extent the subject can remember something about the sound he heard.

In this experiment and others similar in form (e.g., Crossman, 1958; Guttman and Julesz, 1963) the maximum delay at which the clue helps—and therefore the estimate of echoic storage—ranges from 1 second to 15 minutes—quite a range. Because of such variability in the estimates, it is difficult to determine just how long sounds remain in the auditory register. When an estimate as great as 15 minutes is obtained, however, there is also some question about its validity. Note that the estimate depends on the assumption that the subject has retained a raw unidentified sound when the clue is given to him, and that he uses the clue to identify that raw sound. It is possible, however, that the subject has actually made a *partial identification* of the sound. For example, he thinks, "It started with an s-sound and seemed to have two syllables." At that point, he is no longer remembering a mere sound, but his verbal description of it, and he can easily remember the description for 15 minutes.

It is not surprising then, that when he is much later given a clue such as "It is either 'second' or 'perform,'" he can identify the word he heard. It seems that partial identification of this sort could account for the estimates of echoic storage in the 15-minute range. On the other hand, some of the variation in estimates may actually reflect variation in the duration of true echoic storage resulting from differences in the stimuli stored and the conditions of the experiment.

In general, the duration of sensory storage for sounds appears to be greater than that of visual sensory storage. This assumption has been used to explain experiments on what are called modality effects (Crowder and Morton, 1969; Morton, 1970; Murdock and Walker, 1969). One instance of a modality effect is observed in free-recall serial-position curves. If a list of words to be recalled is presented visually (the subject sees the words), his recall differs from recall of the same list presented auditorily (he hears the words). The difference occurs in the recency portion of the serial-position curve. A greater percentage of recent words are recalled when presentation is auditory than when it is visual, but there is no such difference in the primacy portion of the curve. That is, the last several items in the list are better recalled when the list is heard rather than seen. That is the modality effect: the difference in recall corresponding to a difference in the modality (auditory or visual) of presentation.

The modality effects in recall have been interpreted by reference to a difference in the durations of echoic and iconic storage. The argument proposes that for recall of the most recent items in the list, information can be retrieved from the echo if the list was presented in auditory form. (That is because the information about those items' sound persists for several seconds; lasting through the interval between their presentation and recall.) However, iconic information about the same items presented visually does not persist long enough to form any basis for recall. This results in a clear advantage for auditory presentation.

This explanation of modality effects receives some support from data obtained when the presentation rates of lists of items are varied (Murdock and Walker, 1969): greater differences between the auditory and visual presentation modalities are found at fast rates than at slow rates. This is what an explanation of modality effects in terms of the sensory registers would lead us to expect. For at rates that are fast (relative to slow rates), less time elapses between the presentation of an item and its recall; there is thus less time for an item to decay; thus, more items will be represented in the echo when recall of an auditory list begins; and this leads to an advantage for the recall of those items. In contrast, since presentation rates do not greatly affect storage in the icon (partly because iconic information decays so fast, and partly because at fast rates, successive visual stimuli may erase those that preceded them), there is no increase at fast rates in the contribution of the icon toward recall of visually presented lists. Thus, we find a greater advantage for the auditory modality over the visual at fast rates.

The preceding argument about modality effects implies that several words from a free-recall list can be represented in the echo at one time. But that further implies that each new word does not erase the words that preceded it, and leads us to the question of whether echoic erasure exists. The answer to the question depends on what we are willing to accept as erasure. If, by erasure, we mean something equivalent to the visual phenomenon—the actual replacement of one stimulus by another that follows it—the answer is probably no. That is, it does not seem to be true that a sound that follows immediately upon the presentation of some other sound effectively eliminates the first. We already have noted that because sounds occur over time, there must be some mechanism for their preservation. In the same way, the fact that sounds take time to occur must mean that new sounds do not erase just-presented sounds. If they did, we would not be able to understand "seal, not zeal." We would also not be able to hear speech, for even single syllables take some time to produce, and we could not afford for the later portion to erase the first.

On the other hand, there does seem to be an erasure-like phenomenon that affects the echo. To a certain extent, the presentation of new sounds can mask or decrease the storage of previously presented sounds (Massaro, 1972). It seems reasonable to call this phenomenon interference to distinguish it from the quick and total erasure seen more clearly in the case of the icon. This echoic interference is similar to the effect of a light field following the letter array in Sperling's task—it shortens the duration of storage but does not instantaneously end it.

One way in which echoic interference has been demonstrated is with the stimulus-suffix effect. The stimulus-suffix effect is illustrated by the two curves in Figure 3.6. One curve shows the frequency of error for each serial position in serial recall of a brief list of items that had been presented auditorily. The other curve shows the results obtained when the redundant digit "zero" was added as a suffix to the list of items. Although the subjects did not have to respond to the zero in any way, and they knew it would occur, recall was nevertheless much worse than in the control condition, where the items were not followed by zero.

It has been argued (Morton, 1970) that the stimulus-suffix effect occurs

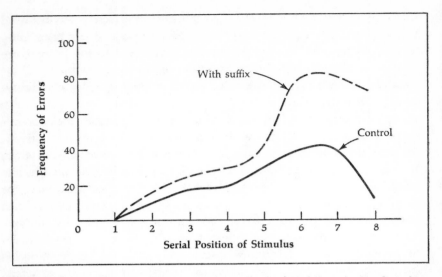

FIGURE
3.6

Effects of an auditory suffix on serial recall of a brief list of stimuli. When there is a suffix, errors increase relative to a control condition, particularly for the recent positions of the list.

because the addition of a suffix interferes with echoic storage. That is, the sound of the spoken "zero" degrades the information already in the echo, thus eliminating some echoic information which would otherwise facilitate the subject's recall of list items. In fact, the suffix reduces performance to the level of recall for a visually presented list, supporting the idea that it is the information in the echo—the very same information that produces the modality effect in recall—which is lost.

The magnitude of the interference effect of a stimulus suffix varies with the relationship of the suffix to the preceding sounds (Morton, Crowder, and Prussin, 1971). For example, if the list of items to be recalled is spoken by a male and the suffix is in a female's voice, the suffix effect is less than when both list and suffix are spoken by the same voice. Also, if the suffix is much louder than the rest of the list, the suffix effect is again reduced. These examples suggest that the interference produced is less when the sound of the suffix is different from that of the items in the list.

These interpretations of (1) modality differences and of (2) stimulus-suffix effects in terms of the echo have both been questioned. In the case of suffix effects, one problem is presented by the fact that there are also *visual* suffix effects. In studying these, Neisser and Kahneman (reported in Kahneman, 1973) had subjects recall brief lists of digits, visually presented for 0.5 seconds. Sometimes they were followed by an irrelevant, *not* to be recalled, zero. (The digit list looked like "1375260," as compared to a list like "137526," which has no suffix). In that case, a suffix effect—decrement in recall—was obtained, even though the lists were easy to see and the subjects knew they could ignore the suffix.

Unlike the auditory-suffix effects, the visual-suffix effects cannot readily be interpreted in terms of sensory storage. Kahneman (1973; p. 133) suggests that all the suffix effects occur because of post–sensory-registration processes that organize the registered inputs into groups. Because the "zero" of the suffix cannot be separated from the rest of the list by these grouping operations, particularly when it is spoken by the same voice, it must be included, and its inclusion interferes with the recall of list items. Thus, Kahneman locates the auditory-suffix effect outside of some mechanism of echoic erasure.

The interpretation of the modality effects found in recall experiments in terms of differences in the durations of the echo and the icon has also been questioned. For example, Murdock and Walker (1969) have pointed out that auditory presentation leads to superior recall for items in the last few serial positions of a list, even when the period over which those items are presented is longer than estimates of the echo's duration. Since the time-course of the modality effect is longer than that of the echo the effect cannot be entirely attributed to echoic memory.

Another problem (Watkins and Watkins, 1973) is that the modality effect occurs for the last few words in a list, regardless of whether those words are of one syllable or four syllables. That is, the serial positions where auditory–presentation superiority is found (each position corresponding to a single word) are the same, regardless of the number of syllables per word. Of course, that means that the span of the modality effect, as measured by the number of serial positions where auditory presentation leads to superior recall, is unaffected by how long it takes to auditorily present the items in those positions (since four-syllable words take longer to present than do words of just one syllable). But that finding suggests that the effect is not in an acoustic store—such as the echo—at all, for the duration of word presentation should surely have an effect on acoustic storage.

In view of the criticisms we have just discussed, it can be seen that theories of echoic storage leave us with a rather incomplete understanding of the echo. There are more general problems with research on the sensory registers as well. To illustrate this point, note that the register that we have been calling the echo has also been called Pre-categorical Acoustic Store (or PAS; Crowder and Morton, 1969). The term precategorical is important, because it implies that information held in the registers is not held there as recognized, categorized, items, but in raw, sensory form. Visually presented stimuli are held as visual patterns, auditorily presented stimuli are held as sounds, and so on. When pattern recognition occurs, the registered information will no longer be held solely in the sensory registers, and shortly after recognition has taken place it will have decayed.

That the sensory registers are precategorical deserves emphasis here, because a central problem in research relating to the registers is the separation of true effects of sensory storage from possible effects of recognized information. In Sperling's experiment, for example, the separation was accomplished by comparing the amount of information that could be held just after stimulus presentation to that stored a few seconds later. In the experiments on the echo, separation was sometimes attempted by giving subjects information they could not recognize—words embedded in noise, for example—and we have observed that there may have been a failure to confine the echoic experiments to raw, sensory data. Possible consequences of that failure may include overestimates of the duration of the echo and misinterpretations of the suffix effect.

More generally, it is often important in research on memory to determine the form, or code, in which items are stored. A single word, for example, may exist in memory as a sound, a sight, a label, or a complex set of meanings. Quite often, psychologists wish to separate the storage of information in some verbal, labeled form from some alternative code. We will see, for example, that some researchers have attempted to discriminate storage in a verbal form from storage in a visual form that is neither sensory nor verbal. It is this latter kind of storage that has been called "mental imagery." Such problems are especially important in the study of *human* memory, for humans are uniquely capable of describing sounds and sights in words. That unique ability to use language to store information enables humans to code the information in several different ways, making discrimination among the various codes an important problem for memory theorists.

4

PATTERN RECOGNITION

When you recognize a pattern, you derive meaning from a sensory experience. The process of pattern recognition is of fundamental importance to human behavior, for it is part of the interplay between the real world and the mind. For a pattern to be recognized, information in one memory store, the sensory register, must be matched with information in another memory store, LTM. The first set of information comes from a stimulus; the second set is previously acquired knowledge about the stimulus. For example, given a stimulus consisting of three lines (/ \ and –), we may recognize a letter, A. In that case, we can assign a label—a word or set of words—to the stimulus event. ("The letter ay" might be such a label.) Pattern recognition need not always mean labeling, for we can often recognize patterns and not name them. (For example, we may recognize that a face is familiar, or a certain smell may remind us of a place where we have experienced it.) In any case, information conveyed by the senses (about lines, faces, smells, or whatever) is matched with and related to what we know about the world.

It is easy to see that the study of pattern recognition is an important part of the study of memory. For one thing, it involves the study of memory stores like the sensory registers and LTM. For another, in discussing the process of recognizing patterns, we will find it is necessary to study the nature of the memorial representation—the code of information in memory. (In general, the memory "code" of some information refers to its representation in memory in an encoded form.) And in addition, we will study some of the processes that work with the memory code. That should become clearer if we consider what is essential to any model, or theory, of pattern recognition.

41

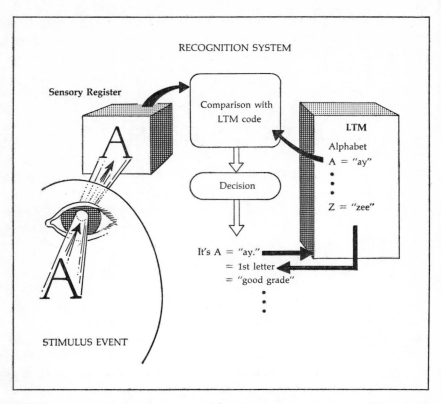

RECOGNITION SYSTEM

Sensory Register

Comparison with LTM code

LTM

Alphabet
A = "ay"
•
•
•
Z = "zee"

Decision

It's A = "ay."
= 1st letter
= "good grade"
•
•
•

STIMULUS EVENT

FIGURE
4.1

Basic components of pattern recognition: the sensory register; a comparison component, which compares sensory information with known patterns; long-term memory, in which known patterns are stored; a decision component, which chooses the best match.

A simplified basic model of pattern recognition is presented in Figure 4.1. It shows that the process of recognizing a pattern has several components. First, the stimulus to be recognized enters the sensory register. Because sensory registration is of short duration, the recognition process must be completed quickly, while the register still contains information about the stimulus. The recognition process itself involves a comparison of the incoming stimulus with codes in LTM: what that implies is that the information in LTM must be in such a form that the stimulus can be compared with it. That is, in some sense, the memory code of a stimulus in LTM must resemble, or describe the appearance or form of, the stimulus. After the stimulus is compared to codes in LTM, a decision is made as to which of the internal (LTM) codes best matches the stimulus. That decision determines the output from the recognition system—the output is the result of the decision. Once the pattern is recognized, of course, more information in LTM concerning that pattern can be evoked. Given the stimulus A, for example, once we have recognized it, we can reconstruct what we know about it—that it is the first letter of the alphabet, the word apple begins with it, it is a grade you might like to obtain, and so on.

The pattern-recognition process can now be seen as a collection of several complex subprocesses. There is the process of sensory registration, discussed in the preceding chapter. There are the processes of comparison and decision. There is also the representational problem—what is the form of the codes in LTM which are compared to an incoming stimulus? How closely does the code of a stimulus resemble the stimulus itself? In the remainder of this chapter, we shall discuss memory codes and some of the comparison and decision processes that can be postulated for pattern recognition.

MEMORY CODES AND RECOGNITION

Templates

We shall begin our discussion of memory codes with the problem of the LTM codes that are used to compare with incoming stimuli. The question is, what kind of codes are they? A code must correspond to or describe a stimulus, or otherwise it could not be used for comparison. One hypothesis we could suggest is that the LTM code is some kind of miniature copy (or "template") of the stimulus. That is, for every stimulus we recognize, there is an internal, literal copy used for recognition. According to this hypothesis, known as the template hypothesis, pattern recognition requires comparing a stimulus with a vast array of templates in LTM. Recognition occurs when the best-matching template is selected by the decision process as *the* matching template, and it determines what the pattern is recognized to be.

But such a template hypothesis is too simple—too naive to serve as the basis for a theory of pattern recognition. For one thing, too many templates would be required. Consider, for example, the recognition of one single stimulus, the letter A. Our template hypothesis stipulates that there is in LTM a copy of the letter A which is compared to it whenever it occurs as a stimulus and which will match it better than any other template. But it follows that we would need a template for every kind of A. Change the size of the stimulus? A different template is needed. If it is rotated slightly (producing a still recognizable A), another template is needed. If we draw it in some peculiar manner, such as A, we need a peculiar template to match. If we didn't have templates for all these versions of the letter A, we could expect errors in pattern recognition. For example, a tilted A might fit a template for R better than A, so we would recognize R when A occurred. To avoid such errors, we would need an immense number of templates, undoubtedly more than LTM could hold.

It is possible to modify the template hypothesis so that it does a much better job. One modification is to add a process to the model, one that occurs prior to comparisons and acts to "clean up" the stimulus input. Such a precomparison processor might act on the stimulus to bring it into a standard orientation and a standard size. This is called "normalizing" the stimulus, for it reduces the irregularities and brings it into a more normal form. For example, if the stimulus looked like A, normalizing would reorient it, reduce it in size, and straighten out the bend on the right; all of this *before* it was compared to a template. Such a process would greatly reduce the number of templates required to recognize an A.

However, a precomparison process that normalizes the stimulus will not solve all our template hypothesis's problems. A logical objection can be raised: in order to know the appropriate orientation and size, must you not *already* know what pattern the stimulus represents? For example, should a stimulus which looks like this: Q, be in this orientation: P, or this one Q? In one case, it looks like a P; in the other, like a Q. In order to know which orientation is appropriate, you must first decide which it is. But that is what the pattern-recognition system is supposed to do, not the precomparison processor. However, this logical problem is not difficult to deal with. For one thing, gross departures from standard orientation would probably result in a truly unrecognizable stimulus. That is, there is no need to postulate that the preprocessor must be able to deal with the stimulus Q, when in fact that is the sort of stimulus that the recognition system could not handle. Moreover, stimuli to be recognized usually occur in some larger *context*, and the stimulus context can help the normalizing process by indicating what the proper orientation or size of a stimulus might be.

More generally, the context greatly aids the recognition process by reducing the number of patterns the stimulus might match. Context effects also help to solve problems like that of the novel stimulus. How do we recognize a stimulus like A, when we have never seen it before? Obviously, we can't have a template in LTM that corresponds to it. Again, what we recognize A to be depends on when and where it occurs.

If it occurs in a discussion of recognizing letters of the alphabet, it might be recognized as an A, whereas if it occurred in this cartoon,

it would not seem much like an A.

Prototypes

Context effects may help to deal with some of the difficulties with the template hypothesis, but they cannot completely solve the problem. The fact is that many stimuli we can recognize do not occur in a special context, and we can still recognize them in spite of variations in size or orientation. It therefore seems necessary to have a template system that allows some variation, or "slop" in patterns coming into it. That is, the recognizer must be able to perform despite minor variations which might remain after some clean-up operation. When you introduce variable patterns into the recognizer, the literal template system becomes more like what is called a prototype, or schema, system.

A schema is simply a set of rules for producing or describing a prototype, which, as the term is used here, is an abstract form that represents the basic elements of a set of stimuli. For example, we might think of the prototypical airplane as a long tube with two wings attached, with all airplanes being some variant of the prototype. A prototypical representation, in other terms, is an essence, a central or average tendency, even a Platonic ideal. According to the prototype hypothesis of pattern recognition, what are stored in LTM are prototypes—central, ideal representatives of sets of stimuli. In theory, any stimulus can be encoded as a prototype plus a list of variations, and incoming stimuli can then be compared to prototypes rather than templates. (Thus, the concept of prototypes replaces that of templates here.) What this suggests is that you have in LTM prototypes of all the categories you recognize—dogs, people's faces, or the letter A—enabling you to recognize unique members of those categories.

Do prototypes exist? There is some experimental evidence that they do; that is, that prototypes are formed for sets of stimuli. For example, Posner and Keele (1968) conducted an experiment in which subjects performed as if they had learned prototypes. First, Posner and Keele constructed prototypical patterns of nine dots each. In some instances, the

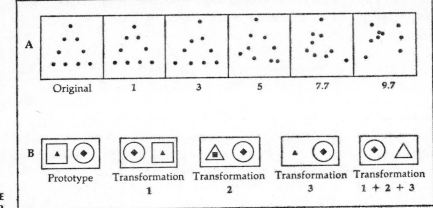

FIGURE
4.2

(A) A prototype pattern—a triangle composed of dots—and distortions of the pattern (increasing in distortion from left to right) as used by Posner and Keele (1968). [From Posner, Goldsmith, and Welton, 1967.] (B) Prototype form and transformations of that form. [From Franks and Bransford, 1971. Copyright 1967, 1971 by the American Psychological Association.]

nine dots formed a geometric pattern such as a triangle; in others, the dots formed a letter; and in still others, the dots were placed in a random pattern. Then Posner and Keele constructed new patterns, which were distortions of the prototypes, by moving some of the dots around a bit (Figure 4.2a). Sometimes the dots were moved in one direction, sometimes the other, so that the original prototype was equivalent to the pattern that would be formed by placing each dot in the position it occupied on the average in the distortions. Having formed prototypes and several distortions of each, the authors had groups of subjects learn about them. Let's consider the case where the prototypes were random collections of dots; the distortions would, of course, also be random sets. Subjects were first shown four distortions of each of three random-dot prototypes, one at a time. The subjects were supposed to classify each distortion; that is, indicate in which of three categories it belonged. All the distortions corresponding to a single prototype were to be put in the same category; however, the subjects were *not* shown any of the prototypes. Eventually the subjects learned to classify the patterns correctly, that is, they learned to classify all the distortions of one prototype into a common category, all distortions of another prototype in another common category, and so on. Next, the subjects were given a new classification task. They were shown a series of patterns and asked to classify each as a member of one of the three categories learned previously.

Some of the patterns were those that the subjects had already seen (old distortions), some were new distortions of the same prototypes, and some were the prototypes themselves, which had not previously been seen by the subjects. The old distortions were, not surprisingly, classified quite well—with 87% accuracy. More surprisingly, the prototypes were classified about equally well, even though they had never been seen. But the new distortions, those the subjects were seeing for the first time but were not prototypical, were classified less well—with about 75% accuracy. Since the prototypes were classified so well, the authors suggested that in the course of learning to classify the first set of distortions, the subjects actually learned the prototypes. In other words, the subjects abstracted a central or average tendency—a prototypical representation—from a set of stimuli which were variations of it.

Related experiments offer still more evidence for prototype theory. In one, Franks and Bransford (1971) constructed prototypes by combining several geometric forms (a triangle, a circle, a star, etc.) into structured groupings (Figure 4.2b). Distortions were then formed by applying one or more transformations to the prototypes. For example, a transformation could consist of deleting one geometric form from the group, another of substituting one form for another, and so on. Subjects were first shown some of the distorted patterns and then given a recognition test. In the test, they were shown a series of patterns—some distortions they had seen, some they had not seen, and the prototypes—and asked to indicate for each whether or not they recognized it. For each recognition, they also indicated how confident they were of having seen or not seen that particular pattern in the originally viewed set. The confidence ratings indicated that subjects were most "confident" of having seen the prototypes, even though they had *not* been shown them during the first part of the experiment. Moreover, for any pattern, the subject's rating on the test was predictable from its degree of transformation from a prototype. The prototypes were most confidently "recognized"; patterns differing from them by one transformation were next most confidently recognized, and so on. The originally seen distortions were recognized no better than new (previously unseen) distortions with the same number of transformations of the prototype!

What these experiments seem to suggest is that experience with a set of related patterns leads to the development of a prototypical representation of that set. Subjects are said to abstract the prototype from the patterns they see. The Franks and Bransford experiment also suggests that subjects may use those prototypes when they identify new patterns. In that experiment, the degree to which the prototype was distorted, or transformed, determined whether or not a pattern was recognized—whether or not it had actually been presented earlier was irrelevant. More generally, according to the prototype hypothesis of pattern recognition, people store in LTM prototypical patterns for every class of information —prototypical letters, faces, or random dot patterns. When a new pattern is presented, it is compared with the prototypes, not with the expectation of an exact (template) match but rather an approximate match, that allows for some variation in the stimulus. The most closely matching prototype determines what the pattern is recognized to be. Such a hypothesis, including the notion of precomparison processing, represents a great improvement over the naive template proposal.

Features

Up to this point, we have been discussing pattern recognition without defining the word "pattern"—a notable omission. According to one definition (Zusne, 1970), a pattern is a configuration of several elements that belong together. Such a definition implies that any pattern may be broken down into more basic subcomponents, or features, and that when those subcomponents are put back together, there is the pattern. For example, we might think of the letters of the alphabet as being composed of such basic features as vertical lines, horizontal lines, 45° lines, and curves: the letter A might thus be represented as / plus \ plus –. Those features, appropriately combined, make up the pattern A. In general, the idea of basic features implies that a relatively small set of features, combined in various ways, can be used to construct all the patterns in some larger set (such as the printed letters of the alphabet).

Another example of a set of patterns that might be composed of features is found in human speech. Speech comprises basic units of sound, called phonemes, analogous to the letters which make up visually presented words. A phoneme can be defined as a sound which by itself can change the meaning of a word. For example, the sounds corresponding to b, p, and g in the following words—but, putt, and gut—are different phonemes because the use of each sound changes the word which is spoken. On the other hand, a single phoneme corresponds to a wide range of sounds, for each speaker pronounces it just a bit differently—and yet we can recognize the same phoneme spoken by different people. What all this means is that we can think of the phoneme as a unit of speech, a concept which encompasses many "sloppy" examples. In that way, it is not unlike a hand-written letter whose shape varies from person to person, and from one writing to another, but is still recognizable.

The problem of finding a set of features that can be used, in different combinations, to make up phonemes (as one might try to use lines, curves, and angles as the basis for printed letters) is extremely difficult, but several attempts have been made. One method examines the production of sounds, attempting to describe each speech-sound according to the way people use their vocal apparatus in producing it. That vocal apparatus includes the tongue, the nose, the teeth and lips, the vocal cords, and the muscles of the diaphragm.

For example, consider the sounds of *s* and *z*. Try saying each, and you may notice that in saying *z* your voice seems to emanate from your throat, whereas the sound of *s* is produced solely in your mouth. This difference between the production of the sounds of *s* and *z* is called voicing. The *s* is unvoiced; the *z* is voiced, meaning that when you say a *z* your vocal cords vibrate whereas during the production of *s* they do not. The two sounds are said to differ by a single feature (voicing). Of course, there are many other features of speech. These include tongue position (forward in the mouth, in the middle, or in the back), whether air passes through the nose or does not, and so on. There is supposedly a unique combination of such features—a specific configuration of the vocal apparatus—which produces each phoneme. What the articulatory-feature analysis of speech attempts to do is to find the set of vocal components which describes each separate phoneme.

Although attempts can be made to specify distinctive features for speech or the printed alphabet, so far no attempt has been thoroughly successful, although some have been moderately so. Nonetheless, the idea that patterns can be described in terms of some basic set of features is intriguing. A fairly detailed specification of the phonemes of English in terms of distinctive features has been proposed (Jakobson, Fant, and Halle, 1961), and distinctive features for limited printed alphabetic sets can be stipulated (Rumelhart, 1971). For example, the alphabet can be described solely in terms of vertical and horizontal lines, if we allow our letters to look like ⊓, ⊟, ⊏, ...

So far, we have considered a naive template hypothesis and found it woefully inadequate. However, we have seen that with the addition of preprocessing—slight modification of the input stimulus to bring it into standard size and orientation—and the concept of the prototype, a hypothesis which is a great improvement over the template system can be formed. Another alternative to the template hypothesis, now to be considered, is the feature hypothesis. This holds that the stimulus to be recognized is first analyzed in terms of its features. A list of features is compiled as the result of the analysis; features which, if combined, would

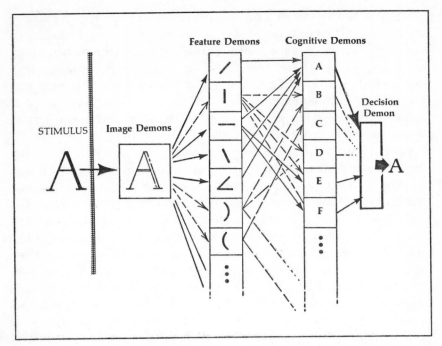

FIGURE
4.3

Selfridge's Pandemonium model of pattern recognition: The stimulus is registered by image demons. Feature demons analyze it to see what features are present. Cognitive demons compare the features to their patterns. A decision demon decides which pattern has occurred.

make up the stimulus. The list is compared to lists in LTM. Thus, this theory holds that the LTM code for a given stimulus is a list of features rather than a template or prototype. The best-matching list is obtained, and the pattern is recognized.

One version of the feature hypothesis is called Pandemonium (Selfridge, 1959). The Pandemonium model is depicted in Figure 4.3. Like our general model (Figure 4.1), it shows that patterns are recognized in stages, or levels. At each level are a set of "demons," who work on the pattern recognition in some way. At the very first level are image demons, who do what we have been calling sensory registration; that is, they record the stimulus as a sensory event. Then, that event is analyzed by feature demons, who break down the pattern into its component features. Each such demon represents a single feature—such as a line at a certain angle, or a curve—and it registers if its feature is present. The feature demons are observed by cognitive demons, who correspond to feature lists. Each cognitive demon's list represents a certain pattern, and the demon's job is to "yell," or signal, as loudly as is justified by how well he is indicated by the feature analysis. That is, a cognitive demon looks at the number of responding feature demons which correspond to features in its list, and it yells loudly if it finds many such feature demons, less loudly if there are fewer. Sitting above all of this is a decision demon (the decision process), who decides which cognitive demon is yelling the loudest, and thereby recognizes the pattern.

If all this has a ring of familiarity it is not surprising, since the feature hypothesis is very similar to the template hypothesis. What is a feature, if not a template? Here, the template corresponds to some part of a stimulus rather than the whole. The advantage of the feature hypothesis is that if a set of features can be obtained which describes a much larger set of patterns (as it could, for example, if we could describe speech in terms of a few basic features), there are many fewer templates to work with. On the other hand, the similarity of the feature hypothesis to the template hypothesis brings with it a host of similar problems.

For example, how would a feature system handle variations in the size of a visual feature? How would novel stimuli, never seen before, be recognizable? What would happen when two stimuli differ only by the presence or absence of a single feature? (An example is the lower line in E which is absent in F. Here, two lists of features in LTM might match the stimulus F, because every feature of F would match features in lists corresponding to both E and F.) In the case of speech recognition, there are even greater complexities. For one thing, it is not always possible to determine just where a unit of speech begins or ends, making the analysis of a pattern into features rather difficult. This is clear when we listen to someone speaking in an unfamiliar language. He seems to speak with incredible speed, and it is next to impossible to tell where one word ends and another begins. In fact, when we listen carefully, we find that speakers of English often pause longer in the middle of a word than between two words.

At this point, there is no definitive solution to all of these problems for a pattern recognizer. That does not mean that the feature hypothesis for pattern recognition should be abandoned, however. After all, alternative hypotheses also have their limitations. Moreover, there is some experimental evidence that a feature-matching process is used for recognizing patterns.

Some of the evidence for the role of features in pattern recognition is physiological. It stems from research indicating that the visual system contains specialized cells whose function it is to recognize particular features. In the past decade or so, physiologists (Hubel and Weisel, 1962; Lettvin, Maturana, McCulloch, and Pitts, 1959) have discovered nerve cells in the visual systems of cats, frogs, and other animals which fire (respond) only when a particular pattern of visual stimulation occurs. Such patterns include horizontal lines, vertical lines, and moving lines. In the frog's brain, cells have been found that fire when moving black dots appear in the visual field; the suggestion has been made that these are bug-detector cells, firing so that the frog can catch his dinner! There is an obvious analogy between the patterns that set off specialized neurons and what we have been calling features. In humans, it might be surmised, there may be cells that fire when specific features appear and that serve as the feature-analyzers for incoming visual stimuli. Moreover, some cells seem to fire independently of specific stimulus characteristics like length. Thus, these cells seem to detect more abstract features (such as a line of any length at a particular angle), and may help to explain why patterns can be recognized despite transformations such as variations in size.

There is other evidence for the importance of features in visual pattern recognition. Young children, for example, often call *b* and *d* by the same name. This may reflect an inability to distinguish between two features— C and ⊃ , say—differing only in their orientation. In adults, a similar effect is obtained if visual stimuli are presented so rapidly that perception may be incomplete. This kind of experiment leads to confusions similar to those found in experiments on the memory span. When a letter, for example, is presented very briefly and the subject is asked to report what it was, he may make a confusion error—the substitution of some other letter in his report. Unlike memory-span confusions, which seem to follow patterns of acoustic similarity, the errors in the experiment just described follow visual patterns (Kinney, Marsetta, and Showman, 1966). Here, D is much more likely to be reported when Q is presented than when B is presented. The D and Q share visual features, whereas the B and D are acoustically similar but visually dissimilar. These confusions may be used to infer that the process of perceiving letters deals with visual features.

From the preceding discussions, it seems that there is evidence both for the formation of prototypes and for the use of features. We have also seen that both prototype and feature hypotheses seem to explain many of the same things about pattern recognition, and to leave many of the same problems unanswered. So which approach is better? At this point, the answer to that question is unclear. There may be room for both hypotheses, for the variety of patterns we recognize may call for different mechanisms of pattern recognition. Then, too, what we call prototypes and features may not be as different as they appear. For one thing, the two ideas can be combined: we can consider a prototype to consist of the features common to all instances of a pattern; the idea of prototypes can thus be as consistent with features as it is with templates. It is also important to recognize that at some level, a feature hypothesis is very like a template hypothesis. One problem in stating a feature hypothesis is that of describing how individual features, like lines of a given angle, are recognized. The answer to that problem may call for a comparison process that matches the feature with an internal template. Thus, we would have a template theory of feature recognition! These considerations illustrate some of the problems with attempting to specify exactly what type of LTM code is used in pattern recognition. Although we may not be able to specify the code exactly, in our discussion of it we have come quite a way from a naive template hypothesis. And in doing so, we have gained some important insights into the recognition process.

RECOGNITION PROCESSES

One topic which has not yet been discussed in any detail is the comparison/decision process of pattern recognition. Consider the template hypothesis. A pattern must be compared with a great number of templates; then the template that best matches the pattern can be selected. It immediately becomes apparent that with all the templates there must be in memory, such a comparison process would be immense. Thousands and thousands of templates would have to be compared before a decision could be made—how could it be done? If the recognizer had to compare the pattern with one template at a time, one after another, it would surely take a very long time to recognize some stimuli—and the same argument applies if "prototypes" or "feature lists" is substituted for "templates." Yet we know that pattern recognition proceeds very quickly.

Serial Versus Parallel Processing

One answer to this question may be that the recognizer does not compare LTM codes to new patterns one after another. The one-after-another process has a name—it is called a *serial* process. The label "serial" derives from series, because the process involves a series of comparisons. The alternative to serial comparisons is called a *parallel* process. The label "parallel" derives from the geometric meaning, referring to two or more separate lines that go on together side by side. That's just what parallel comparisons are like—many separate comparisons going on at once. In pattern recognition, what this means is that a stimulus could be compared to many internal codes at the same time, the whole process taking no longer than a single such comparison. In this fashion, comparisons could proceed very quickly.

Parallel comparisons sound like a potential answer to the problem of saving time during the comparison stage, and we do know of such parallel processes in the physical world. One example (Neisser, 1967) is found in the use of tuning forks. If we take a tuning fork of unknown frequency and strike it (so that it hums) and hold it near a group of forks of known frequency, then one of the known forks will also begin to hum. The fork that hums matches the frequency of the unknown fork: no other fork will hum. In that way we can determine the unknown frequency. That is a parallel-comparison process, for the unknown fork is tested against all the known forks simultaneously.

Experimental evidence for parallel activity in psychological processes has also been found. One example comes from Neisser's (1964) visual-search experiments. In those experiments, subjects were confronted with lists of letters 50 lines long. On each line were several letters, like U F C J. Each subject was instructed to start at the top line and find some target letter, designated by the experimenter, as rapidly as possible. The target was placed at a randomly determined position in the list, and the subject pressed a button when he found it. The total search time, the time between his first seeing the list and finding the target, was recorded. Neisser (Neisser, Novick, and Lazar, 1963) found that when well-practiced subjects were given *ten* targets and asked to respond when they found the one that was present, they responded just as quickly as when they had only one target to consider. That result argues against a serial-search process. For if the subject looked for ten targets sequentially, scanning the entire list for one, then another, it should take him much longer (on the average) to find the target that was present than it would take when he was looking for a single letter. Instead, it seems that the subjects could search the list for ten targets at once—a parallel search.

The visual search tasks also indicated that the speed with which the subjects found the target depended to some extent on how different the target was from the rest of the list. For example, subjects could find a target z hidden in a list made up from the letters o, d, u, g, q, and r, faster than they could find a z hidden in a list composed of i, v, m, x, e, and w. The former list contains curved letters, which resemble the target z much less than the latter list, composed of angular letters. From this, Neisser argued that the subjects were not using a template of the target for comparison with list letters, but that instead they searched for critical features within the list. An angular feature, such as from a z, would be much easier to find in a list of curved letters than among angular letters, so that search times would be affected by the overall appearance of the letters in the list.

In theorizing about these results, Neisser took advantage of the Pandemonium model of Selfridge's that we have previously discussed. Selfridge's model assumes that pattern recognition is in some sense sequential or serial, because one process must follow another (cognitive demons must follow feature demons, and so on). However, parallel processes occur in the Pandemonium model at each level: all the cognitive demons examine the feature demons and yell at the same time, for example.

Context Effects

Parallel processes are only one way—but a good one—of confronting the problem we have proposed. Our problem is how the comparison and decision processes can operate fast enough for patterns to be quickly recognized, given the size of the job they have to do. With parallel processes, recognition can be fast because many operations can go on at the same time, saving time over a sequential process. Another way to save time is to reduce the magnitude of the comparison process—reduce the number of patterns that might match the given stimulus and thereby the number of templates or feature lists to which the stimulus must be compared. At first, this approach to the comparison problem may seem logically impossible. After all, how can we reduce the set of LTM codes to compare to a stimulus without already knowing what the stimulus is? Once again, the answer to that question lies in the effects of context.

In general, the context in which a stimulus occurs is immensely important in determining its ultimate classification. There can be a great number of patterns eliminated from consideration if we know which patterns are likely to occur in the current context of recognition. For example, if we are attempting to recognize the mumbled word in "To be or not to be, that is the *mumble*," and if we hear something that sounds like "session," we will probably be easily able to recognize the mumble as "question." This could occur even if the stimulus itself sounded more like "session" than "question." Thus, the context, in this case a well-known quotation, restricts the number of patterns that are relevant at the site of the mumble, making recognition possible despite an ambiguous input. Context acts to reduce the number of possible patterns the stimulus might match, thus lessening the demands on the system.

Context effects are often found in psychological research. One example is found in experiments that show that a visually presented letter is easier to identify when it is presented within a word than when it is presented by itself (Reicher, 1969; Wheeler, 1970). It has been suggested (Wheeler, 1970) that the word provides a context for the letter, and one effect of the context is to direct the feature-analysis process. For if one letter in the word is identified, the very fact that it is in a word restricts the possible identities of the other letters. That means that some features can be checked while others can be eliminated without being checked.

Similar effects are found when spoken words are identified. In an experiment by Miller, Heise, and Lichten (1951) that showed this, the subjects had to identify words that were heard against a background of noise. When the words formed meaningful sentences, they were much more readily identified than when they were arranged into random strings: the context formed by the sentence facilitated the recognition of the words. It has similarly been suggested (Miller, 1962) that in recognizing speech, we ordinarily recognize whole groups of phonemes—whole words or even phrases—all at once. That implies that decisions can be interdependent and a decision about one phoneme can provide a context for the categorization of other sounds. The same sort of effect can occur when the letters of a printed word are identified in reading. Recognition may not be letter-by-letter but may occur at the level of several letters or words (Smith and Spoehr, 1974), so that even the context of partially recognizing one letter facilitates recognition of others.

The addition of context effects to a pattern-recognition hypothesis makes it much more powerful. We can begin to see how it is possible for us to recognize a pattern with such facility. So far, our discussion has indicated some of the characteristics of an adequate theory of the process. At this point, having considered memory codes and comparison processes, we will turn to a new aspect of pattern recognition. That is the relationship between pattern recognition and attention.

ATTENTION

In an earlier chapter, it was noted that the term "attention" has more than one meaning. One of those meanings will be especially pertinent to our discussion, and it is the one referred to as "selective" attention. Selective attention was illustrated in the context of the cocktail-party phenomenon. It refers to the capacity to tune in certain sources of information, to select certain channels for processing, and to reject, or tune out, others.

Shadowing Experiments

Selective attention has been extensively studied in experiments with dichotic listening and shadowing. Dichotic listening refers to hearing two channels of sound at once. You may recall, from Chapter 3, that a channel is a source of sound. In a typical dichotic-listening-and-shadowing experiment, a subject listens to two spoken messages on two channels, one coming to each ear via headphones. The subject is asked to listen to one of the messages and to "shadow" it (that is, to repeat the words in the message as he hears them). Surprisingly, subjects have little trouble shadowing one message while listening to two. They tune out the unshadowed message and attend to the one they are shadowing.

Dichotic-listening-and-shadowing effects were extensively studied by Cherry (1953). One of his interests was to find out what became of the unattended, unshadowed message. It suffered from being tuned out; nevertheless, certain characteristics of the unattended message came through. For example, the subject did know something about the unattended message: that it occurred (some sound was there), and whether it was human speech or some nonspeech sound, like a buzz. Subjects also noticed when the unshadowed message changed from a male voice to a female voice. On the other hand, the subject could not report any of the specific meaningful content of the unshadowed message. He could not tell whether it was actual speech or nonsense speech-sound, what language was spoken, or whether the language changed in the course of the experiment. He did not know any of the words, even if one word was repeated over and over (Moray, 1959).

Dichotic listening and shadowing is an experimental version of the cocktail-party phenomenon. It is a useful procedure with which to study attention, for in order to perform the task, the subject must selectively attend to one channel, the one shadowed, and not the other. The experimental results have given rise to several models of attention, for they provide some of the critical data that such models have to explain. In particular, a theory of attention must explain *how* just one channel can be focused on and not others. It must also explain what happens to the information in the unattended channel.

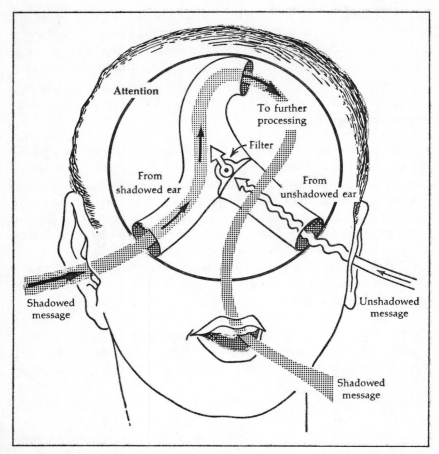

FIGURE
4.4

The dichotic-listening-and-shadowing task as viewed by Broadbent's filter model. The filter selects one message for further processing on the basis of its location, filtering out the other message.

Models of Attention

One of the best-known theoretical models of attention is Broadbent's (1958) filter model. It proposes that selective attention acts like a filter, blocking out some channels and letting only one through. The blocking-out process is made possible by an analysis of the incoming messages on all channels for their physical characteristics. A particular message can then be selected and attended to on a physical basis. For example (see Figure 4.4), in dichotic listening, the two messages can be discriminated on the basis of their origin in space (one on the left, one on the right).

That discrimination forms the basis for the action of the filter. What the filter does is select and tune in just one of the messages—for example, the one on the left. Similarly, a male or female voice could be selected on the basis of its pitch. This also explains why subjects know some of the physical characteristics of the unshadowed message in a dichotic listening experiment. They know them because the physical analysis takes place prior to the filtering.

Broadbent's filter model was shown to be inadequate by experiments demonstrating that attention can jump back and forth between channels to follow the meaning of a message. This can be seen, for example, if we split up a continuous input between the two ears. We could send the message "mice eat cheese" by sending the first and third words to the right ear, and "eat" to the left. At the same time, another message could be split up in the alternate ears. For example, the digit "three" could be spoken to the left ear at the same time "mice" is spoken to the right, the digit "five" could be spoken to the right as the left hears "eat", and the digit "nine" could be spoken to the left ear as the right hears "cheese". Under these conditions (Gray and Wedderburn, 1960), subjects tend to follow the meaningful content of "mice eat cheese," even though it alternates between the two ears, rather than sticking with a single ear and reporting something like "mice five cheese." What that indicates is that attention follows something other than physical characteristics of the input—namely, it follows meaningful sequences.

Similarly, Triesman (1960) has shown that in dichotic listening, the subject's shadowing sometimes follows the message. (See Figure 4.5.) For example, if a subject is shadowing a message coming to the right ear, and if that message suddenly jumps to the left, changing ears with the unshadowed message, then the subject's response may also jump to the left ear. The subject may persist in shadowing the message when it jumps ears, even though he is instructed to continuously shadow the right-ear channel. Thus, the shadowing follows meaning rather than location.

Because of such results, an interpretation of attention as based solely on physical characteristics of the stimulus must be faulty. To compensate for such problems, Broadbent's model was subsequently modified by Triesman (1969), who proposed that attention acts more like an attenu-ator—something that turns down the volume on unattended channels without blocking them out. She proposed that all incoming signals undergo a series of preliminary tests. The tests first analyze the inputs on the basis of rather gross physical characteristics, but there are also more refined tests that can analyze an input in terms of its content. After

FIGURE
4.5

Result of Triesman's shadowing experiment: subjects failed to shadow one ear consistently when the content of the shadowed and unshadowed messages suddenly switched from one ear to the other.

these tests, attention can be directed to one of the channels. The tests determine what is attended to and what is not, because the particular channel that is selected for attention is determined by what the preliminary analysis has revealed. Thus, if I am listening to a message about mice on one channel, and if that same message suddenly continues on a different channel, the preliminary tests will indicate that fact, enabling me to switch channels to the new channel to follow the message.

The problem with Triesman's analysis is that the preliminary tests can become so refined that we find ourselves claiming that a message which has already been analyzed for its meaning has not yet been attended to. This raises the question: can we recognize patterns (as we must, to extract their meaning) before we attend to them?

The relationship between pattern recognition and attention has been made explicit by Norman (1969), following a proposal of Deutsch and Deutsch (1963). Norman's model proposes that all channels impinging on the processing system get some analysis—enough to activate a representation in LTM. (In terms of the Pandemonium model, we might say that all stimuli are analyzed by the feature demons, which arouses some of their counterpart cognitive demons.) At that point, selective attention takes effect, for selective attention corresponds to the full recognition of attended-to patterns. (In Pandemonium terms, cognitive demons that could possibly correspond to incoming patterns are aroused, but only some are recognized.) According to Norman, recognizing a pattern corresponds to attending to it. Context plays an important part in all this, for which patterns are recognized depends on which are most probable in the present context.

Neisser (1967) has similarly related pattern recognition to attention. His theory states that all incoming information undergoes preliminary analysis by "pre-attentive processes." Then, the final recognition of a stimulus can occur only when attention is devoted to it. That is, attention *is* full recognition.

Neisser's theory is of special interest because the nature of the LTM code it postulates is one we have not thus far considered. His idea of the LTM code is derived from "analysis-by-synthesis," a model of speech perception devised by Halle and Stevens (1959; 1964). This model proposes a rather radical notion: namely, that recognizing a pattern of speech is fundamentally the same thing as producing it. We might summarize this notion as follows: First, what is stored in LTM for comparison with an incoming stimulus is not some copy of the stimulus or its features, but a set of rules for producing it. Second, these rules are used to synthesize, or construct, an internal pattern for comparison with the stimulus. Third, context plays an important part in this synthesizing process, because it is used to select some small set of patterns for synthesis. Those patterns are the ones hypothesized as most likely to occur in the present context. In short, pattern recognition includes a process of active stimulus construction. This construction is certainly not random; it is guided by the situation in which the stimulus occurs. The guided construction uses a set of rules stored in LTM. (Thus, this theory suggests that the LTM code used in recognition is a set of rules for producing an internal copy of the stimulus.) The internal stimulus so produced, or synthesized, is compared to the external stimulus, and that comparison determines recognition. In Neisser's theory, then, the process of synthesizing the internal pattern is the same as attention.

A GENERAL MODEL OF PATTERN RECOGNITION

From our discussion of pattern recognition, we have been able to determine some of the basic components of that process. At this point, it seems reasonable to attempt to delineate these basic components and to attempt to integrate them into some general model of pattern recognition. What would we need in such a model? First of all, we would have to have all the components presented in Figure 4.1—representation, or registration, of the stimulus; some internal (LTM) codes to compare it to; and comparison and decision processes. We should also include mechanisms incorporating context effects in pattern recognition. This is particularly important because context can serve to greatly reduce the number of patterns needed in the comparison process. Next, we come to the question of the nature of the LTM code used in comparing patterns. We do not have evidence clearly indicating what kind of code it is; thus, we cannot specify any particular one of the types of codes we have discussed (prototypes or feature lists or rules).

Let us include in our model a mechanism for the preliminary analysis of the stimulus. That preliminary analysis would be guided by context. It could correspond to the precomparison standardization process proposed to correct the naive template hypothesis, or alternatively it could correspond to the feature analysis in Pandemonium-like models. Finally, let's consider context itself. In order to bring context effects into the model, we must include a "feedback" mechanism that provides information about previous recognitions to be used when it comes to recognizing the present stimulus. And let us give the recognition process the capacity to work on several patterns at once—that brings in the idea that recognition of speech does not act at the level of the single phoneme, and that reading is not done one letter at a time.

Figure 4.6 represents the model of the recognition process we might come up with. It shows incoming information about a stimulus (remember, it could be a set or phonemes or letters or whatever) coming into a sensory register. While the information is in the register, a preliminary analysis takes place. Features of the stimulus are noted, and the representation of the stimulus may be changed to some standard form (normalized). That preliminary analysis is affected by information about the total context of recognition, provided by feedback from just-concluded

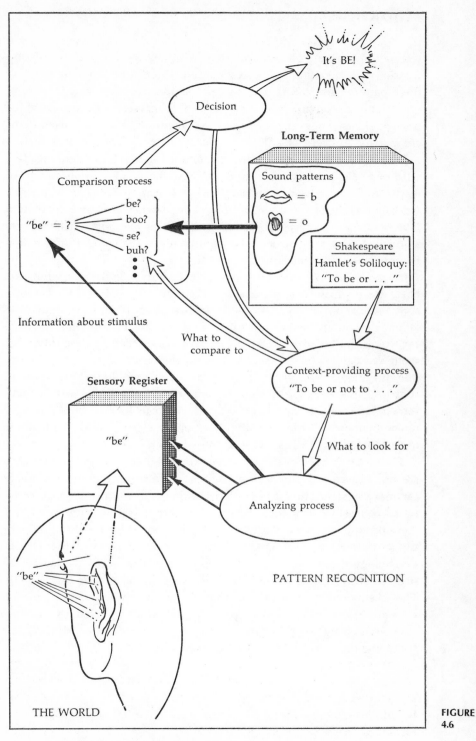

FIGURE
4.6

A general model of pattern recognition.

recognitions. Then, a set of patterns—LTM codes—is provided for comparison with the stimulus representation. We cannot stipulate whether these patterns are feature lists, templates, prototypes, produced by rules or something else; however, it seems clear that the set of codes provided does not consist of every code in LTM. The number of codes used in the comparison process is adjusted according to the context information provided. (We would not try to recognize a Hebrew letter while reading a list of English words, for example.) Then, the set of codes is compared to the analyzed stimulus; in parallel, we might suggest. At that point, a decision is made about which LTM code matches best, and the pattern is recognized as corresponding to that code. This decision is fed back into a "context-provider," which will use it to adjust the context information it provides for the recognitions that follow.

It seems that the model in Figure 4.6 includes almost everything we have gained from our discussion of pattern recognition. It also says something about the kinds of failures this type of recognizer would have. When the system makes mistakes, they will not be random, nor need they be completely predictable on the basis of feature similarity. Our model recognizes patterns not only on the basis of features that are present, but also on the basis of features which would fit in the present context. Thus, we could recognize something that was not actually presented because we expect it to occur. This can lead to the "I accept" phenomenon—at a meeting, the loser of an election may jump up to accept victory when the name of the winner is read!

The system can also fail to recognize things that do exist, because they are not expected in the present context. And of course, the recognizer can make mistakes that lead to particular kinds of confusions, such as the visual confusions that occur when letters are presented very briefly for identification. We would expect such errors to be especially prominent where contextual information is minimal, which is often the case in psychology experiments. The pattern-recognition model we have constructed seems to predict the kinds of errors humans make consistently. That seems only reasonable in a model of human pattern recognition.

In short, our discussion of pattern recognition has led us to some interesting insights, not only about recognizing external stimuli, but about the general nature of human memory.

5

STM:
SHORT-TERM
STORAGE AND
PROCESSING

In previous chapters, our discussion of human memory has been concerned with the storage of precategorical memory codes (codes that have not yet undergone pattern recognition) and how those codes are recognized, a process in which LTM codes are involved. We have followed the course of a stimulus from the "real world" as it undergoes sensory registration, is attended to, and is recognized. We can now consider what happens to those categorized memory codes. According to the general model presented in Chapter 2, what happens to at least some of them is that they are transferred to short-term memory (STM), and it is the role of short-term memory in the information-processing system that we will consider in the present chapter.

It is important to keep in mind throughout this discussion that most research on STM has been conducted with verbal material. For that reason, much more is known about STM as a storehouse for words than is known about its other characteristics. The general picture that has emerged from such research is that of an STM which holds words in an acoustic form—that is, as sounds. In this chapter and in Chapter 6, the discussion will center on STM in the verbal-acoustic capacity. In Chapter 7, we will expand the picture to include the possibility that STM can hold visual and semantic (meaningful) information.

It is also important to note that in our discussion of STM we will adopt the theoretical model presented in Chapter 2, which depicts STM and LTM as distinct memory stores. In that chapter, we noted at least three lines of evidence for the separate existence of STM, but we also noted that not all psychologists accept the duplex model. This discussion will proceed with STM as a generally accepted notion, for the concept of short-term storage serves as a useful tool in explaining some of the important phenomena of human memory.

Perhaps it will be helpful to think of STM as a workbench in a workroom where a carpenter is building a cabinet (Figure 5.1). All his materials are neatly organized on shelves around the walls of the room. Those materials that he is immediately working with—his tools, boards ready to be put into place, and so on—he brings from a shelf and places on the bench before him, leaving a space on the bench where he can work. When the bench gets too messy, he may stack his material in orderly piles, so that he can fit more onto the bench. If the number of stacks increases, some may even fall off, or the carpenter may replace some things on a shelf.

Now, how does this analogy fit our notion of a duplex system? We can think of the shelves in the workroom as LTM; the repository for the large set of material available for the carpenter's work. The bench—divided into the carpenter's work space and a limited-capacity storage area—is STM. When the carpenter stacks things in order to create more space, he is performing a process analogous to one associated with STM: chunking. (We shall see that in the process of memorizing a short list, chunking is often used to combine several items into one, which takes up the space of a single unit in STM.) Things that fall off the bench correspond to the items forgotten from STM, just as the process of bringing things from the shelves and replacing them there is akin to transfer of information from and to LTM. In order to accommodate the idea that LTM is permanent and that material is not actually *removed* from LTM when it is put into STM, we might stretch things a bit and assume that the LTM shelves contain an essentially unlimited supply of any given material, so that when the set or copy of some material is transferred to the workbench, another set still remains on the shelf.

Although it should not be pushed too far, the workbench analogy is a useful one. From it, we get an idea of STM as a rather changeable entity, in which various things may be stored and worked on. Also, we see that there is a trade-off between work space and storage space, so that more of one must mean less of the other. However, the complexities of STM involve more than placing things in stacks or on shelves.

REHEARSAL

One process associated with STM is rehearsal—the cycling of information through the memory store. We have previously considered what

FIGURE 5.1

STM seen as a workbench.

are hypothesized to be the two main functions of rehearsal: to renew information in STM so that it is not forgotten, and to transfer information about the rehearsed items to LTM, thus building up the strength of the information LTM preserves. (The question of just what LTM strength might be will be taken up in later chapters.) Thus, rehearsal might be thought of as one way in which STM is a "working memory"—rehearsal is a type of work, and is essential to both renewal and transfer. Still, it is not at all clear just how rehearsal accomplishes these functions; how it works and precisely what is rehearsed.

Rehearsal as speech

One notion about the rehearsal process is that it is some kind of speech—implicit, or subvocal. This idea is supported by the observations of Sperling (1967), who noted that a subject writing letters in an immediate-memory task often spoke the letters to himself. This tendency, noted Sperling, might reflect the nature of a more general process in STM, that of rehearsal. He suggested that in the course of rehearsing an item, the subject *said* it to himself, *heard* what he said, and then *stored* what he heard in STM—thereby restoring the item to its original strength. The "to himself" part of this description is what is called "implicit" or "subvocal." There may be no sounds actually present, but rehearsal may instead use *mental* representations of sounds, which remain unspoken.

The idea that rehearsal is implicit speech is supported in several ways. One bit of evidence comes from estimates of the rate at which rehearsal takes place. If a subject is asked to rehearse a series of letters to himself ten times, and we measure how long it takes him, we can get an idea of how fast he can rehearse, say, in terms of letters per second. If we compare this rehearsal rate to the rate of vocal, overt speech, we find that the two rates are about the same; usually about three to six letters per second (Landauer, 1962). Thus, rehearsal and speech are alike in that they take about the same amount of time to perform.

We have already mentioned other data that indicate that rehearsal is implicit speech—acoustic confusions in immediate memory experiments (Conrad, 1963; Sperling, 1960; Wickelgren, 1966). Essentially, items that sound alike are likely to be confused in STM, independently of whether they are visually similar or have similar meanings. Sperling and Speelman (1970) suggest that these confusions result because the items stored in STM are stored in acoustic form and may be forgotten phoneme (individual sound) by phoneme. At the time of recall, the subject attempts to reconstruct the items from whatever sounds remain. Thus, if he makes a mistake, his incorrect report will share sounds with the item actually presented—leading to the acoustic pattern in his confusions. In this model, rehearsal is seen as implicit speech that results in the re-entry of the sounds into STM, in a form equivalent to that of their original encoding and storage there. This model has been used with some success to predict subjects' performance in immediate-memory tasks.

Although the notion that rehearsal is implicit speech fits very nicely with the notion that STM codes are acoustic, it does not tell the whole tale. Insofar as rehearsal may be thought of as the mental representation to oneself of an item (for example, the saying to oneself of a letter), rehearsal can also be visual. For example, it is very easy to visualize the letters of the alphabet. To demonstrate this for yourself, go through the alphabet mentally and decide whether or not each letter has a vertical line (A does not, B does, and so on). This visual mental representation, which we will discuss eventually in more detail, is a kind of rehearsal (by the above definition). Estimates of its rate (for example, how long it takes to run through the alphabet visually) indicate that it takes longer than the auditory rehearsal we have referred to as implicit speech (Weber and Castleman, 1970). Does our ability to visualize mean that rehearsal may sometimes take the form of "implicit sight"?

Rehearsal and Transfer to LTM

The rehearsal concept includes more than the maintenance, or revivification, function apparently served by internal speech. It is also assumed to transfer information to LTM, thereby building up LTM strength.

What does it mean to claim that rehearsal results in the building up of strength in LTM? One attempt to answer that question was that of Rundus (Rundus, 1971; Rundus and Atkinson, 1970), who had his subjects rehearse out loud. Typically, in one of his experiments, a subject performed a free-recall task in which a list of words was presented at a rate of one word every five seconds. The subject was instructed to study the list by repeating some of the words aloud during the five-second interval between successive words. He was not told any particular words to recite; instead, he was free to choose whichever words he liked. The set of words the subject chose to speak during a particular five-second period was called his "rehearsal set" for that period (Figure 5.2a). Rundus was concerned with the relationship between the nature of the rehearsal sets and performance on the recall test that followed the list's presentation. Not surprisingly, Rundus found a strong relationship (Figure 5.2b): the more overt rehearsals (recitations) of a word, and the more rehearsal sets it appeared in, the greater the probability that the word would be recalled.

Rundus also found that the items that subjects rehearsed tended to be affected by their long-term knowledge. In particular, a newly presented word was more likely to be rehearsed if its meaning fit in with the current rehearsal set. An incoming word like SPARROW would be likely to be included in a rehearsal set already containing "robin, canary, wren," but it would probably not be rehearsed if the current rehearsal set was "bread, eggs, cheese." Thus, Rundus' work suggests that rehearsal does indeed serve the function of increasing the strength of particular items in LTM

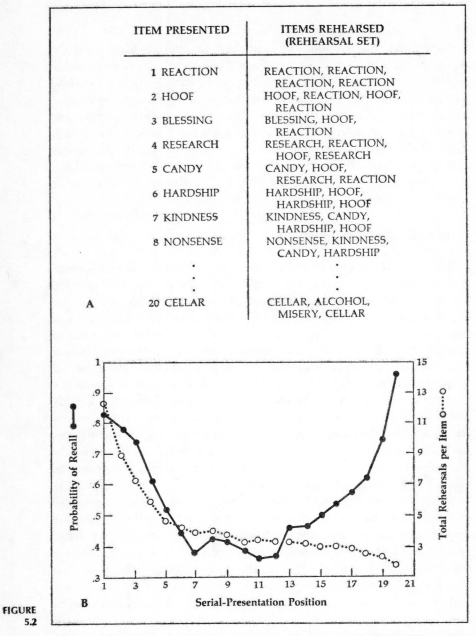

ITEM PRESENTED	ITEMS REHEARSED (REHEARSAL SET)
1 REACTION	REACTION, REACTION, REACTION, REACTION
2 HOOF	HOOF, REACTION, HOOF, REACTION
3 BLESSING	BLESSING, HOOF, REACTION
4 RESEARCH	RESEARCH, REACTION, HOOF, RESEARCH
5 CANDY	CANDY, HOOF, RESEARCH, REACTION
6 HARDSHIP	HARDSHIP, HOOF, HARDSHIP, HOOF
7 KINDNESS	KINDNESS, CANDY, HARDSHIP, HOOF
8 NONSENSE	NONSENSE, KINDNESS, CANDY, HARDSHIP
. . .	. . .
20 CELLAR	CELLAR, ALCOHOL, MISERY, CELLAR

A

B

FIGURE 5.2

(A) Examples of rehearsal sets in Rundus' experiment. The figure shows sets of items that were rehearsed as each new item was presented. (B) The relationship between rehearsal and recall for each position in the recalled list. In general, the more an item is rehearsed, the higher is its probability of recall. Items in the recency portion of the list are assumed to be recalled from short-term memory and thus not to depend on rehearsal for recall. [From R. C. Atkinson and R. M. Shiffrin, "The Control of Short-Term Memory." Copyright © 1971 by Scientific American. All rights reserved.]

(as indicated by the positive relationship between rehearsals and recall), and that organizing processes use information in LTM to determine what is to be rehearsed in STM. In general, the use of LTM to relate previously learned information to information currently being processed is called *mediation.* Thus, Rundus' work shows that rehearsal is linked to mediation.

A criticism of Rundus' experiments on rehearsal is that they are essentially correlational, because the number of rehearsals is controlled by the subject and not the experimenter. Although they show a relationship between number of rehearsals and recall, the direction of the relationship is uncertain: they do not prove that rehearsals determine recall. Instead, it is possible that subjects rehearse those items that they recall most readily and that they would recall later in any case, rather than that rehearsal is the *cause* of recall.

The possibility of drawing an alternative conclusion from Rundus' evidence for the role of rehearsal in long-term storage does not, by itself, invalidate the idea that rehearsal strengthens recall. However, there is other evidence against the notion that rehearsal necessarily results in the transfer of information to LTM. That evidence comes from experiments showing that the amount of rehearsal an item gets does not always affect later recall (Craik and Watkins, 1973; Woodward, Bjork, and Jongeward, 1973). Craik and Watkins induced subjects to hold single words in STM for varying amounts of time. In one experiment, they did so by telling the subject he should report the last word that began with a given letter in a twenty-one-word list. For example, the critical letter might be G, and the list might begin: DAUGHTER, OIL, RIFLE, GARDEN, GRAIN, TABLE, FOOTBALL, ANCHOR, GIRAFFE, . . . As he listened, the subject would hold "garden" in memory until "grain" appeared, then hold "grain" until he heard "giraffe," and so on until the last G-word in the list, which he would report when the list ended. Thus, he would hold single words in STM for varying amounts of time—"garden" much less time than "grain," for example. After twenty-seven such lists, the subject was unexpectedly asked to recall as many of the words as possible, from all lists. Craik and Watkins found that the amount of time a critical word (word beginning with the critical letter) was held in STM, defined by the number of words beginning with noncritical letters which intervened between that word and the next critical word, did not affect performance on the unexpected recall test. Thus, the amount of time a critical word was held in STM did not appear to affect its LTM strength.

In another experiment, Craik and Watkins found that the time an item was held in STM, as measured by overt rehearsals, also did not affect recall. They gave subjects a series of free-recall lists. Some lists were recalled immediately after they were presented; others were recalled twenty seconds after the last word was presented (the delayed-recall condition). The subjects were told that they *must* concentrate on recalling the last four words of each list, and were asked to rehearse aloud, if they felt rehearsal were needed. The experimenters recorded the number of rehearsals each word was given. Not surprisingly, the last four words were rehearsed much more for delayed recall than for immediate recall. After the subjects had recalled a number of lists in this fashion, they were unexpectedly given a test covering all the lists they had seen. On that final test, there was no difference between the immediate and delayed conditions for recall of words that had been the last four of the lists. Thus, the number of overt rehearsals, which was much greater for the last four words in delayed-recall lists, did not affect recall.

Experiments like these cast doubt on any simple interpretation of the role of rehearsal in long-term memory. It seems that sometimes rehearsal can lead to long-term recall. However, Craik and Watkins, and Woodward et al., suggest that rote rehearsal—mere repetition of an item to hold it in STM—does not do so. The kind of rehearsal that does lead to LTM strength may be an elaborative process, one in which the items being rehearsed are also mediated, associated with one another, and enriched through contact with information in LTM. From Rundus' experiments showing that subjects do use LTM information in constructing rehearsal sets, it seems likely that purely rote rehearsal is relatively rare. Instead, subjects may elaborate on rehearsed material as a matter of course, giving rise to the usual finding, that rehearsal does increase recall.

CHUNKING AND THE CAPACITY OF STM

The preceding discussion indicates that the label "working memory" for STM is a good one. It seems that even the rehearsal process, once thought to be a relatively passive repetition of items, may incorporate rather complex "work," such as mediating and elaborating on the information given. This same sort of activity takes place in "chunking"—the process of combining information so that it takes up as little as possible of the limited space in STM. In fact, chunking and the elaborative rehearsal just discussed seem to be opposite sides of a coin: on the one hand, mediation and elaboration of information enable it to take up minimal space in STM; on the other hand, these same processes give rise to increased strength for the information in LTM. A more detailed discussion of the chunking process, and of its relation to STM capacity, may clarify this.

Chunking and STM Capacity

We have already noted a fundamental fact about STM. Its storage capacity is limited; it can hold only so much information at any one time. The basic evidence for this comes from experiments on the immediate-memory span in which, as we have seen, the subject is first presented with a brief list of items (for example, WORK, BAT, FALL, SALT, EDIT, DRESS, BOOK), and then attempts to recall them. If there are just a few items, the task is easy, and the subject can perform perfectly. But if the number of items increases to more than seven, errors will creep into most subjects' performance. The number that can be recalled before errors begin to occur is called the memory span, and it has been interpreted as the limit on the storage space available in STM. The idea is that STM can hold about seven items at once, so that seven can be reported without error. But if more are presented, some of the items cannot be held in STM, and those items will not be recalled, leading to errors.

Although the span of immediate memory can be said to be about seven words, it is also seven letters (if the letters do not form words) or seven nonsense syllables. That is, the memory span is not defined in terms of any particular unit—word, letter, or syllable—but instead seems to be about seven of whatever units are presented. Thus, a subject can remember seven letters if they do not form any particular pattern (x, P, A, F, M, K, I), but he can remember many more letters if they form seven words. That is because he is able to *recode* multiple-letter sequences into single units when the sequences form meaningful words. The ability to recode in this way, to combine single stimuli (the letters) into larger units (the words) is called *chunking.* The units that result are, not surprisingly, called chunks. This term was used by Miller (1956), who coined a now-famous phrase when he claimed that the memory span, as measured in chunks, was "the Magical Number Seven, plus or minus two."

Miller discussed some other spans which fit this magical number range of five to nine, but what is particularly important for our present discussion is his view of STM: The short-term memory span is measured in units that can vary quite widely in their internal structure. A unit of STM's capacity corresponds to a chunk, and a chunk is a rather variable entity, containing more or less information as circumstances permit.

One problem with the concept of the chunk is that its definition is circular. On the one hand, we define a chunk as whatever STM holds seven of; on the other, we claim that the span of STM is seven chunks. That means that the span of STM is seven of whatever STM holds seven of. The claim that STM has a capacity of seven chunks is thus not very meaningful unless there is some way of defining chunk other than as "that which STM holds seven of." Quite often, of course, there is some other way to determine the nature of a chunk. For example, suppose we present to a subject the letters of several three-letter words, in sequence (e.g., C, A, T, D, O, G, F, A, R). We may find that a subject can remember about twenty-one letters—those of seven words—for immediate recall. In that case, a chunk corresponds to a word, if we define a chunk as that which one can recall seven of. But a chunk also corresponds to a word on the basis of our knowledge of words. That is, we could have predicted in advance that the subject could remember twenty-one (not seven) letters, because a chunk should be a word in this case. Thus, there is agreement between two ways of estimating what a chunk might be—the memory span, and our knowledge of what corresponds to a unit.

This approach to the concept of chunks receives support from the fact that as we vary what we might intuitively consider to be a chunk, the memory span remains constant at about seven chunks. One test of this idea was performed by Simon (1974), using himself as subject. He found that the amount of material he could immediately recall without error was about seven one-syllable words, about seven two-syllable words, and about six three-syllable words. So far, so good, for the chunking claim. The span has remained at about seven, despite these variations. However, Simon could recall only about four two-word phrases (such as MILKY WAY, DIFFERENTIAL CALCULUS, or CRIMINAL LAWYER), and only about three longer phrases (such as FOURSCORE AND SEVEN YEARS AGO; ALL'S FAIR IN LOVE AND WAR). He concluded that the claim that the STM span remains constant at about seven is roughly true. However, it is a far from exact proposal, for as we increase the size of what we think to be a chunk, the STM capacity in terms of those chunks decreases. According to the definition of chunk, that capacity should remain constant.

Simon noted that the basic problem with defining a chunk is that the chunk is used to measure the span of immediate memory, but it is also a concept derived from immediate memory tasks. If some other situation could be found in which chunks played a part, then that other situation could be used to provide an independent description of a chunk. If that description could then be applied to validate the role of the chunk in immediate-memory tasks, the chunk would become a more meaningful concept.

Let us consider Simon's reasoning in more detail. First, we note that the span of STM is claimed to be seven chunks, which means that the number of syllables that can be recalled in an immediate-memory task is about seven times the number of syllables in a chunk. (For example, if the chunk is a two-syllable word, we could recall 7 $\times$ 2, or 14 syllables.) Thus, we can say that the number of syllables per chunk (call it S) averages about 1/7 the number of syllables recalled (call it R), or $S = 1/7\ R$. This would give us a way of estimating chunk size (S) for any given stimulus material, from the recall of that material (R). However, this equation alone cannot prove or disprove the hypothesis that STM holds seven chunks, for we could always come up with some estimate of chunk size that would fit the equation perfectly.

Now it is necessary to find something other than an STM task in which chunks play a part, and Simon suggested that rote learning might be such a task. He suggested that the length of time required to learn a list of syllables might depend on how those syllables combine into chunks. For example, the number of syllables that can be learned in a given time depends on how those syllables combine to form words. We might expect that the more readily syllables combine to form chunks, the faster they can be learned. This would apply generally to any type of rote learning, like serial learning or paired-associate learning.

Let us express the learning–chunking hypothesis as follows: $F = kS$, where S is chunk size (in syllables, as before) and F stands for the number of syllables that can be learned in a given time, say a minute. The equation says that the number of syllables that can be learned in a minute is proportional to (or k times, where k is some unknown constant analogous to the seven in "seven chunks") the number of syllables in a chunk, for any given material. Then from our two equations, $S = 1/7\ R$ and $S = 1/k\ F$, we can eliminate chunk size, S, and say $1/7\ R = 1/k\ F$. That equation should hold for any given material (for example, two-syllable words). Moreover, for any material, we could actually measure R, the number of syllables that can be immediately recalled correctly, and F, the number of syllables learned in a minute. (For the latter, just take the total number of syllables learned and divide by learning time.) We could do that for two different types of material—call them Type 1 and Type 2. (Type 1 might be two-syllable words; Type 2 might be nonsense syllables.) We could say $1/7\ R_1 = 1/k\ F_1$, and $1/7\ R_2 = 1/k\ F_2$ (where the subscript denotes the type of material). Dividing to form ratios, we get $R_1/R_2 = F_1/F_2$. We have eliminated the unknown k, and this final equation does not even depend on the assumption that the span of STM is *seven* chunks.

In short, the formula $R_1/R_2 = F_1/F_2$ is a means of testing the consistency of the chunk concept. It has been assumed that chunking is relevant in two different tasks (rote learning and immediate memory) and we can expect that the ratios derived from experiments with those tasks, using any two sets of material (R_1/R_2 and F_1/F_2), should be equal. Simon investigated that proposal, and found that within limits, the ratios were equal. Thus, chunking has been supported as a meaningful concept, and it seems reasonable to say that the span of STM is indeed roughly seven chunks.

We now have good reason to believe that subjects can increase the amount of information they are able to hold at one time in STM by recoding that information into chunks. Of course, a subject will be successful in increasing his memory span only if he can subsequently *de*code the chunk and recall its components. For example, a subject given the four-letter series "R, N, C, T" for immediate recall might recode it into the one-word chunk, "Raincoat." Later, at the time of recall, he could make an error, and perhaps report "R, A, C, T." In that case, chunking would not have aided him in recall. However, chunking generally provides a means of increasing the limited capacity of STM.

The Chunking Process

We have seen that STM is not a storehouse, in which sets of material are simply received and stored indiscriminately, but is instead a system in which information can be acted on and stored in a variety of forms. Clearly, chunking in STM uses information from LTM; for example, the spelling of words. The LTM information is used to impose a structure on otherwise unrelated materials; a necessary condition for forming them into a chunk. Thus, chunking, like rehearsal, involves mediation.

From this characterization of the chunking process, we can suggest some conditions of its occurrence. First, we note that chunking usually occurs as the material enters STM, which means that the material to be chunked must come into STM at approximately the same time. (We would find it hard to chunk three letters into a word if the three letters were randomly interspersed in a series of twenty-one.) Second, chunking should be facilitated to the degree that to-be-chunked items have some inherent relationship that permits them to form a unit. In particular, if a group of stimuli has a structure that matches some code in LTM, we might expect the stimuli to form a chunk that corresponds to that code.

Bower (1970; 1972a; Bower and Springston, 1970) investigated some of these aspects of chunking by manipulating the ways in which items co-occurred and the extent to which items matched information in LTM. In some studies, he varied the ways in which sequences of letters co-occurred. One way in which the letter sequences were manipulated was by temporal separation. Subjects performed a memory-span task in which letters were spoken aloud to them. The experimenter separated the letters by brief pauses, and the positions and durations of his pauses varied selectively. For example, the experimenter might read a letter sequence as: TVF . . BIJF . . KY . . MCA. Subjects hearing that sequence could not remember as many letters as subjects who heard: TV . . FBI . . JFK . . YMCA, even though the number of letters, as well as the number of two-, three-, and four-letter groups was identical in both conditions. Bower found very similar effects when he presented the letters visually and manipulated the letter groups by varying the color of adjacent letters. (Here, capital and lower-case letters signify two different colors.)

TVFbijfKYmca versus TVfbiJFKymca

Bower's experiments indicate that learned spelling patterns such as acronyms can be the basis for chunking, particularly when the inputs are readily perceived as corresponding to those patterns. Chunks can also be formed when dealing with material more complex than letter sequences, although the principles of chunking remain the same. This is illustrated by work on the verbatim recall of lists of words which vary in how closely they resemble sentences. Such lists are said to vary in their "order of approximation to English." The concept of order of approximation, developed by Miller and Selfridge (1950), refers to a property of a list that characterizes its relationship to English text. The order furthest removed from English, called a zero-order approximation to English, is simply a list of randomly selected English words. A first-order approximation is similar to the zero-order, except that the words are drawn from text. Thus, the frequency with which words occur in first-order lists reflects their frequency of use in the language. Second-order lists are generated by particular human subjects. First, one subject is given a common word such as THE and asked to use it in a sentence. His response might be, "The sky is falling," The word which followed the given word (SKY) in his sentence is then passed on to another subject, who uses *that* word in a sentence. The second subject's sentence might be, "In the sky are birds." The word following the given word in his sentence (ARE) is given to another subject, and so on, until a list of words of some chosen length has been generated ("sky are . . ."). For third- and higher-order approximations to English, the same procedure is used, except that each subject is given *two* or more consecutive words to use in forming his sentence. Thus, as the order of approximation increases, the amount of context present when a new word is added to the list increases, and the list increasingly resembles English prose. The highest order, following seventh-order approximation, is text itself. An example of a first-order list is "abilities with that beside I for waltz you the sewing"; a fourth-order list, "saw the football game will end at midnight on January"; and a seventh-order list, "recognize her abilities in music after he scolded him before" (Miller and Selfridge, 1950).

The development of word lists with measurable resemblances to English sentences is useful in the investigation of chunking. First of all, Miller and Selfridge (1950) found that immediate recall of a word list improved as the list increased in order of approximation to English. The improvement was greatest in the range of zero-order to about third-order. This suggests that subjects could use their knowledge of English to facilitate their immediate memory, which suggests in turn that the subjects were using some mediational process, perhaps chunking, to do so.

That the process is in fact chunking is supported by an experiment by Tulving and Patkau (1962). They generated lists of twenty-four words, varying in approximation to English. They then presented the lists to subjects for immediate recall. In examining the subjects' recall performance, Tulving and Patkau defined a unit called the "adopted chunk." This was a grouping of items in output (the subject's recall) that matched a sequence of the input (the list as presented). For example, if an input list included "saw the football game will end at midnight on January," and the subject recalled "the football game saw at midnight will end," he would be judged to be using the adopted chunks: (1) "the football game" (2) "saw" (3) "at midnight" (4) "will end." Such units were labeled chunks because the fact that each was grouped at recall in the same order as it had been presented suggested that the words within the adopted chunk were grouped together (chunked) by the subject at the time of presentation.

The results of the Tulving and Patkau (1962) study provided some interesting evidence for the use of chunking in remembering the word lists. First, they found, just as Miller and Selfridge did, that the order of approximation to English was positively related to the number of words recalled. In addition, they found that the subjects almost invariably recalled about five or six adopted chunks, regardless of the order of approximation. Thus, the observed improvement in recall (the increase in the number of words recalled) as the order of approximation increased was not due to the subject's recalling more chunks. Instead, it reflected the fact that the more the list approximated English prose, the more words were included in the average chunk. That is, it seemed that the more the word list resembled English syntax, the larger a chunk the subject could form and later recall. Since he always recalled about the same number of chunks (a number equalling the memory span), his ability to form larger chunks led to better recall performance. In short, it appears that something about the structure of English leads to chunk formation.

Just what might be the factor in English sentences that leads to increased chunk size is not clear. One possibility is that chunking is based on the rules of English syntax, rules that specify how words can be arranged to form sentences. For example, one rule of syntax says that a sentence contains a noun phrase (the subject) followed by a verb phrase (the predicate). Thus we learn that "the boy ran" is proper English syntax, but "ran the boy" is not. All speakers of English learn the rules of syntax, and it may be the knowledge of those rules that leads to the chunking of English text. As lists of words increase in their approximation to English, they increasingly comply with English syntax, and on that basis chunking could be facilitated.

One set of evidence favoring the view that syntactic rules lead to chunking comes from some experiments by Johnson (1968). In his studies, subjects learned to give whole sentences as responses to digit stimuli, in a paired-associate learning procedure. For example, a subject might be taught to give "The tall boy saved the dying woman" when presented with the stimulus "seven."

Of particular interest in these experiments were the errors that subjects made when they recalled only part of a sentence. Johnson assumed that in learning the sentences, the subjects would recode, or chunk, the words into higher-order units. For example, the sequence *"the"* + *adjective* + *noun* could be chunked as a *noun phrase*. Within any unit, the words should be more dependent upon one another than upon the words in any other unit. This leads to the prediction that recall of one word within a unit should be more highly related to recall of other words within that same unit than it is related to recall of words in some other unit. In particular, the recall of two adjacent words should vary according to whether those two words were in the same unit or in two different units.

To test this hypothesis, Johnson calculated the transitional-error probability (TEP). The TEP is defined as the percentage of the time that some word in a sentence was recalled incorrectly when the preceding word was correctly recalled. For example, in THE TALL BOY SAVED THE DYING WOMAN, the TEP between TALL and BOY refers to the percentage of the time subjects gave something other than "boy", having given "tall" correctly. One would expect low TEPs between closely related words, for if a subject got the first word right, he should also be correct on the highly related second word. According to the hypothesis that subjects learn sentences in chunks, one would therefore predict that the TEP would be higher at a transition between consecutive words in two different chunks than between two words within the same chunk. That would follow from the assumption that a high TEP between words means that they are not closely related.

Because the TEP is a measure of the relation between two adjacent words (with high relatedness corresponding to low TEP), it is possible to test the hypothesis that chunking takes advantage of syntactic rules. We could predict, if that were true, that the TEP should be high *between* syntactic units (like subject and predicate) and low *within* a single unit. That is precisely what Johnson found, as can be seen in Figure 5.3. The TEP is high between words three and four in THE TALL BOY SAVED THE DYING WOMAN, and it is precisely between those words that the major division in the sentence occurs, according to syntactic rules. On the other hand, in sentences like THE HOUSE ACROSS THE STREET BURNED DOWN, the main breaks—and high TEPs—come between STREET and BURNED and between HOUSE and ACROSS. Even the pattern of TEPs *within* a phrase in the sentence (for example, within SAVED THE DYING WOMAN) corresponds to the within-phrase structure predicted by syntactic rules.

The TEP results clearly support the idea that chunking can be based on syntactic rules; however, there is another possibility to consider as well. Chunking could be based on meaning, rather than word order. That is, words that combine properly according to the rules of English syntax also form more meaningful phrases than do randomly ordered words. It may be the meaning factor (called the semantic factor) rather than the syntactic—or word order—rules that facilitates chunking. Johnson has provided evidence that word order does play a role in his results. He compared the TEP patterns for three different types of sentences: normal (meaningful and syntactically proper), such as THE HOUSE ACROSS THE STREET BURNED DOWN; syntactically proper but semantically anomalous, such as THE FALSITY CALLING FLAT SLEEP SANG WHITE; and randomly ordered anomalous (and therefore neither meaningful nor syntactically proper), such as THE SANG WHITE FALSITY SLEEP CALLING FLAT. Not surprisingly, the three types were learned at different rates, with normal learned fastest and randomly ordered anomalous slowest. Moreover, the TEP patterns for the two types that were syntactically proper (meaningful and anomalous) were similar. This suggests that subjects formed chunks according to syntactic rules, whether meaning was present or not. The TEPs for the random anomalous sentences were quite different, and those were precisely the sentences that did not follow syntactic rules.

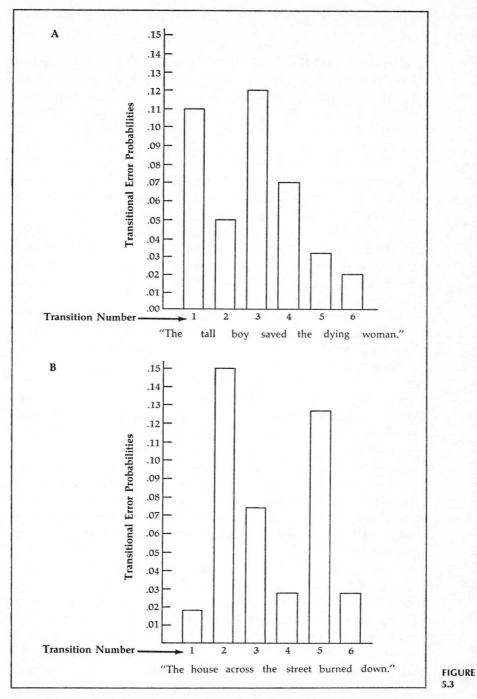

Transitional-error probabilities (TEPs) for two sentence forms: (A) Sentences like "The tall boy saved the dying woman" and (B) "The house across the street burned down." [From Johnson, 1968.]

In short, there is evidence for the role of syntax in chunking. However, the fact that the meaningful sentences were learned much faster than the syntactically correct but anomalous sentences shows that meaning is also very important. Other experiments (Salzinger, Portnoy, and Feldman, 1962; Tejirian, 1968) have indicated that semantic effects are particularly important in the approximation-to-English studies for orders of approximation above the third. Tejirian generated new lists of words from approximations to English by substituting, for words in the original lists, new words of the same grammatical class (noun, verb, adjective, and so on). The substitution of a new word changed the semantic structure of the list but left the syntax unchanged. His results indicated that such changes had no effect on the number of words recalled for orders of three and below. This indicates that semantic content of first- to third-order lists is not an important factor in recall. However, above the third order, semantics were much more important, and word substitutions led to decreases in recall.

The effects of spelling patterns, grammatical rules, and meaning all demonstrate how the process of chunking can utilize well-learned rules. You may have noticed that in discussing those effects we examined several experiments that might be thought of as long-term storage experiments rather than as experiments with short-term storage. For example, the Tulving and Patkau study used lists of twenty-four items, which exceed the memory span, so that LTM storage must be involved. However, it is easy to see that these experiments can be useful in investigating chunking when we consider the similarity between the chunking process and the kind of elaboration of information that leads to successful long-term storage. Since the processing involved in the chunking of material to be stored in STM strengthens the chunked material in LTM, experiments on LTM can provide valuable insights into the short-term storage process as well.

Chunking can also be facilitated when people learn particular rules designed for just that purpose. For example, Miller (1956) reports that subjects learned to recode long strings of zeros and ones into short strings of numerals by first learning to translate three-digit patterns into single numerals as follows: 000 = 0, 001 = 1, 010 = 2, 011 = 3, 100 = 4, 101 = 5, 110 = 6, 111 = 7. Then, given a sequence like 001000110001110, they converted it into three-digit patterns (001,000,110,001,110) and used the above system to convert those into single digits, resulting in 10616. A well-practiced subject could, in this manner, remember sequences of twenty-one or so zeros and ones! The above example of chunking fits into a general category of mediation called mnemonics: the use of a rule to organize input information where the rule has been learned just for this purpose. Such a rule is called a mnemonic device. In short, a mnemonic device is a rule, or system of rules, that has been devised to improve our ability to recall items. Many of these devices are ancient, and some—like the system described by Miller—are rather new. In addition, some mnemonic devices are designed for remembering specific information ("Thirty days hath September . . ."), and some are intended for use with any list of items. An example of the latter is an ancient mnemonic device called the method of loci. With this method, a person first learns to think of a sequence of places; for example, you might think of a sequence of ten positions in your living room (at the TV, at the clock, and so on). Then, the positions can be used to remember lists. Suppose I give you a list of ten items. Using the system, you imagine each item as if it were positioned in one of these places, matching the sequence of items with the sequence of locations. For example, given a list DOG, FIRE, POT, . . ., you think of an image of the dog on the TV, the fire in the clock, and so forth. When recalling, you—the mnemonist—merely travel mentally around the room and think of each location. As you imagine the TV, you will recall the dog; next on to the clock, where you recall the fire, and so on. Thus, you can remember each of the objects, as you come to its position.

CONSCIOUSNESS AND STM

A final consideration in our introductory discussion of STM is the relationship between short-term storage and "consciousness." We have discussed STM as a working memory, because it seems to be the place where items are held while they are worked on—chunked, mediated, or rehearsed. A logical question is whether that kind of work might be synonomous with consciousness, or awareness; that is, whether the act of "working on" is the same as "thinking about."

At present, there seems to be no good answer to such a question. Whatever consciousness might be, it does not seem to be the same as STM "work." To see this, let's consider the cocktail party phenomenon, where you hear your name in someone else's conversation. We could say you become conscious of your name. In that sense, consciousness seems to be equivalent to "paying attention to." But if we consider the definitions of selective attention discussed in Chapter 4, attention and consciousness do not seem synonymous. When you drive a car, for example, it would seem that much of the stimulation from driving undergoes pattern recognition, or you would leave the road. Yet, we often find ourselves driving a car and listening to the conversation of its other occupants. We are conscious of the conversation and unaware of the driving, yet we are devoting at least some attention to the road (Kahneman, 1973). We might propose, however, that driving can be controlled by the pre-attentive processes that precede full recognition, and that consciousness corresponds to full recognition; full attention. This is essentially the same as saying consciousness corresponds to encoding information into STM. However, to say that consciousness corresponds to putting-into-STM is circular. How do we know that something is put into STM? Because we are conscious of it—but then we define consciousness as putting-into-STM. It seems that consciousness is a rather "mystical" problem.

Because of that mystical quality, it seems appropriate to consider here some remarks Freud (1925) made on the nature of consciousness and short- and long-term memories, in connection with something called the "Mystic Writing Pad." This writing pad is a sort of apparatus you may have played with as a child. It consists of a dark waxy pad, covered by a transparent layer of celluloid, and between the two is a translucent thin sheet of waxed paper. One writes on such a pad with a pointed stylus, pressing it down on the celluloid. The celluloid presses in turn onto the thin sheet, which adheres to the wax below, causing the writing to appear on the surface of the pad. The writing can be erased by merely lifting the upper layers of celluloid and waxed paper, leaving the pad available for new writing. Sometimes, if one carefully lifts the upper layers, one can see that the wax below still holds what has just been written, even though it has disappeared from the upper surface.

Such a pad, said Freud, was like the human memory. He proposed a two-part memory: a permanent memory like the wax pad, and a memory that received and held information only briefly, like the middle layer. That renewable, impermanent memory was the locus of consciousness, and as information appeared on it and was erased, consciousness would come and go. All this sounds much like what we call STM and LTM. If so, it seems that Freud felt that transient, short-term memories were part of consciousness. And just as lifting the upper sheets on the Mystic Writing Pad caused information there to vanish, so too might the departure of information from STM cause it to leave our consciousness. Freud may have been right—at least, we cannot prove that he was not right.

6

STM: FORGETTING

Let us suppose that you ask a telephone operator for the phone number of an acquaintance. He gives you the number, and you repeat it to yourself as you reach for the phone. At that point, a friend enters the room and you say hello. When you turn back to the phone, the number seems to have vanished; you can no longer remember it. Information about the number, which was being held in your short-term memory, has been forgotten.

In a sense, we have already talked about STM forgetting. Forgetting is simply the loss of information from the store, and it is precisely that loss which we have presumed to underlie the acoustic confusions in memory-span tasks. That is, we assumed that part of the sound corresponding to an item in STM was forgotten, and when recall was based on the sounds left over, an error was acoustically similar to the original item. It seems that partial forgetting is a normal aspect of STM—that items there can be lost a little at a time.

This chapter, in which we shall discuss the forgetting process in detail, actually has two functions. One is to address the problem of what causes forgetting in STM: this problem has quite a history, and there is some controversy surrounding it. The second function is to focus on some of the experimental variables that affect forgetting, and, in the attempt, to find out more about the short-term storage of information.

THEORIES OF FORGETTING

The what-causes-forgetting problem is generally set up as a dichotomy. Forgetting is said to be the result of either "passive decay" or "interference." To make sense out of these terms, let us try to pose the problem in a rather simple form. We begin by considering an item that resides in STM. When this item is fresh and new, we might say that it is at full strength. (The concept of strength can be a sticky one, but we will use it here in the sense of "amount of information present" or "completeness.") We can say that forgetting occurs when the item is no longer at full strength—for example, if part of the information about its sound is gone. In general, this will occur only when the item is not being rehearsed, because we assume that rehearsal maintains the item at full strength. Forgetting occurs because the item's strength has so declined that it cannot be reconstructed. Our basic question is: what is the cause of the item's decline in strength? We shall now examine the two common answers: (a) passive decay and (b) interference.

To say that the item decays means that the item's strength simply decreases with the passage of time. Only time's passing is necessary for the item to weaken—no other causal factor is specified. Because there is no other specified cause, we say that the decay is passive. In contrast to the decay hypothesis, the interference hypothesis suggests a more active cause of forgetting. It holds that an item declines in strength because new items enter STM. It is the presence of other items, then, that weakens a given item, not just the passing of time.

It would be easy to determine which of these two hypotheses is correct, if only we could perform the following experiment. First, we would present an item to a subject. Then, we would have the subject do nothing for some period of time (this is called the retention interval)—30 seconds or so. That's absolutely *nothing*—no rehearsal (so that the item cannot be maintained at full strength by that means) and no thinking about other things (for that could bring information into STM and cause interference). Then, after the 30-second period, we would ask the subject what the item was. If he could not remember, it would be evidence for passive decay, because the only occurrence during the retention interval would have been the passage of time. Nothing could have produced interference during the interval. On the other hand, if forgetting had *not* occurred in this interval, we could consider it evidence against the decay hypothesis and consistent with the idea of interference.

Unfortunately, we cannot do this "perfect" experiment, because there is no situation in which a subject does absolutely nothing. We shall see, however, that attempts have been made to approximate this experiment, and the results have been rather controversial.

Before we discuss the experiments, let's take a closer look at the alternative hypotheses. First, the interference hypothesis. One version of this hypothesis is what might be called the "simple slot model," or "displacement model." According to this model, STM has a certain number of slots—about seven plus or minus two. Each slot holds a chunk of information. When items come into STM, each item (chunk) occupies a slot. When there are no more empty slots left to put incoming items into, then old items must be moved out to make room for the new. According to this model, each new item that enters a filled STM displaces an item already there, resulting in the latter being forgotten. Each of the old items in STM has some chance of being displaced.

The displacement model is of interest because it helps to clarify the more general hypothesis that says that STM forgetting is caused by interference. One implication of the model is that the first few items to enter STM should not interfere with each other. There should be no forgetting until enough items come into STM to fill up the slots. This means that forgetting occurs only when the number of items is greater than the capacity of STM. Another implication of the simple slot idea is this: because each item, or chunk, occupies a single slot, and the slot either contains the item or does not, then an item should be either all gone (the slot does not contain it) or all there. But this, we know, is not true. The fact that we get acoustic confusions among syllables (for example, letter names) held in STM can be explained by the partial forgetting of the syllables, one phoneme at a time. If a syllable is a chunk, this sort of partial forgetting is inconsistent with the simple slot model.

It is not difficult to modify the simple slot model of STM forgetting so that it is consistent with partial forgetting. We just allow an item in STM to vary in its completeness—to take on several values like "all there," "mostly there," "just a little left," and "all gone." When we modify the model in this way, we are essentially assuming that the item can vary in "strength," equating strength with completeness. Our displacement hypothesis now states that new items entering STM can partially displace other items—that is, can cause the strength of those items to decrease.

The other implication of simple slots, namely, that there should be forgetting in STM only if the number of items to be stored there exceeds its span, also demands modification. That is because the claim that forgetting can occur only when STM is full makes the decay and interference hypotheses compatible. To understand this, consider what it means to a duplex theorist to speculate about forgetting by decay: the decay hypothesis is relevant only to an *unfilled* STM, for implicit in the idea of a limited-capacity STM is the idea that forgetting will occur when more information enters STM than it can hold. Such forgetting cannot be attributed to passive decay; thus, to consider forgetting by decay, we must look at forgetting that occurs when the information in STM does not exceed the memory span.* But if the decay hypothesis is most meaningful when it is applied to below-span forgetting, then the interference hypothesis should be similarly restricted. That is, our interference hypothesis cannot assume that there should be forgetting in STM only if its capacity is exceeded. Otherwise, the source of controversy between the two hypotheses would be eliminated: decay could apply to below-span forgetting, and interference to forgetting that occurs when the span of STM is exceeded. In short, the displacement model needs a second modification—let us say that interference can lead to forgetting in STM even when its capacity is not exceeded. That is, the entry of other items in STM can interfere with a given item, even if there is room in STM for all the items to be held. Such an interference hypothesis contrasts with a decay hypothesis that says that the strength of an item in STM gradually declines, even if there is room in STM to hold the item and if no other items enter.

It is possible to modify the interference hypothesis still further. Some theorists assume that interference is a function of similarity; that is, that new items will interfere with old items to the extent that they are similar. This version of the interference hypothesis we might term "interference by similarity" to contrast it to interference by displacement, which does not assume that similarity determines the extent of forgetting.

Our new, revised, interference hypothesis might go like this: Each item in STM has a certain strength. When the item is newly entered or just rehearsed, it will be at full strength. Forgetting occurs when strength declines sufficiently so that the item cannot be recovered and reported. The cause of forgetting is the entry of other items into STM. We may also assume that the extent of the forgetting depends on the similarity of those new items to the original items. Gradually, as more items enter STM, the strength of those already there fades away, as shown in Figure 6.1a. In contrast, the passive-decay hypothesis, which says that forgetting occurs because time passes and not because of item interference, would predict a strength function like Figure 6.1b.

---

*This limitation on the decay hypothesis, which is dictated by the concept of a short-term store with a limited capacity, differs somewhat from traditional views on decay. That is, outside of the context of the duplex theory, the decay hypothesis can be applied whether the information being forgotten is greater or less than the span of immediate memory. In fact, the memory span can be viewed as the *result* of decay, as follows: when the number of items presented is small, all of the items can be rehearsed before any of them has a chance to decay completely. As a result, there are no errors in recall. When the number of items presented is large, there are too many items to allow for rehearsal of each one before it can decay. Thus, some do decay, and there are errors in recall. The memory span is thus viewed as the point at which the number of items becomes too great to permit rehearsal of all of them in less time than it takes for any one to decay completely.

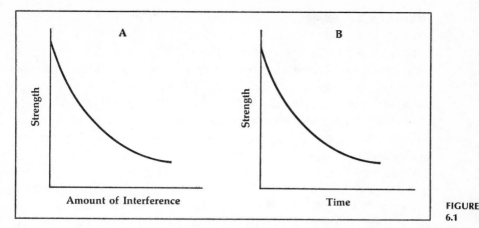

FIGURE
6.1

Theoretical curves predicted by **(A)** the interference hypothesis, **(B)** the decay hypothesis. The former says that the strength of an item in memory gradually decreases with interference; the latter that strength gradually decreases over time.

The two strength functions we have considered in Figure 6.1 clearly differ. For one, the x-axis measures Amount of Interference; for the other, the x-axis represents Time. The way to determine which theory is correct is to translate the theoretical (and internal, unobservable) variable of Strength into something external and measurable. Then we can determine what affects our strength measure. If the measure is affected by time, we have evidence supporting decay theory; if by interfering items, for interference theory. For example, one measure that would presumably reflect strength is the percentage of correct responses on a recall task. Suppose we were to present a small set of items, then generate a series of items specifically designed to interfere, and then ask the subject to recall the initial set. If recall decreases as a function of the number of interfering items, we have evidence for interference.

Unfortunately, this sort of procedure presents a problem. Assuming that the generation of interfering items takes time, as more interfering items are presented, more time passes. The two variables, number of items and amount of time, are confounded. As one increases, so does the other. Thus it would be impossible to tell just what caused the decline in recall—time or interfering items. It is because of this sort of confounding that we need some other procedure to test the two hypotheses. That other procedure is the perfect experiment previously described, in which time passes and nothing interferes. If forgetting occurs under those conditions, time has clearly caused it, and decay theory wins. If there is no forgetting, so much for decay theory.

DISTRACTOR TASKS

We cannot perform the perfect experiment, but that does not mean it cannot be approximated. Experiments that attempt to do so typically use what are called "distractor" procedures. These procedures were first used by Brown (1958) and Peterson and Peterson (1959). The latter researchers are usually credited with giving the impetus to experiments on decay versus interference in STM, as well as giving research on STM an immense boost.

What the Petersons did was quite simple. They had subjects perform in a series of trials like this: First, the subject hears a three-consonant sequence (a trigram), such as PSQ. Then, he hears a three-digit number, say 167. He counts backward from that number by threes: 167, 164, 161, 158, . . . keeping time to the beat of a metronome, for a certain period of time—called the retention interval. Then, a recall cue occurs, indicating that the subject is to recall the three letters.

This task is called a distractor task because the counting backward is supposed to distract the subject, preventing him from rehearsing the letters in the trigram. However, the counting is assumed not to interfere with the letters of the trigram, presumably held in STM, because the numbers do not have to be stored for later recall. Thus, we have an approximation to the case where time passes, in the form of the retention interval, while the subject does nothing—except count backwards, which is presumed to be noninterfering. If the subject forgets the letters, we have support for a theory of decay.

The results of the Petersons' experiment are shown in Figure 6.2. In the range of retention intervals they used, from 3 to 18 seconds, there was a marked decline in the subject's ability to remember the trigram. This was astonishing—such rapid forgetting had not heretofore been obtained in research on memory. For one thing, most of the then current research concerned long lists; the familiar procedures of serial recall, paired associates, and so on. For another thing, with those long lists, forgetting functions were plotted in terms of hours or days. And most astonishing, the results of this experiment were readily interpretable as the result of passive decay in STM.

That the Petersons found experimental evidence favoring the passive decay hypothesis was an important event in the world of memory. It came at a time when a duplex theory of memory had been heard of (Hebb, 1949) but was by no means popular. Moreover, a large body of evidence then in existence pointed to interference as the primary causal factor in long-term forgetting; that is, material appeared to be forgotten

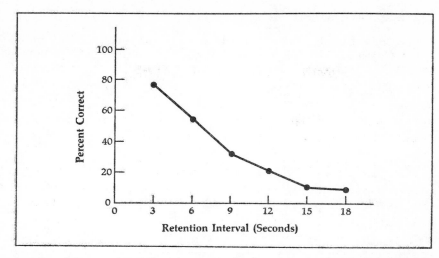

FIGURE 6.2

Results of the experiment on forgetting in short-term memory, showing that recall decreases as a function of the retention interval. [From Peterson and Peterson, 1959. Copyright 1959 by the American Psychological Association.]

over long intervals because other information eroded it. Thus, the distractor experiment suggested that two kinds of forgetting mechanisms were operative—the passive decay *and* LTM interference, strongly suggesting that there may be two kinds of forgetting because there were two systems of memory. That is, (*a*) the finding by the Petersons that decay is operative in the short run and (*b*) the findings of others that interference is operative in the long run could be attributed to forgetting taking place in two different stores, an STM and an LTM.

Thus a goal was set for theorists who felt more comfortable with one kind of memory: to somehow show that the Peterson experiment did not necessarily demonstrate the existence of a previously unknown short-term memory where forgetting occurred through decay. The most likely means of disproving the STM notion was to show that interference was actually responsible for the short-term forgetting. To understand how this might be accomplished, it is necessary that we get an idea of what was known about interference as the cause of forgetting in LTM. Most of the knowledge came from work with paired associates in what are called proactive-inhibition (PI) experiments and retroactive-inhibition (RI) experiments.

The two types of procedure—PI and RI—are diagrammed in Figure 6.3. Of the two, RI is the most closely related to what we have been calling

RETROACTIVE INHIBITION

Experimental Group	Learn List A	Learn List B	Retention Interval	Test List A
Control Group	Learn List A	_____	Retention Interval	Test List A

Time →

PROACTIVE INHIBITION

Experimental Group	Learn List A	Learn List B	Retention Interval	Test List B
Control Group	_____	Learn List B	Retention Interval	Test List B

Time →

FIGURE 6.3

Diagram of the RI and PI procedures. When learning of List B interferes with List A, RI exists. When learning of List A interferes with List B, PI exists.

interference—RI refers to the detrimental effect of recently acquired information on previously learned material. It is retroactive because the new information affects the material previously learned. When we measure RI, we usually use several lists of items rather than one as we might do in an STM experiment. We conduct an RI experiment with two groups of subjects—an experimental group and a control group. The experimental group learns two lists of paired associates: first a "List A," and then a "List B." They learn each list to some criterion level of performance—say, three repetitions of the list without an error. Then, they wait during a retention interval, after which they are tested on the first list they learned, List A. The control group is treated in the same way as the experimental group, except that they do not learn a List B. What is actually found is that the control group performs better than the experimental on the test. Presumably this is because the learning of List B, which was done only by the experimental group, had a detrimental—interfering—effect on the memory for List A.

Could RI have been operating in the Petersons' experiment? Yes—if the counting backward interfered with the trigram stored in memory. This seemed unlikely to investigators at the time, since the counting did not require the storage of new information in memory. Moreover, the numbers used in counting were much different from the letters that were to be remembered. One well-known fact about RI at the time of the Petersons' work was that its effect was large when the to-be-remembered material (List A) and the interfering material (List B) were similar, and small if they were not. Therefore, because the numbers and letters did not seem to be similar, the interference theorists did not try to show that the stored trigram was forgotten because of RI from the counting.

We have mentioned proactive inhibition as another possible way that interference might account for short-term forgetting. The PI procedure is much like the RI procedure, with one crucial difference. In PI, the concern is with forward-acting interference—the detrimental effect of learning a List A on remembering a subsequently learned List B. Thus, the experimental procedure tests the second list learned, List B, after the retention interval. (See Figure 6.3.) Typically, the experimental group, which has learned a List A before learning List B, does worse on recall of List B than a control group which did not learn List A. When this occurs, the experimental group can be said to exhibit PI.

Could PI have been the cause of forgetting in the Petersons' experiment? There is no obvious source of PI, since apparently nothing was learned prior to the presentation of the trigram on each trial. But wait—because each trial did not occur all by itself, but in the context of a long series of trials, it is possible that early trials could interfere with later trials. Such a PI effect would not be readily apparent in the Petersons' data, because their experimental design would obscure it.

The reasoning is this: The Petersons had subjects take part in two practice trials, followed by forty-eight trials (eight trials with each of the six retention intervals used). Now, it is known that PI is something that rapidly builds up to a peak. Thus, although the detrimental effect of learning one prior list on learning and recalling a second may be great, the effect of learning two lists prior to learning and recalling a given list is not that much greater than the effect of learning just one, and the effect of learning five prior lists is not much greater than the effect of learning just four. On this basis we would expect that PI might have rapidly grown to a maximum in the course of the first few trials of the Petersons' experiment. Thus, most of the forty-eight trials would occur with PI at its maximum level, since PI could be expected to be strong after the first few (which would include the two practice trials). To see whether PI were operating here, it would be necessary to look at only the first few trials for each subject, making sure that all the retention intervals were represented equally often at each of the trial numbers.

The above analysis is that of Keppel and Underwood (1962), who went on to perform the experiment it suggests. They attempted to find out whether PI worked in the distractor experiments. To do so, they had to use each subject for only a few trials; also, they had to make sure that each retention interval they used was associated equally often (distributed over subjects) with a first trial, a second trial, and so on. This they did by using three retention intervals, three trials per subject (one for each interval), and a large number of subjects. Their results are shown in Figure 6.4 below.

The results of the Keppel and Underwood study were important to the one-kind-of-memory theorists. The data show that on the first trial, there is no forgetting during an 18-second interval. However, on the subsequent trials, when PI has had a chance to build up, the rapid forgetting observed originally by the Petersons occurs. It seems that laws of LTM forgetting, notably laws of PI, determine when the so-called STM forgetting will occur, and that short-term forgetting is a result of interference.

Keppel and Underwood attributed the short-term forgetting observed in the Petersons' experiment to changes in the amount of PI. In the traditional PI procedure, it was known that PI increased as the retention interval (in Figure 6.3, the time between learning of List B and its recall) increased. This was attributed to recovery of the strength of List A

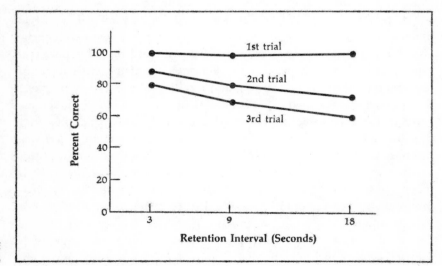

FIGURE 6.4

Results of the experiment on short-term retention by trial number, showing that correct recall depends not only on the retention interval but also on the number of prior trials. [From Keppel and Underwood, 1962.]

(originally reduced by the learning of List B) during the retention interval. Recovery of List A would presumably allow it to interfere more and more with List B. In terms of experiments using the distractor procedure, a similar effect would mean that PI should be greater after an 18-second interval than after a 3-second interval. This would produce the forgetting observed. Of course, this could only happen when there was some PI to increase, that is, when there had been some earlier trials to produce PI. We therefore arrive at the prediction that the amount recalled should decrease as the retention interval increases, but only after the first few trials—exactly the results observed by Keppel and Underwood.

Keppel and Underwood wished to interpret their results in accordance with a unitary theory of memory; they were not duplex theorists. But since we know that other bases for separating STM and LTM exist, for purposes of the present discussion we can interpret their results as favoring the interference hypothesis of short-term forgetting; forgetting in STM is seen to be predictable on the basis of PI.

THE PROBE EXPERIMENT

The next study we shall discuss (Waugh and Norman, 1965) offered a different kind of evidence for interference in STM. It examined the interfering effects of subsequent information on information previously stored in STM. The experiments were not approximations to the perfect experiment discussed above, in that they did not use the distractor technique. Instead, their attack on the problem attempted to unconfound the effects of time and number of intervening items, which, as we have noted, usually vary together. The experiments used what is called the probe technique to accomplish the unconfounding. The probe technique works like this: The subject gets a list of digits, say, sixteen to remember. The sixteenth digit is a special one, in that it has occurred somewhere in the previous fifteen, and it is used to probe the list. The subject is told to recall the digit that followed the first appearance of the probe digit. (The probe digit is accompanied by a tone to signal that it is the last in the list, so that the subject need not count the digits.)

For example, the subject might hear the following list:

1 4 7 9 5 1 2 6 4 3 8 7 2 9 0 5*

(The asterisk denotes the tone.) He is being asked, "What is the digit that followed the first appearance of the digit five?" The correct answer would be "one." The crucial data here concern the percentage of recall (that is, the mean percentage of the time the digit following the first appearance of the probe is correctly recalled, averaged over many trials and subjects) as a function of the number of digits intervening between the initial presentation of the recalled digit and its recall (the appearance of the probe digit). In the above example, there are ten intervening digits (counting the probe). This gives us a way to look at recall as a direct function of intervening digits, which are considered interfering units.

In order to examine the effect of the passage of time, an additional variation can be introduced—we can vary the rate of presentation of the digits from fast (four digits per second) to slow (one per second). We can by this means factorially vary time and number of interfering units. That is, we can separate their effects in such a way that we can look at the amount of *time* between the first and second appearances of the probe digit independent of *number of interfering units*, and vice versa.

This becomes clearer if we consider what the data from this experiment might look like according to the predictions of the two theories—decay and interference. First, if decay were acting, we would predict that recall would depend on elapsed time, regardless of the number of intervening digits. This would mean that the two different rates of presentation would lead to different recall for a given number of intervening items, because the rate would determine the elapsed time between the first and second appearance of the probe. Plotting the percentage of recall as a function of intervening time between the first and second appearance of the probe, we would get Figure 6.5a below. It shows hypothetical data based on the assumption that forgetting occurs gradually as a function of time, regardless of the number of intervening digits that occur within the time. (This is evidenced by the fact that both rates yield the same result, although the fast rate corresponds to more interfering items than the slow for any given time interval.) The same data is plotted a little differently in Figure 6.5b, which uses intervening items on the *x*-axis and shows that the number of items alone does not predict forgetting. It is still the elapsed time corresponding to a given number of items, as dictated by the presentation rate, that is the predictor when the graph is plotted in this way.

Alternatively, we can look at the predictions of interference theory, which says that the important determinant of forgetting is the number of digits intervening between the first and second appearance of the probe. We could plot its predictions in two ways, as in Figures 6.5c and 6.5d. Figure 6.5c shows hypothetical data based on the assumption that, regardless of rate, it is number of intervening items that determines recall. Figure 6.5d shows that if we plot the same forgetting data as a

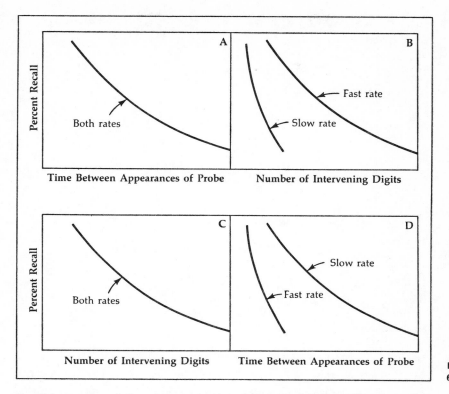

FIGURE
6.5

Possible results of the probe experiment, as predicted by the decay hypothesis (**A** and **B**) and the interference hypothesis (**C** and **D**). The former says that forgetting is a function of time for both presentation rates, and therefore that, for a given number of intervening digits, there is more forgetting for the slow rate. The interference hypothesis predicts that forgetting will depend on the number of intervening digits, and therefore that, for a given amount of time, forgetting will be greater for the fast rate.

function of time, we get different functions for the two rates, because each rate corresponds to a different number of intervening items for a given time (the fast rate leads to more items than the slow rate within any time period).

Now, to see which theory is correct, we compare the predictions to the experimental results obtained by Waugh and Norman (1965), which are shown in Figure 6.6. The results support the interference theory. For both presentation rates, forgetting is determined by the number of digits that occur between the first appearance of the recalled digit and its recall. At this point, we might note that we could have predicted this

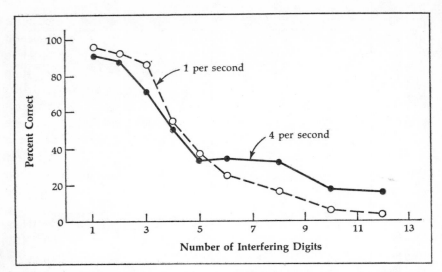

FIGURE
6.6

Results of the probe experiment, consistent with predictions of interference theory, showing that correct recall decreases as a function of the number of intervening digits. [From Waugh and Norman, 1965. Copyright 1965 by the American Psychological Association.]

result from what we know about the free-recall serial-position curve. We know that rate of presentation does not affect the recency portion of that curve, which presumably reflects recall from STM (Figure 2.2c). Thus, the fact that rate does not affect recall from STM in that situation means, just as in the probe-digit experiment, that time is unimportant, whereas number of intervening items (serial position) affects recall.

DISTRACTOR TASKS, REVISITED

The results of the Waugh and Norman probe-digit experiment support the idea that interference is the causal factor in STM forgetting. Adding these results to those obtained by Keppel and Underwood (1962), which show that PI is also related to the rapid forgetting in the Peterson and Peterson task, there seems to be a strong case for interference theory. Keeping this in mind, we shall go on to an approximation to our perfect experiment conducted by Judith Reitman in 1971—the best approximation we have considered up to this point. She performed a distractor experiment in which the distracting task, instead of counting backwards, was a signal-detection task. Subjects in the experiment first were presented with three words to be remembered. Then, for a 15-second period, they listened for the sound of a tone in a background of white noise (the signal detection). They were to press a button when a tone occurred. This task was rather difficult; Reitman set the tone so that subjects could hear it only about 50% of the time. Thus, it was presumably difficult enough to prevent rehearsal. Moreover, it should not have interfered with the three words in STM. It seemed therefore to be a reasonable approximation to the "doing nothing" that we demand for the retention interval in the perfect experiment. After the 15-second interval of signal detection, the subjects attempted to recall the three words.

Reitman was interested, of course, in whether the subjects could remember the three words. She also attempted to insure that the subjects were unable to rehearse during the interval. To determine whether rehearsal had been eliminated, she compared the accuracy and speed of their signal-detection performance to the performance of control subjects who were not attempting to remember three words but only to perform the signal detection. This check revealed no difference between the two groups, suggesting that the experimental subjects were really working at signal detection and not rehearsing. Thus, she believed that the results of her experiment truly could address the question of what happens to information in STM when rehearsal is prevented. The results were quite clear: there was no forgetting during the 15 seconds. That is, unlike the Petersons' findings, she found almost perfect retention of the words after 15 seconds had passed. Thus, there was no evidence that decay had occurred during the interval.

In another version of her experiment, Reitman obtained some rather different results—more like the original findings of the Petersons. The results were found when, instead of signal detection, the distractor task was *syllable* detection: subjects tried to detect when the spoken syllable ⳠOH occurred in a series of DOH's. With this task filling the retention interval, recall of the initially presented words did indeed drop below 100%, to about 75%. It seemed that the nature of the distractor task played a rather important role in short-term forgetting.

Reitman's findings were extended and confirmed by Shiffrin (1973), who used signal-detection periods of 1, 8, and 40 seconds. He also extended the retention interval by adding an arithmetic task after the signal detection on some trials. This was to be used to test for a "ceiling effect." This term refers to the possibility that there could be some decrease in memory strength during the signal-detection interval, but not enough to produce any drop from the 100%-recall "ceiling"—that is, not enough to cause any noticeable decrement in recall.

The typical trial in Shiffrin's experiment went like this: The subject heard a five-consonant quintagram (like RLXBT). He then performed a signal-detection task for 1, 8, or 40 seconds. On some trials, the signal detection was followed by an arithmetic task lasting either 5 seconds or 30 seconds. The task was to add a series of single digits, presented one after another, at 2-second intervals, to a 3-digit starting number (for example, adding 203 + 4 + 7 + 6 + 9 + . . .).

Shiffrin found, as Reitman had, that performance on recall of the quintagram was unaffected by any of the signal-detection intervals; recall was almost perfect following any of the signal-detection periods. But when a period of arithmetic was added to the procedure, it had a detrimental effect on recall, with the 30-second task causing more disruption than the 5-second task. However, there were no differential effects of arithmetic corresponding to differences in the duration of signal detection. That is, neither amount of arithmetic was more disruptive after 40 seconds of detection than after 1 second. This suggested that no decay at all had occurred during the detection interval—that there had been no ceiling effect. For if there had been some lessening of the strength of the quintagram during detection, but not enough to cause forgetting, then the added effects of the arithmetic should "finish the job." This should be particularly true for the longer detection intervals, during which there would be the greatest amount of time between storage of the quintagram and recall, and therefore the most decay. The added arithmetic should lead to noticeable forgetting. So if some decay had occurred, there should be poorer recall of the consonants after 40 seconds of signal detection than after 1 second, given an arithmetic task. The fact that there was no difference in recall after the short and the long detection interval, with or without arithmetic, therefore indicated that there were no weakening effects of signal detection at all.

Following these experiments, there appeared to be no evidence for decay-induced forgetting in STM; all forgetting appeared to be the result of interference. However, this state of affairs was subsequently altered when Reitman replicated her original experiment with new controls for ceiling effects and rehearsal. Her concern with ceiling effects was like that of Shiffrin; that is, she was afraid that subjects might have forgotten some of the information over the retention interval, but not enough to make them unable to reconstruct the three words and show forgetting.

She also felt that her original tests for the possibility that subjects were rehearsing during the retention interval might have been inadequate. And if subjects were surreptitiously rehearsing, that could have been the reason that they showed no forgetting during the retention interval.

For these reasons, Reitman conducted experiments designed to eliminate ceiling effects and accurately assess the possibility of rehearsal. To accomplish the former, she required the subject to retain five words during the retention interval rather than three, as in her original experiment. To accomplish the latter, she instituted an extensive analysis of seven measures of recall and detection performance, designed to indicate whether a subject rehearsed, which of several rehearsal strategies he might have adopted, and how strongly he rehearsed. These measures were applied under the following conditions: (*a*) when the subject was told to rehearse surreptitiously, (*b*) when he was told not to rehearse, (*c*) when he had no items to recall, and (*d*) in a full replication of the original experiment.

Reitman's results confirmed her fears: she found evidence that there had been a ceiling effect in her original data. She also found evidence that subjects were surreptitiously rehearsing during her original experiment, and that her tests for rehearsal had not been strong enough to indicate that fact. In fact, in her new experiments, only ten out of fifty-two subjects appeared actually to avoid rehearsal when told to do so. These ten subjects then formed a critical group for testing the decay-versus-interference question. Did they forget information over a 15-second retention interval during which they performed a detection task *and* avoided rehearsal? The answer is yes: an average of about 25% of the original information was lost during a 15-second tone-detection task. This indicates that the information decayed over the interval. Another fact is also important: when the interpolated task was syllable detection (detecting the syllable ᴛᴏʜ in a series of ᴅᴏʜ's and ᴛᴏʜ's), forgetting was an additional 44% more than for tone detection. Reitman concluded that ceiling effects (in her experiment; but probably not in Shiffrin's, who controlled better for them) and surreptitious rehearsal (in both her original data and Shiffrin's) had given rise to misleading evidence against decay theory, and that forgetting in STM was actually affected by decay.

But Reitman also pointed out that there was evidence for forgetting from interference in her experiment; in this case, interference from the syllable-detection task. She noted that syllable detection produced more forgetting than tone detection. Similarly, Shiffrin found that arithmetic tasks produced forgetting when tone detection did not. It seems that although distractor tasks were originally intended to prevent rehearsal without interfering with the items to be remembered, some distractor tasks do in fact interfere. And it is those tasks which produce the greatest amount of forgetting.

Several experiments indicate that the distractor task actually can be interfering. These include the Reitman and Shiffrin experiments in which it was found that distractor tasks involving verbal skills (skills that require word or syllable manipulation) were more likely to disrupt retention of verbal forms (syllables or words) than nonverbal tasks like signal detection. Watkins, Watkins, Craik, and Mazuryk (1973) showed that difficult nonverbal tasks could also produce short-term forgetting. They had subjects remember five-word sequences. They used for the distractor a task in which the subject listened to a sequence of piano tones and shadowed the sequence by pressing a designated button corresponding to each tone after it appeared. This produced some forgetting of the five words over a 20-second retention interval, though not as much as was obtained in the Petersons' task. (See Figure 6.7.)

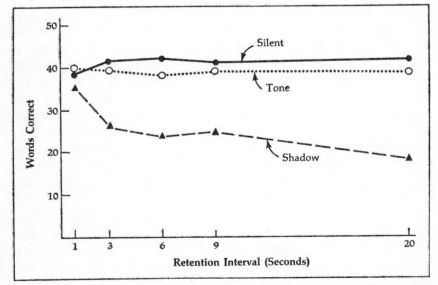

FIGURE
6.7

Number of words correctly recalled as a function of retention interval, for three kinds of interpolated activity: a silent interval; an interval in which a sequence of tones occurred; an interval in which the subject shadowed a sequence of tones. [From Watkins, Watkins, Craik, and Mazuryk, 1973. Copyright 1973 by the American Psychological Association.]

Watkins et al. suggested that two aspects of the distractor task may determine the extent to which it produces forgetting in STM. One is the degree to which the material to be remembered and distractor material are similar. The idea is that of interference by similarity; more similar distractor material generates more interference with the to-be-remembered material, weakening its STM representation so that it cannot be recovered after the retention interval. The experiments we have discussed here (Peterson and Peterson; Reitman; Shiffrin; Watkins et al.) support this. So do others we have not yet mentioned. Wickelgren (1965) found that if the distractor material sounded like the material to be remembered, more forgetting occurred than if it did not. Deutsch (1970) found that retaining a set of tones was more difficult if the tones were followed by an interpolated sequence of tones than if there was an interpolated sequence of numbers. All this suggests that the distractor task can make contact and interfere with the to-be-remembered material in STM. This notion seems to fit in with our idea that STM may be the place where "work" (such as that in the distractor task) is done. Since storage of the material also takes place in STM, it is plausible that the two sets of material could make contact, and that contact could be interfering to the extent the material is similar.

The second factor suggested by Watkins et al. to determine short-term forgetting is the general difficulty of the distractor task. They suggest that to the extent that the distractor task uses processing capacity (or attention, in the sense of capacity), it will create interference. Examples of tasks which do so are (a) shadowing a series of tones, (b) counting backward, and (c) performing addition. This idea receives support from other experiments showing that the difficulty of the distractor task does affect short-term retention (for example, Posner and Konick, 1966; Posner and Rossman, 1965). Given Reitman's results, we might assume that one way that such tasks interfere is by preventing rehearsal, which gives decay a chance to operate. We might also note that this fits in with the idea that STM is a work space as well as a storage space. That is because more difficult tasks could be expected to demand work space, resulting in less space for work such as rehearsal, less room for storage, and therefore more forgetting. Also consistent with this idea is a finding by Murdock (1961) that the amount of information which is to be stored affects recall. In an experiment in which counting backward was the distractor task, he found that forgetting was more rapid when the to-be-remembered material was a consonant trigram or three words than when it was a single word. The former comprised three chunks (and demanded more storage space); the latter only one.

COGNITIVE CONTROL OF FORGETTING

The suggestion that factors such as the type of work done during the retention interval, the amount of information to be stored, and the difficulty of the task affect short-term retention introduces a somewhat familiar idea into our discussion of STM forgetting. The idea is that STM forgetting has a cognitive component, like those that direct the flow of attended-to and recognized information, and control such processes as chunking and rehearsal. Such an idea is supported by the work of Waugh and Norman (1968) in some additional probe-digit experiments. They found that STM forgetting was affected not only by the number of items intervening between the presentation of a given item and its test, but also by the content of those items. In fact, their results indicate that it is not the number of intervening items that is important but the number of those items that will interfere. Some items will not cause interference, most notably those that are predictable in the context of the experiment.

To see this, consider what would happen if we were given a sequence of numbers that repeated each digit in the sequence three times: 555, 666, 333, and so on. Would each of those repetitions count as an interfering unit? This seems unlikely on a purely intuitive basis, since we could simply remember the rule that each was repeated three times, rather than remembering every single repetition. This is precisely what happens; Waugh and Norman found that items that are predictable do not interfere in the same way as unexpected items. Once again, we are forced to conclude that the information-processing system is not passive, but involves some mechanism of cognitive control.

At this point, we will leave the discussion of short-term forgetting. We can conclude that all in all, the evidence seems to call for a theory that includes both passive decay and interference: decay occurs in the absence of rehearsal; interference can be produced by the storage of new information, or by performing some task (work) while the original information is to be retained. The amount of interference generated by a given task seems to vary with its relationship to the material stored in STM and also with the processing capacity it requires. The more interference that task generates, the more forgetting of competing material it will induce. And last but not least, we should note that control processes act to direct the nature of forgetting. These processes determine such things as what is stored, what work is done, and whether rehearsal occurs. In short, they determine the allocation of storage space and processing capacity to given information, thus playing an important role in what information is retained in STM.

7

STM:
NONACOUSTIC
STORAGE

In Chapter 2, we discussed a general model of the human information-processing system. Of necessity, the description of that model was simplified; one simplification was the claim that information in STM is coded acoustically, whereas information in LTM is coded semantically. At the chapter's end, we noted that our depiction of STM excluded some complicating factors. In the present chapter, we will find out what some of the complications are, and we will round out our discussion of STM and its related processes.

One of the most important problems with our earlier simplified description is its depiction of STM as a storehouse for acoustically coded items. Certainly much of the original work in this area (for example, the acoustic confusions noted by Conrad, 1964) indicated that STM was an acoustic store. However, there is also evidence for visual and semantic encoding of items in STM. For example, our earlier description of STM assumes that if a letter is presented visually, it is labeled and encoded acoustically for storage in STM (thus, A becomes the sound "ay"), but there is some evidence that a visually presented letter can be stored visually in STM (thus, A is stored as "A"). It is the evidence for such nonacoustic storage that will form the focus of the present chapter.

Before we pursue the topic of nonacoustic short-term codes, it is important to clarify just what it means that say that information is represented visually or semantically in STM. We have arbitrarily *defined* STM as the place where verbal descriptions of items (that is, syllables and words) are held in acoustic form, but this definition excludes the possibility of visual or semantic STM codes. Instead, in order to investigate the nature of information in STM, we must now define STM independently of a particular type of code.

One way to define STM is to use the duration of its storage. That is, we could say that STM is the store where items are held over the short term—on the order of seconds, if there is no rehearsal. We could also say that the information stored there may come from the senses (and sensory registers) or from LTM. With this definition, it is possible to consider STM information in any form. However, it now becomes particularly important to distinguish between the sensory registers and STM, for information in the sensory registers is also held for a short time. Therefore, we must add another characteristic. Let us say that items in STM coming from the sensory registers (as opposed to those coming from LTM) are not held as raw *sensory* information, but have passed the crucial point of pattern recognition in which they make contact with their corresponding LTM representation. They are no longer precategorical. What we would like to consider, then, is evidence that information can be held for short intervals in nonsensory form, in a code that is nonacoustic (specifically, visual or semantic).

VISUAL CODES IN STM

The first nonacoustic, nonsensory, short-term codes we will consider are visual codes. In particular, we will discuss research indicating that visual information can persist for a short time after a stimulus has vanished, even though the information does not seem to be stored in the sensory register. We will also discuss evidence that visually coded information can be called from LTM and held for short periods of time. The research to be reviewed, then, constitutes evidence that there can be visual storage having the same characteristics as the acoustic storage which has been our primary interest in previous discussions of STM.

Posner's Letter-Matching Experiments

One body of evidence for the existence of visual STM codes comes from a procedure developed by Posner (Posner, 1969; Posner, Boies, Eichelman, and Taylor, 1969; Posner and Mitchell, 1967). Posner's work strongly supports the ideas: (1) that visual information can persist, after a visual stimulus has occurred, under conditions which are incompatible with iconic storage, and (2) that visual information can also be generated from LTM for short periods. His basic procedure is as follows (see Figure

7.1): A subject takes part in a long series of trials, each lasting for a brief time. On each trial, the subject sees two letters. He is to indicate whether the two letters have the same name (for example, A and A or B and b) or have different names (such as A and B). He does this by pressing one of two buttons which are before him. One has been designated the "same" button, one the "different" button.

Now, it is obvious that unlike most tasks we have discussed before, this task is one a subject can do without making any mistakes. Thus, the data collected by the experimenter cannot be merely percent correct or percent error. Instead, the dependent variable is the subject's reaction time (RT)—the time it takes him to respond "same" or "different" after seeing the letters. Specifically, RT is the time that elapses between the onset of the letters and the subject's response.

In theory, using RT in this way will give an indication of how long it takes for internal events to occur. In Posner's task, RT includes the time required for the subject to perceive the letters, compare them and decide whether or not they are the same, and press the button. The RT should be longer or shorter as the subject takes more or less time to perform these actions. But the use of RT in psychological experimentation is not restricted to just one task. In fact, it has a rather long history. Posner's use of RT is actually developed from the work of Donders (1862), who devised a "subtractive procedure" for using RT to investigate psychological processes. The technique is quite simple: Suppose we have two tasks, X and Y, and suppose that task Y includes all of task X plus some other component, Q (that is, $Y = X + Q$). Now if we measure RT for the completion of tasks X and Y, then we can subtract the RT for task X from

Type of trial	Example of What Subject Sees	Subject's Correct Response
Identity match	A A	"Same"
Name match	A a	"Same"
Negative trial	A b	"Different"
← RT interval →		

FIGURE 7.1

Possible trial types—identity match, name match, and negative trial—and corresponding events in Posner's letter-matching procedure.

that for Y and derive the time it took for component Q. By this means, we can investigate the nature of Q, even though it may not be directly observable in isolation. More generally, by using RT, we can isolate task components and discover some of the properties of mental performance.

Now let us return to the Posner experiments. From Figure 7.1, it is clear that there is more than one situation where the subject will say "same." He will do so if the two letters are identical (say, A and A); this will be called an identity match. He will also say "same" if the letters are not identical but nevertheless have the same name (as in A and a); this is called a name match. When these conditions are violated, he will say "different." ("Same" responses and "different" responses are also called positive and negative responses, respectively.) Typically, the various types of responses—identity match, name match, and negative—do not lead to identical RTs. Instead, the subject is able to respond faster by about .1 second (which is quite a lot of time in a RT experiment) in making an identity match than in making a name match or a negative response. This suggests that there is some difference in how the subject is internally performing the task.

In order to find out what the difference might be, we must break down the subject's task into components, each of which takes part of the total amount of time. In doing so, we attempt to isolate the component or components that contribute to the added time in those conditions that take longer than identity matching. We might tentatively break down the task as follows: First the subject must perceive the letters (visually encode them). Then, he must name the letters. Then, he decides whether or not they have the same name. Then he responds by pressing the button. These activities use up the entire RT from the onset of the letters to the response. There is no compelling reason to suppose that the time it takes to perceive the letters varies from one condition to another, nor does it seem reasonable to suppose that the time it takes to push the button varies. It seems that the most likely source of the difference in RT lies in the naming and comparison processes. It must take less time to perform these components of the task when the letters are identical than when they are not.

In fact, Posner suggested that the difference in the RTs arose because there was no reason to name the two letters when they were identical. He suggested that two identical letters could be judged the same on the basis of their physical, visual forms. Only when the letters were not identical would it be necessary to name them and compare names. In short, for identity matches (A A), the task was to perceive and encode visually, compare physical images, and respond; whereas for name matches (A a) and negative responses (A B), the task was to perceive and encode visually, encode verbally (name), compare names, and respond. Name matches, having more components, would take more time, thus leading to the observed differences in RT. In short, Posner suggested that identity matches were based on visual information and that name matches were based on verbal labels. (See Figure 7.2.)

Now, to suggest that visual information is used for comparisons in the case of identity matches implies that the information must be available. This implication is unequivocal when two letters are simultaneously presented and stay in view until the subject responds—precisely the case we have been discussing. What we seek is evidence that there is visual

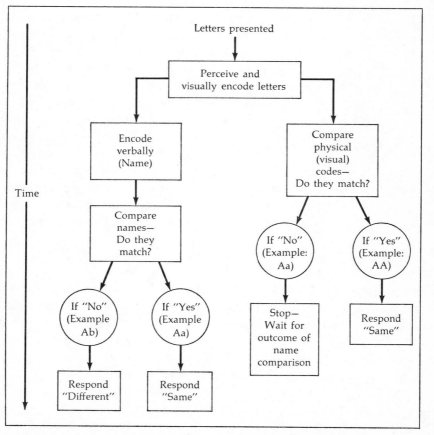

FIGURE 7.2

Diagram showing possible mental events in the letter-matching task.

information available in memory after the stimulus has vanished. More-over, we want to demonstrate that the information is not in the icon, but beyond it, in STM.

In order to show that this visual information exists in memory, the Posner task can be modified so that the two letters are presented not simultaneously, but sequentially. The typical trial goes like this: First, a letter appears for a half-second or so. Then, there is an interstimulus interval (ISI) in which the subject sees a blank field. Next, a second letter appears. The subject, as before, indicates whether the two letters are the "same" or "different." Reaction time is here defined as the inter-val between the onset of the second letter and the subject's response.

In this task, the first letter must be in memory when the subject makes his response because it vanishes from the display before the ISI. Thus, the comparison of the two letters must use information in memory. Is there still evidence that visual information is used in the comparison? That is, do identity matches still take less time than name matches? The answer is yes—at least under some conditions. If the ISI is less than a second or so, the identity matches take less time, but as the ISI ap-proaches 2 seconds, there is no longer a difference in RT (see Figure 7.3). Using the same reasoning as before, we can infer that when RT for iden-tity matches is less than that for name matches, visual information is being used for identity matching. But in this case, since the first letter is not physically present when the match is made, the visual information being used must be in memory. Thus, we have evidence that visual information about the first letter persists for a period of about 2 seconds after the letter has vanished. The gradual decrease in the advantage (shorter RT) of identity matches over name matches can be interpreted as a gradual decay of the visual information about the first letter in memory.

In summary, we now have evidence that visual information can persist in memory for a brief time after the stimulus has vanished. However, that leaves an important problem: how do we know that the visual in-formation is in STM, rather than the icon? From the experiments that have been described, we cannot be sure that it is not iconic information that contributes to matching two identical letters. However, there is evidence that indicates that the information is not in the sensory register, but is more appropriately labeled "short-term" (according to the criteria we set out at the beginning of this discussion).

One bit of evidence for the nonsensory nature of this visual memory is that it seems to exist even when the iconic representation is erased (Posner et al., 1969). For example, suppose the two letters are separated

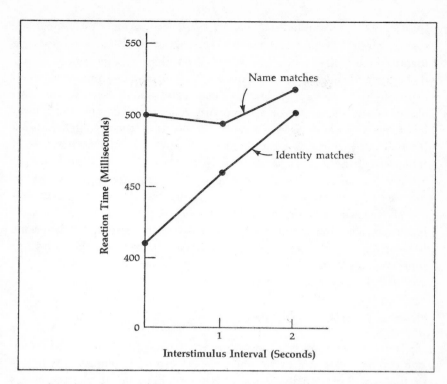

FIGURE
7.3

Reaction time for matching successively presented letters as a function of the interstimulus interval (ISI). Functions for identity matches and name matches are shown. [After Posner, 1969.]

by an ISI that is filled with a masking field, like a random black-and-white pattern. Under those conditions, we would expect the random pattern to erase the iconic representation of the first letter. In this case, identity matches are still made faster than name matches (although both take longer than when there is no pattern during the ISI). Thus, it seems that visual information about the first letter is present even after presentation of a masking pattern, which means that the visual information is held in some store other than the sensory register.

Another indication that this visual memory we are discussing is not sensory comes from evidence that it can be generated from LTM. One piece of evidence follows (Posner et al., 1969): Suppose that instead of giving the first letter visually, we say to the subject, "It is a capital A." Then we have a blank ISI, followed either by a capital A or some other letter. Under these conditions, RT for positive responses (those in which the second letter is what has been announced) is comparable to RT for identity matches (under the usual, both-letters-visual conditions) for ISIs of about 1 second and greater. For ISIs of less than 1 second, the identity matches are made a bit faster. What these results suggest is that the subject uses the spoken announcement to produce an internal visual copy of the announced letter. (He uses rules about letter sounds and appearances to do so.) He then compares his internal copy to the second letter, when it appears. When he has a second or more to generate his internal copy, the internal copy is roughly comparable to what would then exist if the first letter had been presented visually. With less than a second to do so, he produces a generated copy that is inferior to the memory of a visually presented letter. Thus, the subject can generate a visual representation from LTM rules, or he can retain a comparable representation after a stimulus has actually been presented. This seems to be strong evidence that the visual memory that persists after the stimulus is not sensory, for it can also be produced from LTM, not just received directly via the senses.

"Mental Rotation" Experiments

The representation the subject produces from LTM is not unlike the one you may have produced when you attempted to rehearse the letters of the alphabet visually. More is known about such representations through the work of Roger Shepard, Lynn Cooper, and their co-workers (Cooper and Shepard, 1973; Shepard and Metzler, 1971). Their research is concerned with something called "mental rotation"—the rotation of visual images like those we have been discussing. They had subjects perform tasks similar to Posner's. In one experiment, subjects were instructed to press one button if a letter stimulus was normal and another button if it was a mirror image. Particularly interesting is the fact that the stimulus could differ from its upright position by a rotation in the plane of presentation. For example, ⃔ was to be considered normal (for it is, within a rotation), whereas ⃕ was to be considered a mirror image. The degrees of rotation separating the stimulus from its upright position varied from 0 to 360. Shepard et al. found that the RT for deciding a letter was normal or mirror-reversed was a regular function of the amount (in degrees) of angular separation of the letter from the upright (Figure 7.4). As the letter was rotated more degrees from 0 to 180, RT increased; then from 180 to 360 degrees of rotation (which is 0 to 180 in the opposite direction), it decreased just as regularly. This RT pattern suggests that the subject was mentally rotating the stimulus into its normal orientation (clockwise or counterclockwise, whichever direction was

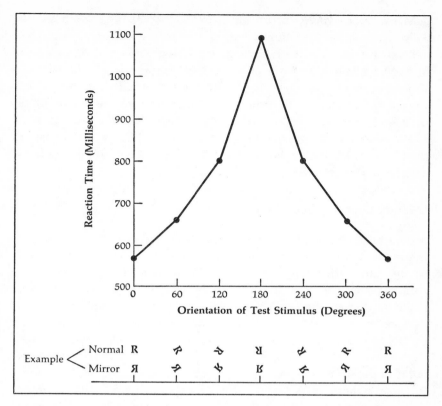

FIGURE
7.4

Reaction time for deciding whether a letter is presented in its normal form or as a mirror image of its normal form, as a function of the degrees of rotation of the letter in the plane of presentation. Below the graph are examples of letters at each rotation value [After Cooper and Shepard, 1973.]

closer to upright; for example, rotating **Ϧ** clockwise into **B**) and then deciding on a visual basis whether it was normal. Each degree the stimulus had to be rotated would add to the RT, thus giving a regular increase in RT with degrees of separation from normal. Thus, these results indicate that subjects could rotate some mental representation of the stimulus; some short-term visual code. This also tells us something about the nature of that visual code. Whatever form it takes, it must be rotatable, which implies that the code is not simply a list of features. How could a list of features be rotated? How could rotation of a list produce such a regular change in RT? Instead, Shepard et al. suggest that the visual code is rather faithful to the original stimulus.

Many other recent experiments strongly support the hypothesis that STM need not be acoustic—that visual representations may exist, either generated from LTM or following an external stimulus, which persist in STM for several seconds or as long as they are being "worked on." In fact, there are too many studies to review here. Before we end our discussion of visual STM, however, let us introduce another set of experiments that are relevant to the hypothesis that visual codes exist. These experiments were not designed with visual STM in mind. Instead, the focus of the original work, that of Saul Sternberg, was the retrieval of information in STM.

Memory Scanning and Visual STM

Sternberg's basic (1966) experiment was designed to investigate how information in STM might be retrieved—looked at, scanned, or read. Can all the information there be examined simultaneously, by means of a parallel scanning process? Or is scanning serial, with each item, or chunk, read one after another? In order to address these and other questions, he designed a task like this: Each subject took part in a series of trials. On each trial, he was first given a "memory set," for example, a set of one to five digits (a typical set of four might be "2, 4, 7, 3"). The number of items in the set was below the span of STM, and the subject was asked to commit them to memory. Then, he saw a "test stimulus," a single digit that might or might not have been a member of the set. He was to respond "yes" if the test stimulus matched one of the memory-set items, and "no" if it did not. As in the Posner experiments, the subjects could perform this task with very few errors, so the measured variable was RT. RT was defined in this task as the interval between the onset of the test stimulus and the subject's response (usually, pushing a button). (See Figure 7.5a.)

What kind of processing goes on during the RT interval? The task can be broken up into components of the type we used in analyzing Posner's experiments. (See Figure 7.5b.) We assume that when the test stimulus appears, the subject has the memory set stored in STM. Let us say that the subsequent processing includes three stages. First, the subject perceives and encodes the test stimulus—gets it into some mental form. Then, he compares that test stimulus to the members of the memory set. Finally, he responds on the basis of those comparisons. The total time taken by these stages is his RT.

Sternberg was particularly interested in the variations in RT that correspond to variations in the memory-set size—that is, the number of

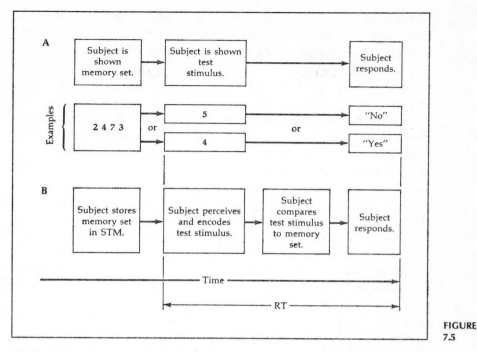

FIGURE
7.5

Sternberg's memory-scanning task: **(A)** Events of a typical trial. **(B)** Proposed mental events during the trial.

items in the set. From those RT variations, we can make inferences about the comparison process the subject goes through in the second stage of his task. To see this, consider what happens if we increase the memory set by one digit. This means that the subject will have more comparing to do, because he must compare the test stimulus to the elements in the memory set. The effects on RT of adding a single digit will vary according to how the subject does the task. Therefore, finding out what those effects are gives us a tool to find out how he is processing this information.

As an example, suppose we had a simple *parallel* hypothesis about the STM comparison process; namely, that the subject has a limitless processing capacity and can examine everything in STM at one time with no more effort than it takes him to look at some part of it. This hypothesis enables us to make certain predictions about the pattern of RT to be obtained. Specifically, we can predict that adding a single digit to the memory set will have no effect on RT. Whether the memory items number two, or three, or four, RT in the task should not vary, because it takes the subject no more time to compare one element of the memory set to the test stimulus than to compare several. This prediction is illustrated in Figure 7.6a, showing RT plotted against the number of items in the memory set.

Alternatively, suppose *serial* scanning occurs, that is, the subject can examine only one item in the memory set at a time. In this case, each item added to the set should increase the time it takes to perform the task. We would predict an increase in RT with memory-set size, the amount of increase depending on just how long it takes to scan an additional digit and compare it to the test stimulus. We would expect to find data like those shown in Figure 7.6b.

Now let us look at this serial-scanning hypothesis in more detail. We have proposed that the subject's task has three stages, each taking up part of the total amount of time. Let us now assign times to these stages. Suppose it takes the subject e milliseconds to encode the test stimulus; c milliseconds to compare a single item in the memory set with the test stimulus; and r milliseconds to perform the third (response) stage. If the memory set had only one digit, he could perform the task in $e + c + r$ milliseconds—that would be his RT. Now, suppose there were five elements in the memory set and none of them matched the test stimulus. The subject would make a negative response, and he would have RT of $e + c + c + c + c + c + r$ milliseconds. In general, the time it would take the subject to say "no" in the negative-response situation would be $e + s \times c + r$, where s is the memory-set size. His data would thus form a straight line on our graph plotting RT against s. The line could be expressed as $RT = (e + r) + (s \times c)$. Thus, the slope of that line would be c. What this means is that if we had a subject perform the task, and we plotted his RTs for negative responses against the size of the memory sets, we would get a straight line. The slope of that line would correspond, in theory, to the time (c) it took the subject to make a single comparison. The zero-intercept of that line (that is, the point on the line corresponding to s = 0) would include the time required to encode the stimulus (e) and respond (r).

At this point, you might be wondering why we have been focusing on negative responses. The reason is that the negative response can be made only after the subject has compared every member of the memory set to the test stimulus; otherwise, how would he know the test stimulus was not in the set? The picture gets more complicated for positive responses, because the subject might stop when he finds a match between some memory-set item and the test item. He would not necessarily make all the possible comparisons. This particular hypothesis of what the subject

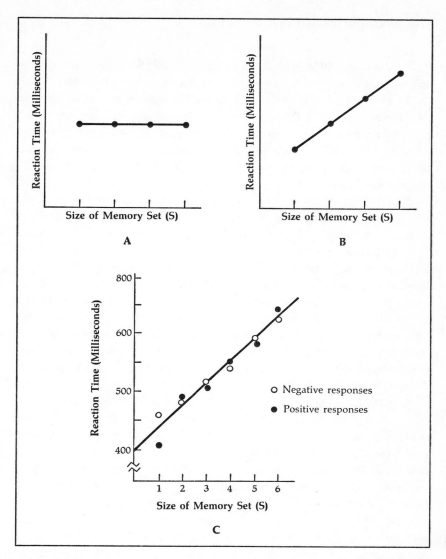

FIGURE 7.6

Sternberg's memory-scanning task: **(A)** Results, showing reaction time as a function of size of memory set, as predicted by the parallel model. **(B)** Results as in **A,** but as predicted by the serial model. **(C)** Actual results of the scanning task. [After Sternberg, 1966. Copyright 1966 by the American Association for the Advancement of Science.]

might do is called the "self-terminating" hypothesis, because it implies that the subject terminates (ends) his scanning whenever he finds a match. Alternatively, we could propose what is called the "exhaustive" hypothesis. This says that whether or not the subject has found a match, he exhausts the memory set in his comparison stage. He does not stop with the match, but goes on to finish the comparisons. The latter hypothesis may not even seem reasonable intuitively, but it should be tested.

The crucial test of the self-terminating hypothesis versus the exhaustive hypothesis lies in the value of the slope of the RT function (which plots RT against memory-set size) for positive responses. On the average, whenever the subject does find a match between the test stimulus and some item in the memory set, he should find that matching item halfway through his examination of the set. According to the self-terminating theory, this means he will stop (on the average) half-way through the set when he makes a positive response, but will go all the way through when he makes a negative response. On the average, he will make $(s + 1)/2$ comparisons for positive responses if he self-terminates. His RT for positive responses will include $e + r + ([s + 1]/2) \times c$. If we rearrange these terms to show RT as a function of s (obtaining: $RT = (e + r + c/2) + (c/2)s$), we find that the slope of the function will be half as great for positives as negatives ($c/2$ for positives, c for negatives). The exhaustive hypothesis, however, says that the comparison stage does not differ for positives and negatives—both involve all possible comparisons—and therefore implies no such difference in the slopes of their RT functions (both slopes should be c).

We now have three hypotheses. One is the parallel-scanning hypothesis, which predicts that the RT function (relating RT to s) will be flat for both positives and negatives (Figure 7.6a). The other two are versions of the serial hypothesis, which says that comparisons go on one by one and predicts RT will increase with memory-set size (Figure 7.6b). One version says that scanning is self-terminating. It predicts that the RT function for positive responses will have a slope half as great as the function for negative responses. The other version says that scanning is exhaustive, and predicts no difference in the RT functions for positives and negatives.

In order to assess the validity of the hypotheses, we must conduct an experiment. We must collect RT data from several subjects, each performing many trials. We must include both positive and negative trials with several memory-set sizes. We must then obtain the average RT for each type of trial—positive and negative—and each memory-set size. Then we must plot graphs of the RT functions; RT versus s. This is what Sternberg did, and his results are plotted in Figure 7.6c. According to the arguments just presented, these data support the serial, exhaustive hypothesis.

That Sternberg's results support exhaustive scanning is of special interest because, as we have noted, the exhaustive hypothesis runs counter to our intuition. Recall that it states that whether or not the subject finds a match between the test stimulus and the memory set, he will always compare every memory-set item to the test stimulus. He will not stop if he finds the match. This seems to imply that in the case of positive responses, those where a match is made, the subject makes many unnecessary comparisons. However, it is possible to explain why exhaustive scans might occur. To do so, we first divide the comparison process of the scanning task into two components. One is the act of *comparison* itself; the other is *deciding* what the results of the comparison are. If the comparison shows correspondence between a memory-set item and the test stimulus, that decision will be positive, leading to a positive response. Otherwise, the response will be negative. Now consider what would happen if the time for the subject to compare the test stimulus to a memory item were very fast, and the time for the subject to decide whether or not that comparison was positive (a match) relatively slow. If the process were self-terminating, his progress through the memory set would go: compare, decide, compare, decide, and so on, until a match was made (the decision would be "yes") or the set was completed. On the other hand, the subject could perform exhaustively, and his progress might be: compare, compare, compare, and so on, and—when the memory set was exhausted—decide. If decisions took a long time relative to comparisons, it is easy to see that an exhaustive search could be more expedient. It would require only one decision. In short, an exhaustive search would be efficient if the subject could compare at an extremely fast rate—so fast it would be difficult to stop for decisions. Instead, the subject would just "shoot on through" the comparisons, all of them, and only then decide and respond.

If the above explanation of exhaustive scanning is accurate, we should find that the comparison time is very fast. We can learn this from the RT data by computing the slope of the function plotting RT against memory–set size, which in theory represents the time it takes to compare the test stimulus to one item in the memory set. Such computation shows the rapid-comparison notion to be supported by the data. From the data in Figure 7.6c, we find that the value of our variable c, the slope of the RT function for negative responses, is about 35 milliseconds (.035 seconds). We infer that it takes the subject .035 seconds to compare the test stimulus to one memory-set element. Converting .035 seconds per comparison to the number of comparisons per second, we find out the subject can make about thirty such comparisons in a single second. That's surprisingly fast!

This finding brings us back to the original topic of this chapter. The inferred speed of comparison suggests that comparisons are *not* based on verbal labels that are acoustically represented in STM. Sternberg

(1966) could say this because of what he knew (and we know) about the relatively slow rate of implicit speech. Measurements of that rate, as well as that of explicit speech (which we discussed in Chapter 5), suggest that a subject can rehearse acoustically only about six items per second. If comparisons were based on acoustic representations in Sternberg's task (and the stimuli were therefore implicitly spoken), we would expect no more than six comparisons per second. This would lead to a slope of the RT functions of about 170 milliseconds, instead of the 35-millisecond slope actually observed. So, it seems the comparisons are not acoustic.

Sternberg (1967) therefore suggested that instead of acoustic codes, visual codes were being compared, and that visually-based comparisons could be performed faster than verbal comparisons. (We should note here that this might seem to contradict our previous suggestion that visual rehearsal is slower than verbal. However, in that rehearsal letters were produced from LTM. Here, the letters presumably exist in STM at the start of the scanning process, and the slope reflects comparison time.) As we shall see, there has been some support for the idea that visual representations are processed in Sternberg's task.

Sternberg (1967) tested the proposition that memory scanning uses visual representations by presenting the test stimulus either in degraded or normal form. In the degraded condition, the test stimulus was presented with a checkerboard pattern superimposed on it; in the normal condition, the checkerboard pattern was absent. Sternberg found that when RT was plotted as a function of memory-set size, the intercept of the resulting function for the degraded condition was higher than for the normal. This effect can be attributed to the fact that it takes longer to perceive and encode the stimulus behind the checkerboard pattern (increasing the "e" component of the total RT). More important is the fact that the *slope* of the RT function (which we assume to represent comparison time) was also higher for the degraded condition. The effect was small, and for well-practiced subjects there was no difference in slope for the two conditions. His interpretation of these results was as follows: The fact that there is some effect on the slope of the RT function owing to degrading the test stimulus indicates that the representation used for comparisons is visual. For if that representation were a label (that is, if the subject perceived and named the stimulus and then compared that name with the memory-set items), then degrading the stimulus might make it more difficult to perceive and name, but once it was named there should be no effect on using that name for comparisons. Thus, there should be no difference in the comparison time of degraded and normal stimuli; no effect of degradation on the slope. That there is such an effect must indicate that it is not names that are compared, but visual representations. On the other hand, the slope effect is quite small, and even negligible for practiced subjects. That indicates that the representation used for comparisons is not a raw, sensory image. For if it were a sensory image, degrading the test stimulus should badly degrade that image and produce a huge increase in comparison time. Thus, that there is such a small effect on the slope, indicating a small effect on comparison time, implies that it is not a sensory image that is compared to the memory set. In short, it seems that the stimulus representation used in Sternberg's task is visual, yet not sensory—in our current terminology, a short-term visual code.

In another experiment, Clifton and Tash (1973) conducted Sternberg tasks in which the memory set and test stimuli could consist of letters, three-syllable words of six letters (for example, POLICY), or one-syllable words of six letters (for example, STREET). For each type of stimuli, they computed slopes of the RT functions obtained with the tasks. They found that all the slopes were about the same. Thus, we can infer that the number of syllables in the memory-set items and test stimulus did not affect comparison time. But this implies that the comparison times were unaffected by how long it took to say the items, a result that would make little sense if comparisons were based on acoustic codes. On the other hand, the fact that the slopes were all equal also indicates that the comparison times were unaffected by the visual length of the items. If the representations used for comparison are visual, then, they must be far from the sensory level, where visual size would be expected to affect RT. This experiment thus suggests that nonsensory, nonacoustic codes are the basis for comparison in Sternberg's tasks, although whether those codes are visual remains unclear from these data.

Somewhat stronger evidence for visual coding in Sternberg's task comes from an experiment by Klatzky and Atkinson (1971). They focused on what is known about the special processing capacities of the two halves (hemispheres) of the brain, namely, that the left half (in most people) is specialized for verbal processing and the right half is specialized for visuo-spatial processing. Using this as a basis for the research, they conducted a scanning experiment that was similar to Sternberg's except that the test stimulus could be presented either in the left or right half of the subject's visual field. The connections between the human eye and brain are such that for both eyes, information presented in the left visual field goes directly to the right hemisphere of the brain, and information presented in the right field goes to the left hemisphere. Thus,

Klatzky and Atkinson could direct the test stimulus to either hemisphere, and they obtained for each hemisphere a function relating RT to memory-set size. They found that directing the stimulus to the left hemisphere raised the intercept of the RT function relative to right-hemisphere presentation, but the slopes of the functions were the same. They interpreted this RT effect as one of interhemispheric transfer. That is, they reasoned that when the test stimulus was presented to the left hemisphere, it had to be transferred to the right before comparisons could occur, resulting in an increase in the intercept of the RT function, the amount of which corresponded to the transfer time. In contrast, directing the stimulus to the right hemisphere required no transfer. This implies that the comparison process occurred in the right hemisphere, the one specialized for processing spatial, not verbal, information. This strongly supports the idea that comparisons do not involve verbal information but rather use visual representations. Thus, this experiment, like that of Sternberg (1967), supports the idea that STM can use visual codes and that the claim that STM is an acoustic store badly needs qualification.* Next, we turn to another challenge to that statement, finding evidence that STM can store semantic codes as well.

---

*It is important to note here that the presentation of Sternberg's experiment and related research has of necessity been simplified. Some of the major points of simplification deserve mention here. One is that the serial exhaustive model is not the only model that can explain the classic results—RT increases linearly with memory-set size. It is possible to devise a parallel model that will do the same (Townsend, 1972). Such a model differs from the simple parallel model we first discussed (the one that predicts no effect of memory-set size on RT) in that it proposes that the subject has available only a limited amount of processing capacity. This is to be distributed over all the items to be processed. When there are a small number, then each item gets relatively more capacity and can be processed quickly. When the number of items in the memory set is greater, then the processing capacity must be distributed more "thinly"; each item receives less and thus takes longer to process. This sort of model is parallel, because it assumes that all the items can be scanned at the same time. Yet it predicts that RT will increase with memory-set size because it assumes limited capacity. Still another model that can predict the Sternberg results represents memory scanning as a serial, self-terminating process (Theios, Smith, Haviland, Traupmann, and Moy, 1973).

Another major point to make about the task concerns the serial-position curves that are obtained. It is possible to plot RT as a function of the serial position of the matching stimulus for positive responses. (For example, if the memory set were "XPQ," and the test stimulus P, the serial position would be 2; if Q, it would be 3, etc.) The serial-exhaustive model predicts that such serial-position functions should be flat, for the subject always exhausts the memory set regardless of the position within the set at which he makes a match. Yet, there are data from the task showing that RT increases with serial position, other data showing that RT decreases, and still other data that produce inverted-U shaped functions. These and other aspects of the task have been reviewed by Nickerson (1972). A detailed analysis by Sternberg is also of interest (Sternberg, 1969).

SEMANTIC CODES IN STM

Because the idea that storage in STM must be acoustic came in part from patterns of confusion errors, it seems like poetic justice that our first demonstration of semantic content in STM is also based on confusions. Shulman (1972) demonstrated that STM confusions could follow a pattern predictable on the basis of meaning. In his experiments, subjects performed in a series of trials, during each of which they first received a ten-word list. The tenth word was followed by a probe word. The subject was instructed to say whether or not the probe "matched" a word that was in the list. On some trials, "match" meant "is identical to"; on others it meant "means the same as" (or "is a synonym of"). The subject was signaled just before the probe occurred during each trial as to which meaning of "match" applied for that trial.

The conditions of particular interest are those in which the probe was a synonym of a word that had been in the list and the subject was instructed to match on the basis of identity. If the subject says "yes" under these conditions, even though the probe is not identical with a word in the list, it indicates semantic confusion. That is, we suspect that the subject made this particular error (mistakenly identifying a word as having been in the list when it is actually a synonym of a list word) because he confused the two words—the one in the list and the probe—on the basis of semantic similarity. To do so, he must have in STM some knowledge about the semantic content of the list words. The reason that Shulman included trials in which a match was defined in terms of synonymy was to induce the subject to make such semantic information available, if he could.

Shulman's results provided evidence for semantic representations in STM. He found that a subject made the error of mistakenly identifying a probe word as a member of the list more often when the probe word was a synonym of a list word than when it was unrelated to the list words. This effect was manifest even when the probe was a synonym of one of the most recently presented words (for example, a word in one of the last three serial positions); the words that almost certainly are present in STM (as in the free-recall serial-position curve; see Chapter 2). Thus, we find short-term confusions that follow semantic patterns.

Evidence for semantic representations in STM has been found in other ways (reviewed by Shulman, 1971). Among the most thorough of these investigations has been that of Wickens and his associates (reviewed in Wickens, 1972), using a release-from-PI paradigm.

In order to understand Wickens' work, we must recall two experiments from our discussion of short-term forgetting in Chapter 6. The experiments are those of Peterson and Peterson (1959) and Keppel and Underwood (1962). Briefly, the Petersons found rapid forgetting of a consonant trigram in an 18-second interval between presentation and recall. Keppel and Underwood then showed that such forgetting occurred only when proactive inhibition (PI) had had a chance to build up, after the first trials of the task. With this background, Wickens, Born, and Allen (1963) conducted an experiment like the following: Suppose we have a subject perform three trials of a Peterson task, using various consonant trigrams as the to-be-remembered items and an 11-second retention interval, during which the subject performs a distractor task. During this time, PI builds up, and as the trials progress, the subject remembers fewer and fewer consonants on each trial. Now, on the fourth trial, we switch the material to be remembered. Instead of three consonants, we use three digits as the memory items. The typical results of such an experiment are shown in Figure 7.7. Relative to subjects in a control group, who have no switch in the material to be remembered, subjects in the experimental group, who switched to digits, show a sudden increase in their ability to remember. In fact, their performance on this fourth trial resembles their performance with the consonants on the first trial. It seems that the PI that had built up during the first trials is specific to the particular class of material to be remembered (here, consonants) and does not affect the new material (digits). Thus, the switch to digits is a switch to PI-free performance—performance notably higher than that with PI present.

The fundamentally important feature of this result is that PI is specific to the class of material that is being remembered. Situations in which PI release is obtained tell us that "new" material is being used. The release phenomenon can therefore serve as a tool for determining what aspects of stimuli are represented in STM. Perhaps an example will clarify this. Suppose we let PI build up by having a subject do several trials in the task with three-word groups as the item to be remembered. In the first three trials, all our word groups deal with food. Trial 1 uses BREAD-EGGS-MILK; Trial 2 uses MEAT-FISH-CHEESE; Trial 3 uses BUTTER-FRUIT-CEREAL. Now, on Trial 4 we introduce a new type of trigram, using the animal names DOG-CAT-HORSE. Will we observe release from PI? Will performance show a sudden improvement on this trial? Consider the possibilities.

Suppose no release is observed. This means that we have not changed the class of to-be-remembered material. Going a step further, what this

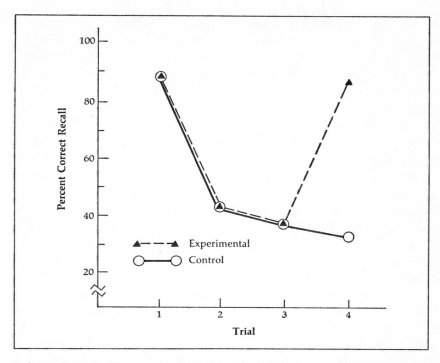

FIGURE
7.7

Release from PI: The graph shows idealized data for the percent of items correctly recalled as a function of trial number. The fourth trial corresponds to the release trial (where for the experimental group, the category of the to-be-remembered items differs from that of previous trials). [After Wickens, 1972.]

means is that we have not changed the class of material from the subject's point of view, the information he encodes and stores during the trial Apparently, he did not store the fact that the words on the first three trials were all names of foods, nor that the next words were names of animals.

On the other hand, suppose now that we did observe release from PI—a sudden leap in the ability to recall on the fourth trial. It would mean we had switched the class of material. That means that our switch from food to animals was meaningful in the context of what the subject was storing about the material to be remembered. But *that* means that the subject must have been encoding and storing something about the *meaning* of those items—that the first group of words referred to types of food, and the second did not. In short, we would have evidence that meanings were stored in STM.

In fact, Wickens has found that shifts in performance do follow changes in semantic content. Category shifts like the one just described (from foods to animals) are a case in point; these shifts lead to the release-from-PI effect. So do shifts in language (e.g., from French to English); masculine nouns (butler, rooster, tuxedo) to feminine (queen, nylons, cow); abstract nouns (advantage, boredom, position) to concrete (palace, acrobat, factory), and many others. We can conclude that semantic aspects of the to-be-remembered items, and not just acoustic representations, are stored in STM.

Although the experiments just cited appear to support the idea of semantic encoding in STM, they are subject to alternative interpretations. Baddeley (1972) has challenged these findings and others relating to semantic STM. He argues that the evidence for semantic STM actually results from the subject's use of retrieval strategies—techniques and rules that are stored in LTM. For example, when a subject performs a memory-span task in which he is to remember a series of letters, he would be unlikely to report a digit as a confusion error. Instead, if the information in STM at the time of recall were the vowel sound "ay", he might report "H" rather than "8", simply because he knows that the sequence consisted of letters. Similarly, the subject could use LTM information in STM experiments to produce results compatible with the theory that STM can be semantic.

Consider the release-from-PI phenomenon. Baddeley argues that those effects reflect LTM processing rather than STM processing. On a given trial, the subject is trying to recall the most recent items in a series (the last set of items to be remembered). The retention interval is long enough so that the information might not be in STM at all. Moreover, the source of interference is the material presented over several earlier trials. If this material is similar to the material to be recalled (for example, if all items come from a single category of words, such as names of animals), then the only retrieval rule that will enable the subject to select the most recent items is some knowledge about the order or time at which items were presented. On the other hand, if the material to be recalled differs from the material previously presented (which is what happens on the release trial), then that difference provides an additional retrieval rule to assist the subject in picking out the most recent items. (For example, if the previous trials used animal names, and the current trial uses food names, then the difference in categories can form the basis for retrieval of the most recent items—those on the current trial.) The aid of this difference leads to better recall—and to the release phenomenon.

Empirical evidence favoring a retrieval-from-LTM explanation of PI release has been provided by Gardiner, Craik, and Birtwistle (1972). They conducted a release-from-PI study in which the material to be remembered was shifted on the release trial from one subset of a category to another subset of the same category. For example, to-be-remembered items on the prerelease trials might all consist of types of wild flowers; then, on the release trial, they might be switched to garden flowers. The experimenters found that the typical release from PI occurred under some conditions and not others. It did *not* occur when the general category name (for example, FLOWERS) was given to the subject as a cue. However, release from PI was obtained when the more specific category name (for example, WILD FLOWERS) was given, either at the time of presentation or the time of recall. There are two particularly important implications of these results: First, release from PI was found, for the same material, under some cue conditions but not others. This indicates that a change in the nature of the to-be-remembered material does not by itself cause PI release. Second, release from PI was obtained when the appropriate cue, the specific category name, was presented at the time of recall. This provides strong evidence for the hypothesis that the release phenomenon takes effect at the time of retrieval. That is because the fact that the cue was effective in the situation where it was presented only at the time of recall (not at the time the material was encoded) indicates that the release effect does not depend on encoding. Instead, it seems that the cue can take effect at the time of retrieval, and its presence or absence determines whether PI release will occur. Thus, the evidence favors a view of release from PI as dependent on retrieval operations in LTM.

The critique by Baddeley and the above results certainly seem to weaken the case for semantic representations existing in STM. On the other hand, our conception of STM may help to resolve the problem. If we consider simply the storage portion of STM, where material is held in some rote manner, it seems unlikely that semantic content plays an important part. On the other hand, if we consider the STM work space, and particularly the role that LTM plays in performing such work as chunking, then we are considering an essentially semantic portion of STM. Our STM concept indicates that many tasks that require short-term storage also require a strong LTM component. The idea of interaction between the stores helps to accommodate the proposal that semantic information could be encoded for STM storage, and the act of short-term encoding, which involves LTM, can be considered a form of STM "work."

One thing seems clear at this point. The picture of STM we have arrived at in three chapters of discussion no longer resembles very closely the simple theory presented in Chapter 2. Well, we knew all along that an adequate theory really couldn't be that simple. Theories of STM have become complex because the findings indicate that STM really is that complex.

ANOTHER LOOK AT DUPLEX THEORY

Turning from our discussion of short-term memory, let us take a closer look at one prominent version of the duplex theory, the theory of Atkinson and Shiffrin (1968), called "the buffer model." This theory is notable because it attempts to present the idea that a complex, cognitive STM can fit in the now familiar context of a two-memory framework. It was Atkinson and Shiffrin who proposed that the distinction between "control processes" and "structural components" be applied to memory, and it is their discussion of the control processes of STM that is of particular interest in the present context.

You may recall that a control process is not built in, but is something that is applied to built-in structures. It represents a decision on the part of the subject, not necessarily conscious, to operate the memory system in a particular way. We might ask what choices an information processor has in controlling STM. One set of control processes has to do with the size of the STM storage space, which in this model is called the "rehearsal buffer." To Atkinson and Shiffrin, this space represents a place where a small number of chunks could undergo rote repetition, or rehearsal, as opposed to more complex "work." The choices here include: What size buffer should be used (within limits imposed by the memory span, of course)? Should there be many items in the buffer, with little work space? Or should there be few items and a lot more room to work? This decision might depend on the rehearsal process itself. A person might choose to rehearse a small number of items because they fit together well—perhaps because they all have the same rhythm: "pattern," "duplex," "level," "hunger." (We would not add the word "incongruity" to this rehearsal set.) Or a person might choose to stop rehearsing something and to eliminate it from the buffer.

Yet, if this begins to sound again like our simple slot model, it is not. For this model of STM also includes control processes that apply to the work-space portion of STM, and states that the form of the information transferred to LTM from STM depends on these processes. Atkinson and Shiffrin have the notion that many items may be rehearsed in a rote manner, but this will cause them to be transferred only in some minimally enriched way. Perhaps only the fact that they were in STM can be transferred to LTM in this way. This is to be contrasted with information that can be sent to LTM about worked-on items. Items can be mediated, associated to, or chunked; information can then be sent to LTM in an enriched form. This enrichment process is costly, however—it reduces the number of items that can be accommodated in STM.

We have now developed the idea that a trade-off occurs between working memory and storage space (like that discussed in Chapter 6), but we have something else as well. This model carries with it the sense of close and complex ties between STM and LTM, as well as the possibility that STM storage can use semantic and visual information. As demanded by the experiments we have been discussing, this is a model that is far more complex than a theory of STM as a set of slots.

8

LTM: STRUCTURE AND SEMANTIC PROCESSING

Long-term memory, we have said, stores our knowledge of the world. It is material in LTM that enables us to recall events, solve problems, recognize patterns—in short, to think. All the knowledge that underlies human cognitive abilities is stored in LTM.

Some aspects of LTM have already been mentioned in previous chapters. We know that abstract representations of patterns are stored in LTM, and that these representations can be matched with incoming stimuli and can thus lead to recognition of those stimuli. We have seen that information can be chunked with the help of various rules—rules of spelling, rules for recoding digit series, rules of English syntax—all stored in LTM. We have seen that word meanings and facts are stored in LTM. Shiffrin's (1973) experiment on STM forgetting made use of the rules for arithmetic that are stored in LTM. Who wrote *Macbeth*? The answer is probably in your LTM. If John runs faster than Mary, and Sally runs faster than John, who runs fastest? As you answer the question, you are working with information in LTM. The sheer amount of information in LTM is astounding. According to some theorists (for example, Penfield, 1959), everything you ever stored in LTM is still there. If so, your LTM is holding a lot of information.

The format of information in LTM is of interest as well as its quantity. Information in LTM seems to be stored in a very orderly fashion. Facts are connected to other facts in a nonrandom way; one word is connected to other words related to it in meaning. It may be this orderly format that enables us to retrieve information from LTM—such as who wrote *Macbeth*—in a matter of seconds. Certainly we do not seem to search randomly throughout LTM for the author of *Macbeth*, for that could take years.

THE STRUCTURE OF LTM

Brown and McNeill (1966) demonstrated and attempted to describe some of the regularities in LTM storage in an experiment that dealt with the tip-of-the-tongue (TOT) phenomenon we have all experienced when we could almost—but not quite—remember a word or a name. They gave subjects definitions of words and asked the subjects to tell what the words were. For example, a subject might be given "a small boat used in the harbors and rivers of Japan and China, rowed with a scull from the stern and often having a sail." What Brown and McNeill were looking for was the "TOT state," in which a subject felt he knew the word (it was "on the tip of his tongue") but just couldn't recall it. Of course, on many trials this would not occur—either the subject would recall the world immediately, or he might feel that he did not know the word at all. Thus, the TOT state was rather elusive, but the authors were able to catch it reasonably often (presumably, by choosing a good batch of definitions). When the state occurred, it had a number of characteristics: Not only did the subject feel he knew the word, he could sometimes report the number of syllables, or the initial sound, or where the accent occurred. (He might say, "It has two syllables, accent on the first, and starts with s.") He knew, often, which words were not correct (it was not a sandal, nor a schooner) and could give words that were related in meaning. This type of recall, in which the subject can identify the general characteristics of the word, is called generic recall.

In accounting for the existence of generic recall, Brown and McNeill described some aspects of LTM structure. They suggested that a word is stored in LTM at some location. Its representation there includes auditory information (its sound) as well as semantic information (its meaning). The word can be retrieved from LTM, then, by its sound (for example, I say the word DOG and you tell me its meaning) or by its meaning (I give you MAN'S BEST FRIEND and you say "dog."). In the TOT state, total retrieval by meaning has failed, but a subject has partially retrieved the word. He has some knowledge of its sound but apparently does not have a complete acoustic representation. The authors also suggested that stored with each word were associations—marked pathways—to other words in LTM, so that the subject could come up with words that meant almost the same thing. Thus, Brown and McNeill depicted LTM as a large set of interconnected storage locations, each holding a complex collection of information related to a single word or fact.

The structure of LTM will be of central importance in this chapter. The TOT research gives us the idea that LTM may be depicted as a network of associated bundles of information. That notion bears a direct relationship to the S–R theory discussed in Chapter 1. Several more recent models of LTM structure are also associationistic (Anderson and Bower, 1973; Quillian, 1969; Rumelhart, Lindsay, and Norman, 1972), but there are other ways to consider the structure of LTM as well. These include conceptions of LTM as composed of sets of information (Meyer, 1970) and as bundles of meaningful features (Rips, Shoben, and Smith, 1973; Smith, Shoben, and Rips, 1974). Each of these approaches has something to offer, and we shall consider each in turn. And for each model of LTM structure, there are associated explanations of LTM processes—the ways in which structured information is put to use.

Before we consider models of LTM in some detail, there are a few things to note. One point is that current models of LTM are quite complex. This is dictated by the complexities of LTM, some of which we have noted: (1) The uses of LTM information include problem solving, logical deduction, question answering, recall of facts, and many others. (2) The amount of information in LTM is astounding. (3) Its organization is orderly, not haphazard. In attempting to account for the many uses to which LTM information is put, the mass of LTM information, and its organization, no model of LTM, however complete, is at present totally adequate. However, models are constantly undergoing modification to enable them to account for more data.

A second point is one that may seem to compound the complexities of LTM. It is in fact useful to talk not only about one LTM, but two. The two-LTM idea has been suggested by Tulving (1972), who sets forth a distinction between *semantic* memory and *episodic* memory. Both memories are long-term stores for information; however, the kind of information they hold differs.

It is semantic memory that holds all the information we need in order to use language. It includes not only words and the symbols for them, their meaning and their referents (what they represent), but also the rules for manipulating them. Semantic memory holds such things as the rules of English grammar, chemical formulas, rules for adding and multiplying, knowledge that autumn follows summer—facts that do not depend on a particular time or place, but are just facts. Episodic memory, in contrast, holds temporally coded information and events, information about how things appeared and when they occurred. It is our memory for autobiographical information, such as "I broke my leg in the winter of 1970." It stores things that depend on context—"It is not every night that I have fish for dinner, but I had it last night."

In addition to differences in what they store, semantic and episodic memories differ in their susceptibility to forgetting. Information in episodic memory can become inaccessible rather easily, for new information is constantly coming in. When you retrieve something from either memory—for example, you multiply 3 × 4 (which uses information from semantic memory), or recall what you did last summer (from episodic memory)—the actual act of retrieving is itself an event. As such, it must be entered into episodic memory, and you will store the knowledge that you multiplied 3 × 4, or that you recalled what you did last summer. Thus, episodic memory is in a constant state of change, and information there is often transformed or made unretrievable. In contrast to episodic memory, semantic memory probably changes much less often. It is not affected by the act of retrieval, and information in it is more likely to stay there.

Of special importance in Tulving's distinction is what it says about the traditional study of human memory, particularly the experimental procedures that use word lists (discussed in Chapter 1). Undoubtedly, such lists of words are held in episodic memory. For example, if I give you a twenty-word list containing the word FROG, I am not actually teaching you the word "frog." The word will be stored in your semantic memory before, during, and after you learn the list. But I am teaching you that "frog" is currently in your list—a fact that depends on this time and this situation. That fact will be stored in episodic memory. What this means is that traditional psychology experiments are studying episodic memory, not semantic memory. The study of semantic memory has been grossly neglected since the time of Ebbinghaus.

Only in the last decade or so has semantic memory become the focus of a great deal of research. That research concentrates primarily on how our semantic knowledge of the world is structured, and how that knowledge is used in various tasks. Several models of semantic memory will be discussed in this chapter (some models include episodic memory as well), and it is their depictions of LTM structure and process to which we now turn. As mentioned above, models of semantic memory can be roughly classified as network models, set models, or semantic-feature models. None of these categories is totally distinct from the others; all are closely related, which is not surprising in view of the fact that all attempt to account for the same human abilities. However, each type of model has some distinctive properties, and the following discussion will consider the nature of each type, some of the data it attempts to explain, and some of the problems it encounters.

NETWORK MODELS OF LTM

Network models of semantic memory, like the theory of Brown and McNeill, depict LTM as a vast network of associated concepts. Network models are not unlike the S–R conception of memory as a bundle of associations. However, these models differ from traditional associationism in some fundamental ways. For one thing, most such models assume that different kinds of associations can be formed—that not all associations are the same. This means that when two concepts are associated, the relationship between the two is known; the association is more than a simple bond. This approach has been called "neo-associationism" (Anderson and Bower, 1973). This view of LTM also includes the idea that the associative network is as orderly and compact as possible. Things that are close together conceptually may be expected to be closely associated in the LTM network. In that sense, LTM is like a dictionary, but its organization is not alphabetical, for the alphabetical organization of the typical dictionary we use is not conceptually useful. Consider, for example, aardvark and zebra, both rather unusual animals. They are closely related in concept, but maximally separated in the dictionary. In LTM, they would presumably be more closely associated than in the dictionary.

Given that LTM is an orderly network of this sort, we might wonder just what "orderly" means. We might ask for a more detailed description of the network, and that is precisely the aim of the models we shall consider. One thing we shall discover is that the connections among concepts are circular. What does this mean? Well, consider our dictionary example once again. Suppose we were to look up the meaning of the word "client" in the dictionary. We might find "**client,** n., (klī´ ĕnt) 1. A dependent; one under the protection of another. 2. One who employs the services of any professional man, as a lawyer." What we have found is a rather detailed description of the word: "client" falls in the class noun, meaning it is a "thing." It has more than one meaning, or sense, and we are given the meanings. Suppose, however, we were unfamiliar with English— it would be unfortunate that the word "client" is defined in terms of other words we do not know, such as "professional." We might look up "professional," and find, "adj., of or pertaining to a profession." Not much help. We might look up "lawyer," and find, in part, ". . . lawyer, the general term, applies to anyone in the profession; attorney and solicitor are strictly applied to the lawyer transacting business for his client." In short, we find a mess: "client" is defined with the terms "lawyer" and "professional"; "lawyer" is defined with the terms "professional" and "client"; "professional" is defined with the term "lawyer," and so on. That's what we mean by circular. Words are defined with other words. And, as we shall see, in network theories of LTM, concepts are thought to have meaning by virtue of their associations to other concepts.

A final preliminary point should be made concerning the language of current models of LTM. You may think that their terminology comes straight out of your junior-high English grammar, including such terms as subject, predicate, noun, and so on, in describing LTM. Why should this be? It is really not surprising when you think about it for a moment. Take, for example, the terms "subject" and "predicate." A subject is a thing, some concept that can be represented by a noun or a noun phrase. A predicate is a concept that tells something about the corresponding subject. Subject and predicate, "thingness" and the predication of things, seem to be distinct concepts as well as distinct terms. As such, they have psychological reality as well as grammatical reality, and they presumably exist as separable elements in LTM. Thus, to the extent that grammatical concepts have psychological reality, we will find grammatical terms in models of LTM. Furthermore, current models of the structure of semantic LTM place primary emphasis on how it represents the kind of knowledge that is transmitted by language. This makes grammatical terms especially useful in describing LTM. The emphasis on language is appropriate, for it is the great linguistic capacity of humans that distinguishes them from other animals. Indeed, it is probable that the human linguistic ability is what makes their huge memorial capacity possible. For these reasons, the structure of language is central in descriptions of LTM.

Quillian's TLC

There are several models of LTM in which language and associative networks play an important part. The first was that suggested by Quillian (1969; Collins and Quillian, 1969), called TLC (for Teachable Language Comprehender). This model is embodied in a computer program that attempts to simulate the ability of a person to comprehend and use language in a natural way. In essence, it is an attempt to program the computer to speak. Quillian's model is more encompassing than the version presented here, since its description of LTM is just one feature of the model. We shall confine ourselves to the model's statements about the structure of LTM, processes that act on that structure, and experimental results that are relevant to it.

First, what is the structure of LTM according to Quillian's model? The format of factual information in LTM is made up of three types of structures—units, properties, and pointers. The first two we can think of as locations, in Brown and McNeill's sense: units and properties are places in LTM that correspond to information about concepts. The difference between units and properties lies in the kinds of concepts they represent. A unit is a structure that corresponds to an object, event, or idea; things that in English would be represented by nouns or noun phrases, or—if sufficiently complex—even sentences. Essentially, a unit represents what we have called "thingness." (Examples of units include the concepts "dog," "America," "father," "beautiful weather," "good vibes," and so on.) In contrast, a property is a structure that tells about a unit; in English grammar it would correspond to the predicate of a sentence, or an adjective, adverb, and so on. (Examples would include "solid," "graceful," "quickly," and "loves cats." We should note that although we use English words here as examples, units and properties are more abstract structures than words. They are the LTM entries that correspond to these words, not the words themselves. However, using the English term is a convenient way to refer to the unit or property in LTM.)

In order to see how pointers, together with units and properties, form the structure of LTM, it will be useful to refer to Figure 8.1, where we find the structure in memory corresponding to just one concept, that of the word "client." Thus, the figure depicts just one tiny portion of LTM. We can see from the figure that the word "client" is external to the LTM network structure; it resides outside the network in a mental dictionary. However, it points to the place in the network that corresponds to the word "client." That place is the unit for "client." The association between the mental dictionary word "client" and the unit "client" is called a pointer. Essentially, pointers are TLC's associations. They serve to associate dictionary labels with concepts in LTM, and they also associate units and properties inside the LTM network with one another. In doing so, they serve to define those units and properties; in fact, definitions correspond to the patterns of associations.

According to the TLC model, the nature of units and properties is described by a small number of rules. Let us look at the rules for making up a unit. (See Figure 8.1.) They say that a unit consists of an ordered list of pointers. The first pointer of the unit must point to a second

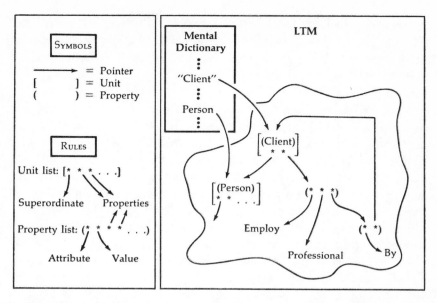

FIGURE 8.1

Information in TLC's memory corresponding to the concept "Client." [After Quillian, *Communications of the ACM,* Vol. 12, August 1969. Copyright 1969, Association for Computing Machinery, Inc.]

unit—specifically, the immediate superordinate of the first unit. (For example, in the unit for "client," the first pointer points at the unit corresponding to "person," because person is a concept that includes "client." In fact, it is the immediate superset of "client"—the smallest higher-order category that includes the category "client.") The remaining pointers of the unit point to properties. There can be any number of such pointers. In the present example, however, we cite only one—it goes to a property called "employs professional."

To understand properties, we should look at the rules for making up properties according to TLC. Like units, properties consist of ordered lists of pointers. As we shall see in a moment, the first two pointers are required, or obligatory. To see what they point to, we must first consider the nature of properties in general. Take a typical property; something that might describe a unit. It might be something like "Its color is white." This property has an *attribute*—whatever the property refers to has the attribute of color—and a *value* of that attribute—white. In general, a property can be thought of as some attribute plus a value of that attribute. It could be something other than an adjective like "white"; it could be a prepositional phrase like "on hill." In that phrase, "on" is the attribute; "hill" is the value of that attribute. Another kind of property might be more like a predicate, such as "throws basketballs." Thus, we can see that the attribute-value form is general enough to include just about any kind of property.

Now, back to the rules for constructing properties. We have said that they include two obligatory pointers. It should be clear that the first points to an attribute; the second to the attribute's value. The property of client shown in Figure 8.1 has its first pointer to "employs" (the attribute); its second to "professional" (the value). Thus, we see that a property of clients is that they employ professionals. In addition to the two required pointers corresponding to its attribute and value, a property can include any number of pointers to other properties. Our current property includes such an extra pointer. It points to the property "by client." Thus, we see that a client is a person who employs a professional; a professional is employed by a client. We could easily expand Figure 8.1 so that it filled this book. We would show the properties of the unit "person" and the properties of the units and properties involved in its definition. "Person" might include "living thing" in its definition; think of all the pointers it would take to define that, and in defining the things they point to. What would evolve is a huge, interconnected set of concepts—that is TLC's memory.

In summary, the structure that evolves is a huge network of concepts. They are of two types, units and properties, and the pattern of interconnections serves to give them meaning. Units are defined by other units and properties; properties are defined by other properties and units. It should also be noted, although the TLC model does not make it specific, that concepts must also be defined by their connections to the world through the sensory system. LTM cannot be totally self-contained. For example, what good would it do to define a concept like "white" by its relationships with such concepts as hospitals, daisies, most bedsheets, hats worn by "good guys," and so on, unless we had a memory of seeing it? Thus, ultimately, the models of LTM must explain how it interacts with the world, as well as how its internal parts are interelated. Those of its internal relationships that define concepts by their connections to other concepts make LTM seem much like our dictionary. We have seen that words are defined in dictionaries by other words, and if we look those other words up we find that they, too, are defined by words. Each word in a dictionary gets its meaning only through the complex interconnections among dictionary entries, with occasional pictures that tie words to visual sensory experience.

We might say that Quillian's model of LTM depicts a vast associated network. What is associated are concepts—ideas like "client," or "having color," or acting in various ways. What ties them together are pointers, which are essentially associations. These associations differ from the traditional S–R bonds in that there are distinct types of associations: the superordinate association, the property association, the attribute association, and the value association. The depiction of LTM as a set of locations connected by labeled associations is the fundamental characteristic of network models of LTM.

Anderson and Bower's HAM

Quillian's model was one of the first to depict LTM as a network containing all of a person's knowledge about the world, and to attempt to simulate human language by programming a detailed structure into a computer. It was followed by other network models, each having its own unique features as well as the general characteristics of a network. To expand the network idea, it will be useful to consider another such model. Developed by Anderson and Bower (1973), it is called "HAM" (for Human Associative Memory).*

Although HAM bears a general resemblance to Quillian's TLC, it is quite different in the detailed structure it proposes for LTM. Of course, as a network model, HAM describes LTM as a vast collection of locations and labeled associations. In HAM, however, the basic component—the "molecule" of LTM—is called a proposition. HAM's propositions resemble English sentences, except that they are more abstract. That is, a proposition can represent a linguistic structure such as a sentence, but it is not that sentence itself. (Propositions are not restricted to representing linguistic information; they can represent nonlinguistic information in LTM as well. For example, according to Anderson and Bower, descriptions of visual scenes could be represented in LTM by propositions.)

In general, a proposition is a small set of associations and locations (much as a unit in TLC is a small set of units and properties). Each association is binary; that means it combines, or associates, two concepts. The associations are of several types. The types of associations, and the way in which they combine to form a proposition, are illustrated in Figure 8.2. There are four basic types of associations to consider, each

---

*A related model, developed by Rumelhart, Lindsay, and Norman (1972), is discussed extensively in a book by Lindsay and Norman (1972). For further reading on network models, the latter source is recommended.

combining two simpler ideas. (1) One association combines a context and a fact. The context tells where and when the fact occurred, and the fact carries information about what happened in that context. (2) Another association combines a location and a time; this combination forms a context. The location tells the "where" of the context; the time tells the "when." (3) A third association combines a subject with a predicate; this association forms a fact. The subject tells what the fact is about; the predicate tells what happens to the subject. (4) A predicate itself can be a binary, or two-part, association: a predicate often tells the relationship between a subject and an object. Thus, the predicate can be said to associate a relation (a verb-like form, such as "is taller than," "hits," or "is the father of") and its object.

When they are combined appropriately, these four types of associations—context–fact, location–time, subject–predicate, relation–object—form a proposition. A proposition is best illustrated with a tree diagram, which shows the way the various concepts can combine in a proposition. In Figure 8.2 such a tree is shown, representing the sentence "In the classroom the professor questioned Bill." At the very top of the tree, we have the concept of the proposition itself. It is labeled A. The point A is called a "node" of the tree, as is every point where two associated entities combine. The proposition node is actually the result of a binary (two-part) association between a context and a fact; they are shown one level down in the tree. Now, continuing down the tree, we see that the context node (B) is the association between a location (D, in the classroom) and a time (E, in the past, since the verb says the professor questioned Bill). The fact node (C), like the others, can be broken down into two parts, a subject (F) and a predicate (G). But the predicate node is also composed of two parts. It is made up of the association between the relation (H, the verb "question") and its object (I, Bill).

That is the form of a proposition. It is composed of a context plus a fact (although in some cases, such as "Mice eat cheese," the context may be absent). The context (if present) is in turn made up of a location plus a time. The fact is a subject plus a predicate. The predicate is a relation plus an object. And the very bottom line of the tree contains what is not broken down at all. The entities there are called "terminal nodes" (terminal because the tree diagram terminates there). These nodes are the basic concepts of LTM, represented here by words (just as we could represent the units and properties of TLC with words). They serve to "anchor" the proposition to LTM; they essentially serve as fixed locations to which any number of trees might be attached. Thus, we see that LTM is like a network of propositional trees that serve to associate

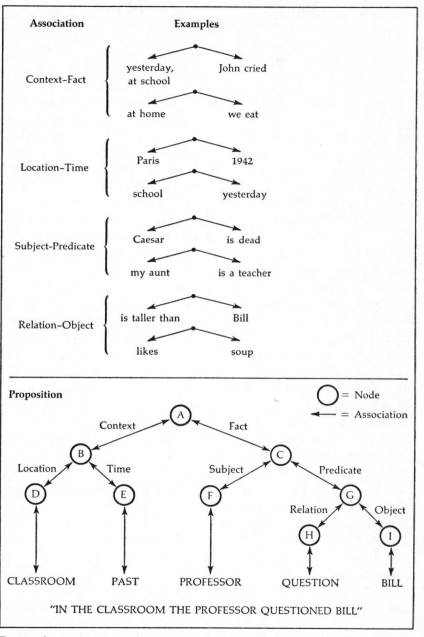

FIGURE 8.2

Types of associations and examples of each type *(above)* and a proposition tree corresponding to the proposition "In the classroom the professor questioned Bill" *(below)*, as represented in the HAM model of Anderson and Bower (1973).

various locations (corresponding to the terminal nodes of the proposition trees).

Processes of TLC and HAM

So far, we have learned that network models have an associationistic structure proposed for LTM, but that is only part of the picture. These models, or any model of LTM, would not go far with structure alone. In order to simulate human behavior, or make predictions about experimental data pertaining to semantic memory (which we shall discuss shortly), a model must also stipulate *processes*. Processes act on the structure and work with it to encode, store, and retrieve information.

In Quillian's model, for example, it is necessary to explain how TLC acquires new information, comprehends linguistic inputs (which is essential for its acquisition of new information), and answers questions. The most important process used in these tasks is called the "intersection search." Suppose TLC is trying to comprehend a sentence that we give it as input, such as A WOLF CAN BITE. In the sentence, certain concepts are named (such as "wolf" and "bite"). The search process simultaneously enters LTM at the location of each concept named, then proceeds outward from those concepts along the pointers or paths leading from them. Each time a pointer leads the search to a new concept, that concept is given a mark to indicate it has been passed in the search and from what concept it was reached. At some point, it is probable that a pathway being followed will lead to a concept that has already been marked (that is, has been reached previously in the search). At that point, we have an intersection. Finding an intersection means that the same point (the intersection) has been reached from two concepts. Thus, it indicates the two concepts are related. By checking the marker at the point, and tracing back the steps leading to the intersection, the process determines just which concepts intersected and how those concepts are related. If the relation between the concepts in LTM is compatible with the relation in the input sentence, the sentence can be said to be comprehended.

The TLC intersection search is illustrated in Figure 8.3. It shows a portion of the LTM network (in a somewhat neater form than Figure 8.1, with units and properties labeled), including the concepts of certain animals and their properties. Suppose we give TLC a sentence like A CANARY IS A FISH. The search process will enter the network at "canary" and "fish." From "canary," the concepts "bird," "sing," and "yellow" will be marked. From "fish," the concepts will include "fins," "swim,"

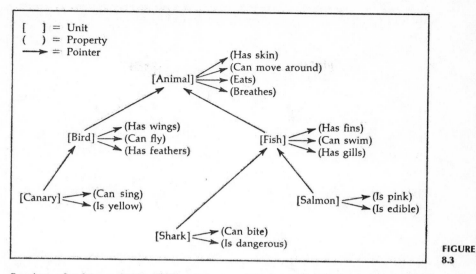

FIGURE
8.3

Portion of a hierarchy in TLC's memory, showing relationships among the units and properties within the category "Animal." [After Collins and Quillian, 1969.]

and "animal." Finally, when the search emanating from "canary" hits the concept "animal," it will find a marker from "fish" there. By tracing back along the paths which led to "animal," the relationship between "fish" and "canary" will be found. It is not compatible with the relation in the sentence, which says "a canary is a fish." However, if the sentence said that "canary is related to fish," it would be verified. Similarly, the search could verify that "a canary has skin" (by finding the path from "canary" to "bird," "bird" to "animal," and "animal" to "skin"), or find that "a canary can fly" (from the path saying "a canary is a bird," "a bird can fly").

HAM's process corresponding to TLC's intersection search is called a "Match" process. It is depicted in Figure 8.4. The process is designed to connect input information with memory, thus enabling HAM to interpret the information. First, HAM attempts to encode the input (for example, a sentence) into a proposition tree, an encoding process called "parsing" the input. Then, it matches the terminal, bottom-most nodes of the tree with their corresponding locations in LTM. (If an unfamiliar word is in the input, however, it cannot be matched with an LTM location. Instead, a new node representing the word will be formed in LTM, and information will begin being collected about that node, such as the word's spelling, and what words it was associated with in the sentence,

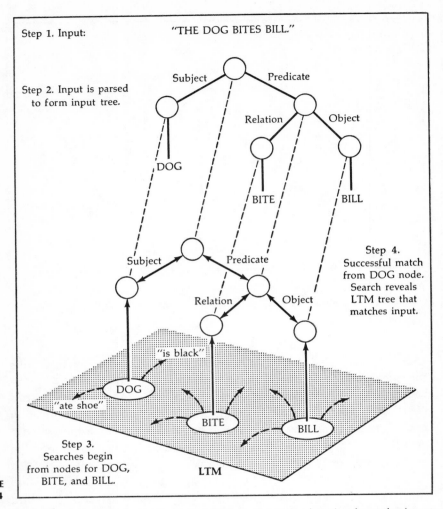

Step 1. Input: "THE DOG BITES BILL."

Step 2. Input is parsed to form input tree.

Subject

Predicate

Relation

Object

DOG

BITE

BILL

Subject

Predicate

Relation

Object

Step 4. Successful match from DOG node. Search reveals LTM tree that matches input.

"is black"

DOG

"ate shoe"

BITE

BILL

Step 3. Searches begin from nodes for DOG, BITE, and BILL.

LTM

FIGURE 8.4

The Match process in Anderson and Bower's HAM, showing how the input sentence "The dog bites Bill" is matched with information in LTM.

and in what manner.) Next, the Match process attempts to find in LTM a tree that looks like the input tree. It does so by starting a search from each LTM location corresponding to a word in the sentence—a search for pathways through the LTM network that connect terminal nodes in the same way as they were connected in the input. This means it looks for an LTM tree that connects the same concepts, and in the same way, as the input. Once this is accomplished, there is a match between the input and the LTM network, and the sentence is comprehended.

144

The same process can be used with many different kinds of input, for example, questions. Given a question such as WHO HIT BILL?, the Match process would parse the question and set up an input tree in which "Who" was treated as a blank. It would attempt to match the nonblank portions of the tree with information in memory. If it found "John hit Bill" in memory, it could fill in the blank and answer the question. (This example is rather trivial, but the same technique can be extended to more complex question-answering.) Another important aspect of HAM's Match process is that it can be extended to nonlinguistic inputs, for example, scenes. Some of HAM's processes are designed to parse, or provide descriptions of such inputs, making trees that tell what they look like. Corresponding descriptions in memory may be matched with the input, thus enabling HAM to recognize what is being seen. In short, the Match process serves many functions, for it provides the basic mechanism for relating current experience to knowledge about the world, thus playing a central role in encoding and retrieval.

SEMANTIC MEMORY DATA

At this point, having discussed one type of model for LTM (namely, network models), it seems appropriate to consider some of the data that these models attempt to explain. In this chapter, we will consider data pertaining to semantic memory (leaving episodic memory to later chapters). We will be able to evaluate the explanatory power of TLC, HAM, and other models by seeing how well they account for the data.

In general, research on semantic memory tries to tap nonepisodic knowledge, knowledge that exists independently of the time or place it was acquired. One of the best examples of this kind of knowledge is found in word definitions. Almost everyone knows that "A canary is a bird" and that "All diamonds are stones." It is not surprising, then, that word definitions have served as a source of many semantic-memory experiments. One of the most commonly used research procedures in such experiments is the sentence-verification task. A subject is given a sentence and is asked whether it is true or false. For example, the sentence might be A CANARY IS A BIRD (true) or A CANARY IS A FISH (false). Not surprisingly, subjects can perform sentence-verification tasks with very few errors. The dependent variable in such a task is reaction time (RT), usually the time between presentation of the sentence and the subject's response.

The Category-Size Effect

Perhaps the most-researched single phenomenon of semantic memory is what is called the category-size effect. Typically, the investigation of this effect uses a sentence-verification task in which sentences are of the form "A subject (S) is a predicate (P)." The independent variable is the category size of the predicate, P. By the size of a category is meant the number of members it contains. Often, it is impossible to say just how many members are contained in a category (but an example of a situation in which category size is readily apparent is the category "seasons of the year," which has four members). Nevertheless, it is still possible to determine relative category size—that is, to say that one category is larger than another. Usually, we can say that if one category is contained in another, then the latter must be larger than the former. For example, since the category "bird" is contained in the category "animal," then "animal" contains all "birds" plus something else, so it must be the larger category. The principal result of these verification experiments is that RT for responding "true" increases as the P-category size increases. For example, it takes longer to verify that "A canary is an animal" than to verify "A canary is a bird" (for example, Collins and Quillian, 1969; Meyer, 1970). Generally, the RT for *false* statements also increases with the category size of P (for example, Landauer and Freedman, 1968; Meyer, 1970).

The category-size effect is of great importance to anyone building a model of semantic memory. Essentially, what it says is that in verifying that some instance (such as "canary") is a member of some category (such as "bird"), the size of the category determines the verification time. This in turn says something about the nature of semantic LTM, and any reasonable model must explain the category-size effect. In Quillian's model, a reasonable explanation is easy to find. The model assumes that a given instance is connected by a single pointer to its immediate superordinate. The superordinate is connected to its superordinate, and so on. That simply follows from the nature of LTM, as dictated by the model. Now in order to verify that "A canary is a bird," only one pointer-path must be followed. To get to a more remote superordinate category, like "animal," two pointers intervene. (See Figure 8.3.) Assuming that following each pointer takes time, it should take more time to follow two pointer-paths than one. Thus, we should get the category-size effect—the higher up the P category is in the superordinate hierarchy, the more pointers there are to follow, and the more time it takes.

It is a bit more difficult to explain why a size effect should occur for false sentences, like A DAISY IS A FISH, in TLC. Yet, the effect is there—RT is greater if "an animal" is substituted for "a fish" in the above sentence, for example. Collins and Quillian (1970) have suggested an explanation. Most of the time, they claim, there is no size effect. It will occur only when the S-word and the P-word are related. If they are related (for example, daisy, fish, and animal are all living things), then the effect will occur. The explanation is this: if the S and P-words are related, they will generally be more closely related when P is large than when it is a small category. You can see this from Figure 8.3, for example—daisy is more closely related (is closer in the hierarchy) to animal than to fish. Moreover, when the S and P words are related, some confusion will result in the search process. The search may find a relation—but one that is inappropriate. The larger the P category, the closer the relation, the more confusion, and the longer it takes to decide that even despite the relatedness of the two words, the sentence is false. This explanation is inadequate, however, for it has been shown (Landauer and Meyer, 1972) that even when relatedness of the two words is held constant, RT for false statements shows a category-size effect. This would be more up-setting if the other models could readily handle their finding, but they cannot. The phenomenon of category-size effects for false statements poses a problem for many models. For the time being, then, we will accept the idea that the Collins and Quillian explanation can generally account for the category-size effect.

Effects of Semantic Relatedness

The issue of relatedness, mentioned above as a possible explanation for the category-size effect in false sentences, is a major area of research on semantic memory in its own right, particularly for true sentences. In typical studies of this phenomenon, subjects are first presented a set of word pairs. Each pair has one word that is a category instance and one that is the name of the category; for example, "robin" is an instance and "bird" is a category. The subject is asked to rate how typical the instance is of the category, or how closely related the two words are (Rips et al., 1973; Rosch, 1973). There is quite a variation in how typical various instances are rated with respect to their category. For example, "robin" is judged much more typical of the category "bird" than is "chicken." This fact, namely, that typicality ratings vary, is one piece of data that semantic-memory theorists should explain.

In fact, typicality presents a bit of a problem for a network model like TLC. In TLC, each instance of a category is separated from its immediate superordinate by a single pointer. Since that same one-pointer distance separates all category members from the category name, it is difficult to see just where the variation in typicality ratings arises. Anderson and Bower's HAM can better account for this and other effects we will note as inconsistent with network models. In this case, HAM can explain the typicality or relatedness result through the operation of the search (Match) process in LTM. You will recall that the Match process begins by starting a search from each LTM location that is mentioned in the input, and it looks for a tree that matches the input. Searches are started from the various locations in parallel (that is, searches from all locations go on simultaneously); however, from a given location, only one pathway can be followed at a time. Since there are usually many pathways leading from any one location in LTM, it is assumed that those pathways are given a priority ordering. The priorities indicate the order in which pathways from a given location are searched. The most important ones will be given high priority. This enables HAM to account for the effect of relatedness on true RTs, for relatedness can be equated with the priorities. We can say that the more closely related an instance is to a category, the more likely the pathway connecting the two is to be high on the priority list. By assuming that judgments of relatedness are based on the priority list, it is easy for this model to account for variations in those judgments.

Not surprisingly, relatedness is found to affect RT in verification tasks (Smith, 1967; Wilkins, 1971). The closer the relatedness between S and P, the faster a sentence of the form "An S is a P" is verified. For example, subjects can verify that "A pigeon is a bird" faster than "A chicken is a bird." What is more surprising is that the relatedness effects can predict situations in which category-size effects do not hold. Consider the following example (Rips et al., 1973). The category "mammal" is included in the category "animal"; thus, "animal" has a greater size. However, subjects rate animal instances (for example, "bear" or "cat") as more closely related to or typical of the category "animal" than that of "mammal." And if the RT to verify sentences such as "A bear is an animal" is compared to the RT for "A bear is a mammal," the first sentence is verified faster. This violates the prediction of category size (for "animal" being the larger category, the associated RT should be greater) but follows the typicality ratings. Again, this result poses a problem for TLC (but not for HAM, which accounts for it with priority of searches—the closer the relatedness of S and P, the higher the priority of their pathway in the Match process, the sooner it will be checked, and the faster the sentence can be verified).

A SET-THEORETIC MODEL OF LTM

Thus far, we have considered only one set of models of semantic LTM. There are alternatives to network models, however, and we shall now discuss one called the "set-theoretic" approach (Meyer, 1970). This approach assumes that semantic categories are represented in LTM as sets, or collections, of information. They can include sets of instances of a category (for example, the category "bird" includes such instances as robins, nightingales, sparrows, and so on). They can also include sets of attributes or properties of the category (for example, "birds" have wings, have feathers, can fly, and so on). In other words, a category is represented in LTM as a set of information.

Meyer (1970) used a set model to account for the time it took subjects to verify or disconfirm sentences of the form "All S are P" or "Some S are P" (for example, ALL STONES ARE RUBIES or SOME STONES ARE RUBIES). To account for the RT data, he proposed a two-stage model describing the processes used in the task. The model says that when confronted with a sentence of the given form, the subject first looks through the names of all sets that overlap (have some members in common with, or intersect with) the P-category. For example, if the sentence is of the form "All S are writers," the subject would look for sets that overlap with "writers." He might find "females," "males," "humans," "professors," and so on, all of which have some members who are writers. If the search through these sets comes up with (finds overlap with) the S-category, then the first stage of the process ends with a match. If the search does not produce a match for the S category, the outcome of the first stage is a negative response.

Given a match in the first stage of the verification process, it is known that S and P have some members in common. That would be sufficient to verify a statement of the form "Some S are P," but it is not enough for the "All S are P" form. For the latter, a second stage must be executed: the comparison of all attributes of P with attributes of S. If every attribute of P is also an attribute of S, then the sentence can be verified. If not, the subject makes a negative response.

Let's consider an example. Suppose P is "gems." Now, consider the sentence "Some stones are gems." In the first stage, the verification process looks through sets that overlap with "gems," that is, have some members in common with "gems." This will include such categories as "diamonds." It will also include "stones," for many stones are also gems. Thus, the sentence can be verified. If the S-word were "birds" ("Some birds are gems"), stage one would result in a negative response, for none of the members of the "bird" category are also members of "gems." If the sentence to be verified were "All rubies are gems," then stage one would come up with a match. However, the use of "all" means that stage two would also have to be executed. This would require comparing all attributes of gems—they are valuable, used in jewelry, and so on—with the attributes of rubies. If the attributes of gems match those of rubies— and they do in this case, for rubies also are valuable, used in jewelry, and so on—the sentence is verified. If they do not, as in "All writers are female," the sentence would be disconfirmed. In the latter case, stage one would produce a match, for "writers" overlaps with "females," but stage two would not be positive.

A set-theoretic model like Meyer's can account for category-size effects like those we have discussed. To see how, we should first note that in that model, it is assumed that the stage-one search for overlapping categories is not random. Instead, the categories that overlap with the P-word are searched through in order of overlap, with the more overlapping categories checked first. What this means is that the fewer instances that S and P do *not* share, the faster S will be found to overlap with P in stage one, for it will be found earlier in the search through all categories that overlap with P. Category-size effects are accounted for: the larger P is, relative to S, the less they will overlap, and the longer it will take to find S in the stage-one search. For example, if S is "canary" and P is "bird," S and P overlap more than if P is "animal" (which is larger than "bird"). Thus, "canary" would be found faster in a search through P's overlapping categories if P is "bird," and RT would be less than for "animal." This would yield the usual category-size effect. However, Meyer's model does not explain the reversal of category-size effects when size is not consistent with relatedness (as in Rips et al., 1973); for example, why does cat–mammal take longer to verify than cat–animal?

A SEMANTIC-FEATURE MODEL OF LTM

A model that derives from the set-theoretic approach is the semantic-feature model of Smith, Shoben, and Rips (Rips et al., 1973; Smith et al., 1974). It has the advantage of being able to account for the relatedness effects we have discussed, namely, that relatedness can be a better predictor of verification RT than category size, and that the relatedness of various instances to a given category, as measured by subjects' ratings, can vary. The feature model assumes that a semantic category can be represented in LTM as a set of attributes, or features. Moreover, the set of features is very broad, including features that are essential in defining the category and some that are relatively unimportant. In fact, the set of features for a given category probably varies along a continuum of importance, from very-important-in-defining to unimportant-in-defining. For example, consider the word "robin." This might be represented in LTM as a collection of the following features: "are bipeds," "have wings," "have red breast," "perch in trees," "are untamed." The first three of these features are probably more important in defining "robin" than are the last two. (Obviously, this list is incomplete, but given a complete set, we could have a set of features that characterized the meaning of "robin.")

In general, on such a continuum of features, we can select an arbitrary cutoff point to separate more important features (called *defining features*) from less important features (called *characteristic features*). In the feature model, defining features are given greater emphasis in verification tasks than are characteristic features. (In our "robin" example, the first three features might be defining, the remainder characteristic.)

Now consider how features might vary as we go from a category name like "robin" to its superordinate, "bird." Since "bird" is the more abstract, or general, term, it will have fewer defining features. In fact, since all robins happen to be birds, then all the defining features of "bird" will also have to apply to "robin," and robin will have more besides. In general, the more abstract the category, the fewer defining features it will have.

The preceding discussion describes the basic assumptions about the structure of LTM that are made in the feature model. Its basic idea—that semantic features exist that might combine to yield the meaning of concepts—is not a new one, either to linguists or psychologists (for example, Katz and Fodor, 1963; Miller, 1972; Osgood, 1952). The model of Smith, Shoben, and Rips is novel in the assumptions it makes about the nature of these features, and in its manner of bringing the assumptions to bear on the data of semantic-memory research. In addition, Smith, Shoben, and Rips have attempted to provide some experimental evidence for the feature idea. Rips et al. (1973) first collected ratings for sets of concepts, that is, ratings of how closely related each of several instances (like chicken, duck, sparrow, etc.) was to its category name (bird) and to other instances of the category. These ratings might be thought of as reflecting distance. For example, a high relatedness rating could be thought of as representing small distance between the two rated concepts. In fact, computerized methods exist for converting such similarity ratings into distances. Such methods represent the various concepts as points in a hypothetical multidimensional space. Distances between the points in the space can then be interpreted as "mental" distances between the corresponding concepts; indeed, those distances actually reflect (are inversely related to) the initial similarity ratings. That is, the closer two points are in the space, the more similar they are seen to be. Moreover, the dimensions of the space derived from the ratings are indicative of the underlying mental bias of the ratings.

In Figure 8.5, the two-dimensional spaces derived from the ratings of bird and mammal concepts are shown. Rips et al. interpret the figure as follows: They assume that in making the initial relatedness judgments, subjects were relying on semantic features in LTM. To the extent that two concepts had features in common, they would be judged as related. That means in turn that the dimensions of the derived two-dimensional spaces could serve to indicate the semantic features the subjects used in making the ratings of relatedness. It seems reasonable, looking at the figure, to give the horizontal axis the name "size." In the bird space, hawk and eagle, the large birds, are at one end of that dimension and small birds like robins are at the other. In the mammal space, the large mammals like deer and bear are at one end of the horizontal dimension,

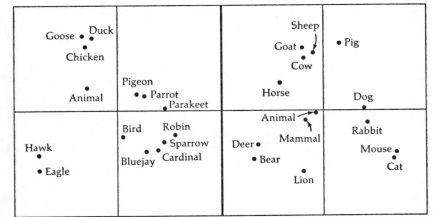

FIGURE 8.5

Two-dimensional spaces derived from subjects' ratings of the relatedness of members of the categories "Birds" *(left)* and "Mammals" *(right).* [From Rips, Shoben, and Smith, 1973.]

and mouse is at the other. The vertical dimension in both spaces can be called something like "predacity"—the extent to which the animals prey on others. Wild mammals and farm animals are at opposite ends of this dimension in the mammal space; predatory birds are separated from tame birds in the bird space. Since the two spaces were derived independently, the consistency of the dimensions is remarkable, and it supports the idea that the dimensions represent some consistent basis for relatedness. In this case, it seems that judgments of relatedness were based on semantic features related to size and predacity.

The feature model can account for many of the data on semantic memory that we have discussed. In order to show how it does so, we must indicate the assumptions the model makes about the processes involved in verification tasks. First, however, recall what the model assumes about the *structure* of information in LTM. It assumes that each concept is represented by a list of features. The features fall along a continuum of importance; let us call the position of a feature on the continuum its weight. (Thus, the weight indicates how important the feature is in defining the concept, with highly weighted features more important.) We can select some arbitrary cutoff weight and call features with greater weights "defining features," features with lower weights "characteristic features." Now, the model assumes that verifying a sentence like "All S are P" proceeds as follows. There is a first stage with three subprocesses. First, lists of features corresponding to the S and P categories are retrieved from LTM. Though not necessarily complete lists, they include both defining and characteristic features. Next, all features listed in the two lists—one for S and one for P—are compared. The number of matching features is used to derive a measure of overall similarity—call it x. Finally, x is used to make a decision about the output of this first stage. Specifically, if x is very high, higher than some fixed criterion value, the two terms are so similar that a quick "true" response can be produced from stage one. If x is very low, indicating no similarity between S and P, a fast "false" response can be put out. If x is in-between, neither high nor low, a second stage is executed.

In the second stage, only the defining features of S and P are used. This stage is like a second check; it operates on the assumption of moderate similarity between S and P, and its purpose is to check on the nature of that similarity. If the defining features of P agree with the defining features of S, then a positive response can be made; otherwise, there is a negative response. What this says is that the RTs for responses in verification tasks are actually a mixture of fast (for very similar or very dissimilar S and P), and slow (when stage two must be executed).

One advantage of the feature model is that it can readily account for the effects of typicality, or relatedness, on RT. That is because it states that the more typical an instance is of a category, the more features they share. Hence, the value of x, the similarity measure which is based on feature overlap between S and P, will be higher as typicality increases. A higher x-value increases the likelihood that a fast "true" response, based only on the first stage of the process, can be produced. That means that RT will be less as typicality increases.

The model also handles category-size effects by assuming that these effects are actually secondary to relatedness. In most cases, increasing the category-size of the P-word will decrease the relatedness of S and P, increasing RT. For example, if S is "sparrow," and P changes from "bird" to "animal," the similarity of S and P decreases. This causes RT to increase. In other cases, such as an increase in P-size from "mammal" to "animal," the size change will actually increase the relatedness of S and P. This will produce a decrease in RT with category size. Thus, Smith, Shoben, and Rips conclude that the category-size effect is not as strong as it is assumed to be. It is quite variable and more readily attributed to concomitant changes in the relatedness of S and P as category size changes.

At this point, we have discussed three kinds of models of semantic memory: network models, set models, and a semantic-feature model. We have considered each type in the context of two major areas of research—category-size and relatedness effects. By now it should be clear that in many ways the models are similar. All of them present a theory of meaning, for example, in which a concept derives its semantic content from its relation to others—whether by virtue of associations, by containing the other concepts as subsets in its definition, or by having those other concepts as features. All the models can explain much of the data we presented about semantic memory, though their specific capabilities differ. It should also be clear that network models and set models differ in some fundamental ways, one of the most important differences being what the models are trying to explain. The set models of Meyer, and of Smith, Shoben, and Rips, are designed to deal with the data collected in specific semantic-memory experiments. The network models, on the other hand, are capable of handling a larger body of data. The HAM model, for example, attempts to deal with such varied topics as linguistic ability, forgetting, perception, pattern recognition, learning, and more. Because of their greater scope, the network models are relevant to many of the phenomena of episodic memory, as well as semantic memory. We shall take advantage of that fact by explaining many topics in the next three chapters in the context of such models.

The set-theoretic framework is, at this point, not equipped to explain episodic processes readily. The phrase "at this point" is an important one. It indicates that the field of semantic-memory research is growing extremely rapidly. No discussion of the area, or of the specific models presented in this chapter, can take into account the constant changes that are occurring. Furthermore, new experiments are continually being devised to challenge the models. All this activity makes semantic-memory research one of the most dynamic, exciting areas of research in psychology.

9

LTM:
FORGETTING

What does it mean to say that something in LTM is forgotten? There is no simple answer, in part because forgetting seems to take so many forms. Consider, for example, the fact that you cannot remember what your first birthday was like, although you may even have had a birthday party. In general, you cannot remember the details of your infancy, or early childhood, at all. Since you were at that time a preverbal organism, and you had no verbal codes to store in LTM, the phenomenon of forgetting your infancy may be quite different from the forgetting you do as an adult. Even in adult life, forgetting has many meanings. For example, there is what we may think of as "ordinary" forgetting; you fail to bring something home from the market, or miss an appointment, or cannot fill in a blank during a test. There is also forgetting as a result of physical trauma—amnesia. Then, there is repression—the deliberate forgetting of information that might be emotionally painful to recall.

In view of this variety of meanings, we should define forgetting in some way before we proceed to discuss it. Let us say that forgetting is what occurs when material that was once encoded, and that is now sought, cannot be retrieved. (We need to stipulate that the material was once encoded so that we exclude from "forgetting" the inability to remember events that have not even undergone the process of pattern recognition.) This is a fairly broad definition, but its breadth is necessary to enable it to include all of the various kinds of forgetting that can be observed. In some circumstances, no part of the forgotten material can be retrieved (as, for example, when we cannot remember the French equivalent of "book" after memorizing it for a test); forgetting can also be partial (as in the tip-of-the-tongue phenomenon); forgetting can even be a form of distortion (as when what we remember is not what actually occurred—for example, one driver in a traffic accident may "remember" after the event that the other driver was driving outrageously, although witnesses may tend to disagree). All of these occurrences fit our general definition of forgetting, for in each case what can be retrieved from LTM does not accord with what is to be remembered.

THE PI AND RI PARADIGMS

Traditionally, forgetting in LTM has been studied with the two procedures described in Chapter 6, PI and RI. At this point, let us consider those procedures in more detail. You may recall that proactive inhibition, or PI, refers to the forgetting of some given material caused by interference from material learned previously. Retroactive inhibition, or RI, refers to forgetting caused by material learned after the to-be-remembered information. (Let us adopt the abbreviation TBR for to-be-remembered.) These two types of interference have been primarily studied in the context of experiments using paired associates as stimuli.

A bit of notational information is in order here, before we continue. We will use the notation the "A–B" list to refer to a paired-associate list in which stimulus terms are taken from a set A and responses from a set B. For example, if the A terms were CVCs and the B terms were digits, DAX–7 and CEB–3 would be typical members of an A–B list. An A–C list, similarly, refers to a list of paired associates using as stimuli the same A terms as the A–B list, but different responses—from a set C. For example, if the C terms were letters of the alphabet, DAX–B and CEB–X might be in an A–C list. Using this notation, the PI and RI procedures are as follows (see Figure 9.1).

For both PI and RI, an experimental group of subjects learns an A–B list of paired associates to a certain criterion, usually several perfect runs through the list. Then, they learn an A–C list; it has the same stimulus terms as the first list but different response terms. After a retention interval, the group is again tested. In the PI procedure, the test is on the A–C list. A control group learns only the A–C list (or sometimes learns an unrelated X–Y list before the A–C list), waits for the same retention interval, and then gets the A–C test. We then define PI as the interference generated in the experimental group by the learning of the A–B list. We can actually quantify PI (numerically measure it) in this situation. We do so by finding out how much worse the experimental group does than

PROACTIVE INHIBITION

Experimental Group	Learn A–B	Learn A–C	Retention Interval	Test A–C
Control Group	————	Learn A–C	Retention Interval	Test A–C

Time →

RETROACTIVE INHIBITION

Experimental Group	Learn A–B	Learn A–C	Retention Interval	Test A–B
Control Group	Learn A–B	————	Retention Interval	Test A–B

FIGURE
9.1

Time →

The PI and RI procedures. The course of an experiment with paired-associate lists is shown.

the control group. The actual measure is: PI = percent correct on A–C test for the control group, minus percent correct for the experimental group, all divided by percent correct for the control group. That is, we take the difference in the mean percentage of correct responses for the two groups, and divide by the performance of the control group (the division makes it possible for us to take into account the difficulty of the A–C list in general; it is a device for making the PI measure here roughly comparable to others). For example, if we find the average percent correct for the control group is 75%, whereas the average for the experimental group is only 50%, we have

$$PI = (75 - 50)/75 = 1/3 = 33\%$$

The procedure for measuring RI is just the same as the measure of PI, except that the experimental group is tested on the first list learned and not the second. That is because we are interested in the decrement in first-list performance caused by learning the second list. So the experimental group learns an A–B list, then an A–C, and is then tested on the A–B list. The control group learns the A–B, then does nothing (or sometimes learns an unrelated X–Y list, depending on the experiment) and is later tested on the A–B list. Again, the experimental group will do worse than the control on the A–B test, and just how much worse is measured by: RI = Percent correct for control group, minus percent correct for experimental group, all divided by percent correct for control group. This is much the same as the PI measure; all that differs, essentially, is that in RI the tested list is the first one learned, whereas in PI the tested list is the second.

The most basic fact about the PI and RI procedures is that they both lead to decrements in performance on the part of the experimental group. That is, we can think of these procedures as manipulations that induce forgetting; in fact, many theorists believe that this laboratory-induced forgetting is fundamentally the same as the forgetting of information outside the laboratory. A second basic fact about the PI and RI procedures is that the amount of interference depends systematically on the number of trials with the interfering list (Briggs, 1957; Underwood and Ekstrand, 1966); an interfering list is one that the experimental group receives and the control does not. To restate, the amount of PI or RI varies with the number of trials that the experimental group has on the interfering list. For the PI procedure, that is the A–B list; for RI, the A–C list.

INTERFERENCE AND FORGETTING

Hypotheses about why the PI and RI procedures produce forgetting have usually been assumed to apply to all forgetting. They form a general class called the interference theory of forgetting. There are several such hypotheses, and we will discuss some of them in this chapter. Before we do, however, there are two points to keep in mind. The first is that these hypotheses are, for the most part, grounded in the S–R tradition, and some try to explain forgetting in terms of "habit strength." For this reason, they will at times appear alien to our information-processing model of memory. However, that does *not* mean that interference has no explanatory value in the eyes of information-processing theorists; it does *not* mean that forgetting in LTM cannot be explained by interference. All it means is that the terminology used by interference theorists will at times seem inappropriate; we shall attempt to reconcile that language with the information-processing approach when confusion seems likely. Second, it is also important to keep in mind that most of the experiments to be discussed concern forgetting in episodic memory. Tulving (1972) suggests that semantic knowledge will not be so easily forgotten. So we must keep in mind that forgetting that the response "frog" goes with the stimulus DAX may not be the same as forgetting what a frog is.

Response Competition

One of the first hypotheses about LTM forgetting was McGeoch's (1942) response-competition hypothesis. It formulated forgetting in rather straightforward S–R terms in the context of the PI and RI paradigms. Essentially, McGeoch said that when we learn an A–B and an A–C list, we set up associations of varying strength: we get two associations for each stimulus term, and one will be stronger. When the subject is given the stimulus term on a test, the two responses compete and the stronger one wins; it intrudes and prevents the weaker response from occurring. For example, if a paired associate on the A–B list is DAX–7, and DAX–8 occurs on the A–C list, there might be an internal structure like this:

At the time of testing, when the subject is given DAX–?, he will report the 8. In the PI or RI procedure, it is possible that the stronger response will come from the interfering list rather than from the tested list.

The basic problem with McGeoch's hypothesis is that it predicts that errors that the subject makes should take the form of intrusions from the interfering list. That is, if the subject errs, he should respond "eight" given DAX, when the correct response is "seven," because DAX–8 came from the interfering list. He should *not* say "two" or "sixteen" or any other random response. However, errors do not follow the pattern predicted on this basis (Melton and Irwin, 1940). To see this, look at Figure 9.2. It shows that RI, and correspondingly, errors on the tested list, increases and then decreases slightly with the number of trials on the interfering list. However, intrusion errors do not follow this pattern: Where RI attributable to intrusions is decreasing with trials on the interfering list, total RI still increases.

Extinction and Unlearning

Another hypothesis proposed to account for PI and RI is extinction, or "unlearning" (Melton and Irwin, 1940; Underwood, 1948a, b): It proposes that a major determinant of forgetting is the unlearning of associations because of interference. The form of this unlearning is sometimes said to be analogous to the extinction that occurs in simple

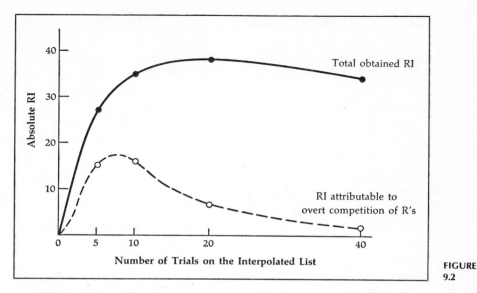

FIGURE
9.2

Total RI and RI attributable to response intrusions, as a function of the number of trials with the interfering list. [After Melton and Irwin, 1940.]

conditioning procedures. So, in order to get an idea of just what un-learning might be, let's briefly review classical conditioning.

A typical conditioning procedure might be used to train a dog to salivate when he hears a specific tone. We start out by taking an unconditioned stimulus (UCS) that produces the desired response without training (this might be some food, to produce salivation). We pair the UCS with a conditioned stimulus (CS)—in this case, the tone. We present the CS, then the UCS, and then the response occurs. (The occurrence of the UCS and the response after the CS is called the reinforcement.) This procedure, when repeated several times, constitutes the conditioning phase of the paradigm. It will ultimately result in the occurrence of the response following the CS alone. That is, without presentation of any food, the sound of the tone will produce salivation. The response is now said to be conditioned to the CS. But is this conditioning permanent? Suppose we repeatedly present the CS without the UCS, so there is no reinforcement. At first, the CS alone will produce the salivation, but eventually the response will diminish and then vanish. It is said to be extinguished, for lack of reinforcement. A third phase of conditioning can now take place: spontaneous recovery. Suppose we allow the dog to rest for a while, presenting neither CS nor UCS. We then present the tone again and find that the dog again responds by salivating. It seems as if the extinction phase was not really complete. The conditioned response is said to have spontaneously recovered from extinction, resulting in its reappearance in response to the tone. The response will re-extinguish if we continue to present the tone without any reinforcement or will be reacquired if we present reinforcement.

These three phases of conditioning—the acquisition of the response, extinction, and spontaneous recovery—are applied to paired-associate learning in the unlearning hypothesis. To see how they are applied, examine Figure 9.3, which depicts the *theoretical* time-course of an experiment with the PI or the RI procedure. First, the subject learns an A–B list. He is supposedly acquiring the responses to the stimuli in that list, much as the dog is acquiring the salivary response to the tone. Then, he learns the A–C list—the C responses are now conditioned, and the B responses previously learned are extinguished because they are not reinforced by presentation. During the retention interval, however, the A–B responses will undergo spontaneous recovery. The result will be that if tested on A–C, the subject will show PI, the relative improvement

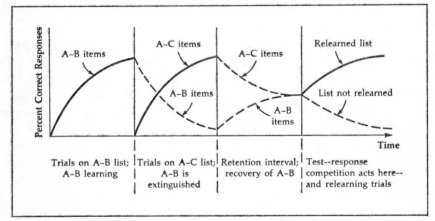

FIGURE 9.3

Theoretical functions corresponding to performance during an experiment with the PI and RI paradigms. During A–B learning *(first panel, at left)*, performance with the A–B list improves. During A–C learning *(second panel)*, A–C performance improves, and A–B performance is assumed to decrease because of extinction of the A–B associations. During the retention interval *(third panel)*, spontaneous recovery of the A–B associations occurs, causing decrements in A–C performance (PI) and improvement in A–B performance, but not to its initial level (RI). Relearning of the tested list *(last panel)* results in improved performance with its items at the expense of the others.

of A–B over the retention interval having led to a relative decrement in A–C performance. This decrement is presumably due to competition between B and C responses to A stimuli. On the other hand, if we test A–B, there will certainly be a decrement due to A–C learning, which has resulted in A–B extinction. Thus, RI will be observed.

To summarize, the extinction hypothesis proposes that in the A–B, A–C situation, A–B associations are extinguished, or unlearned, during A–C learning. Presumably this occurs because the presentation of A terms during the A–C phase leads to the awakening of the B responses, which are then not reinforced. During the retention interval, however, the B responses will show some spontaneous recovery. At the time of test, the B and C responses will compete when A terms are presented (much as in the McGeoch hypothesis), with the competition and its outcome depending on the relative strengths of the terms. (Because response competition is assumed to be a second factor contributing to forgetting, in addition to the unlearning, the hypothesis is sometimes called the two-factor hypothesis.)

The two-factor hypothesis has generated an immense amount of experimental work, far too much for us to attempt a comprehensive overview. However, there are certain experiments as well as theoretical views that have become "classics" in this area; we will try to cover the classics instead of reviewing the field as a whole. (For a recent review, see Postman and Underwood, 1973; their bibliography will also be helpful to interested readers.

One obvious prediction of the hypothesis is that the amount of PI and RI observed at the time of test will depend on the retention interval. Since A–B strength increases as the retention interval goes on, it will lead to progressively greater decrements in A–C performance. In addition, the more time that A–B associations are given to recover, the better the performance on a subsequent A–B test should be. This means that with longer retention intervals there should be greater amounts of PI, and less RI. Underwood (1948a,b) found this pattern of results.

Other strong empirical support for unlearning came from two experiments: the MFR experiment (Briggs, 1954) and the MMFR experiment (Barnes and Underwood, 1959). Both of these experiments tried to make the unlearning of A–B associations during A–C learning observable—to get inside the extinction process. Both used the A–B, A–C procedure; what varied were the instructions given the subject. In the MFR (modified free recall) experiment, subjects went through A–B, then A–C learning, and then were presented with each A item and asked to give the first response that came to mind. That is, they were not asked to give responses from a particular list, but whatever response they thought of first. Underlying this experiment is the assumption that the responses that were most strongly associated with the stimuli would be recalled first. Thus, the percentage of responses coming from a given list would be a measure of the strength of that list's stimulus-response associations. The results of the Briggs experiment, shown in Figure 9.4, provide strong evidence for unlearning. As learning of the A–B (or A–C) list progressed, the percentage of responses from the A–B (or A–C) list increased. And when a final test was given after a short retention interval, more responses came from the C list than the B list. But with longer intervals the advantage of the C list declined, and there was actually a B-list advantage for retention intervals greater than twenty-four hours.

One problem with Briggs' study is that although it supports the unlearning idea, it does not show that the A–C learning actually resulted in the *un*-learning of B responses. It could have been that the B responses

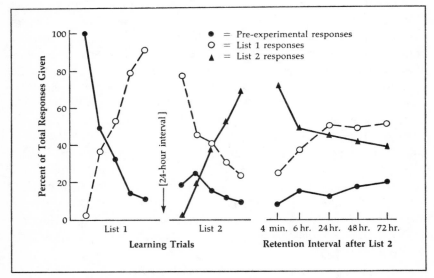

FIGURE 9.4

Results of the MFR experiment. The first and second panels *(starting at the left)* show the percent of responses coming from each list during learning trials with the first and second lists, respectively. The third panel shows performance with responses from each list on the MFR test, as a function of the retention interval after the second list. Also shown in each panel is the percent of responses that were preexperimental—those attached to the stimulus terms at the beginning of the experiment. These responses exhibit extinction and some spontaneous recovery. [After Briggs, 1954. Copyright 1954 by the American Psychological Association.]

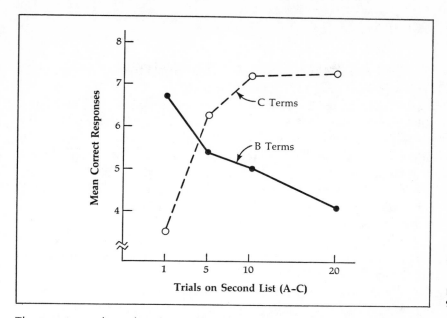

FIGURE
9.5

The mean number of correct responses on the MMFR test for both lists
as a function of the number of trials with the second list. [After Barnes
and Underwood, 1959. Copyright 1959 by the American Psychological
Association.]

were still in memory, but the subject merely did not report them because
he thought of the C responses first. To correct this problem—that is, to
find out if the unreported responses were still available—Barnes and
Underwood (1959) used the MMFR ("modified modified free recall")
procedure—subjects were presented each A item and asked to recall
both B and C responses, if possible. The results, shown in Figure 9.5,
suggest that the responses were actually *un*-learned. As the A–C learning
progressed, fewer and fewer B responses were given, even though subjects were asked to report them if they could: the B responses seemed
to be gone from memory.

Although the experiments just described support the two-factor hypothesis of long-term forgetting, other research is not as supportive.
Let us consider two aspects of the hypothesis that have not been verified
experimentally. First, there has been equivocal evidence for what is
called the elicitation hypothesis—namely, that A–B associations become
extinguished because during learning of the A–C list, the B responses
are first elicited (awakened) and then not reinforced. Second, there has
been some question about the occurrence of spontaneous recovery of
B responses during the retention interval.

First, for the elicitation hypothesis. One form of this hypothesis might propose that, during A–C learning, if a subject actually says aloud the B responses, and the B responses are not then reinforced, the B responses will be extinguished. However, overt (aloud) intrusions from the first-list responses during the second-list learning are relatively infrequent, so unlearning cannot occur only on this basis. We must consider covert, or internal, attempts to use B responses, and their subsequent non-reinforcement. Even here, however, the evidence is mixed. In general, we would expect that any time a manipulation induced either overt or covert intrusions from the A–B list during A–C learning, there would be a great deal of RI, because more intrusions mean more unreinforced B-list responses and therefore more extinction. Thus, it is a result favoring the theory when we find that the more similar the B responses are to the C responses, the more covert if not overt B–list intrusions occur during A–C learning, and the more RI is found. It seems that similarity tends to elicit the B responses, resulting in more extinction—and more RI from the A–C learning (Friedman and Reynolds, 1967; Postman, Keppel, and Stark, 1965). The other side of the coin is that if the A–C responses are learned with little effort, there should be little extinction of the A–B list (and less RI) because there are fewer opportunities for elicitation of B responses during A–C learning and therefore few opportunities for those responses to be unreinforced. Yet, this idea receives unimpressive experimental support (Postman and Underwood, 1973), weakening the case for the elicitation hypothesis.

The spontaneous-recovery portion of the unlearning hypothesis has even less evidence to support it. An obvious way to study spontaneous recovery would be to use the MMFR paradigm. We could give subjects an A–B list, then an A–C list, and then administer MMFR tests after several different retention intervals. We would expect to find an increase in B responses as the retention intervals grew longer, because the A–B associations should be recovering in the course of time. Yet, experiments which attempted to catch spontaneous recovery in action (Ceraso and Henderson, 1965; Houston, 1966; Koppenaal, 1963) found no increase in A–B recall over time. Perhaps the best attempts were those of Postman et al. (Postman, Stark, and Fraser, 1968; Postman, Stark, and Henschel, 1969)—"best" at least in terms of finding some evidence for recovery. They found that there was some recovery of B responses in about twenty-five minutes, a rather short retention interval in this paradigm. This is especially strange when we consider the fact that rather little PI is found at twenty-minute retention intervals (e.g., Underwood, 1949), and that PI is supposedly caused by spontaneous recovery The theory places the

PI mechanism in the spontaneous recovery of B responses—how can we get strong PI when testing at intervals in which there is no recovery, and recovery at short intervals where PI is at a minimum?

A rather telling blow to the most basic assumption of the two-factor hypothesis—namely, that interfered-with associations are actually unlearned—comes from an experiment of Postman and Stark (1969). One condition of their experiment used a recognition test in the A–B, A–C paradigm. When tested on the A–B list after A–C learning, the subject was given a set of B terms and instructed to pick the one corresponding to a given A term. The subject did not have to recall the B terms, merely to recognize which ones matched the A terms. The results of this manipulation were startling—there was an insignificant amount of RI. It seemed that far from being unlearned, responses from the A–B list were available for testing with the recognition method. It was the generation of the B-list response terms, rather than association of those terms with the A stimuli, that was difficult in the A–B, A–C paradigm. That is, the subjects did not have trouble remembering that DAX-7 was a paired associate on the first list so much as they had trouble recalling 7 when given DAX.

The idea that paired-associate learning involves, in part, learning to recall the response terms was not new. However, the idea that resulted from the Postman and Stark experiment—that PI and RI depend on the failure to recall response terms, rather than on the forgetting of associative links—is relatively new. Nor are the response terms actually lost, it seems. Instead, they are *unavailable* at the time of recall. If they were actually lost from memory, we would not expect the recognition test to lead to such extraordinary performance.

Response-Set Interference

The last hypothesis we shall discuss, called response-set interference (Postman, Stark, and Fraser, 1968), is compatible with the Postman and Stark results. It suggests that interference is a form of response competition, but that the competition is not between individual responses. Instead, whole sets of responses compete with one another. For example, one set of responses might be the B terms of an A–B list—all of them. These would compete with the entire set of C responses on the A–C list.

Basically, the response-set hypothesis works like this (in the context of A–B, A–C learning). First, learning the A–B list activates the set of B responses. This activation includes the setting of a selector mechanism that makes B terms available at the expense of other responses. Then, during A–C learning, the selector shifts over to activate the C responses, inhibiting the B terms. Moreover, the selector mechanism has some inertia; it thus takes a little time to shift from one set to another. We will therefore observe RI if we test the A–B list shortly after A–C learning, for the selector is still activating the set of C responses.

The basic statement of the response-set interference hypothesis says that interference occurs at the level of whole response systems, not single associations. In addition to this basic claim, it includes other assumptions. First, it says that under appropriate conditions—those that manage to bypass the selector mechanism, for example—RI will not be observed. Presumably, the application of a recognition test (as in Postman and Stark, 1969) will do just that—bypass the selector by making responses available immediately through presenting the responses during the test. Second, the theory says that the amount of RI should decrease during the retention interval, because the inertia of the selector mechanism will be maximal immediately after A–C learning. With time, however, it will be easier for the selector mechanism to shift back to the A–B system. (This is related to spontaneous recovery.) Third, the hypothesis can handle the finding that RI increases as similarity among response sets increases. (That is, the more the C terms resemble the B terms, the more inter-ference is generated.) This fact is explained by noting that the selector mechanism is sensitive to intralist similarities. Specifically, it is assumed that setting the response-selection mechanism will be effective only so far as there is a distinct response set to apply it to; that is, distinct criteria for its selection. When the mechanism is shifted, it must be directed by new criteria for response-set membership. Thus, if two response sets are not much different, the response selector may include responses from both in its current set.

The response-set hypothesis should not be construed as antagonistic to the two-factor hypothesis, because it includes many of the same ideas—for example, response competition (although it is presumed to be at a different level). It is time now to ask how well interference theory, as a whole, accounts for long-term forgetting outside of the List 1–List 2 situa-tion. The answer is not too encouraging, but it is not too discouraging either.

Some of the attempts to address this question have tried to induce forgetting, outside of the laboratory, of information learned within the laboratory. For example, Underwood and Postman (1960) had subjects learn lists of frequent words (that is, words commonly used) and infre-quent words. They reasoned that the forgetting of the lists of frequent words should be greater, because the subjects would be more likely to use the words in common parlance. The extra-laboratory associations corresponding to habitual use of the frequent words would interfere and lead to forgetting of the laboratory lists. Although somewhat supportive of this idea, the results were certainly not conclusive.

In a situation that was the reverse of the Underwood and Postman (1960) idea, Slamecka (1966) tried to have subjects unlearn associations they brought to the laboratory. First, he elicited responses to stimuli in free-association tasks. (In free-association, a subject is given an item like CAT and asked to give the first word that comes to mind—like "dog"). When the stimuli that had been used to elicit the associations were used in paired-associate lists with new responses (such as CAT-RELY, instead of CAT-DOG), little interference was demonstrated. Tested for their free-association responses, the subjects had not forgotten a thing. In short, if you bring "cat-dog" into the laboratory, a few trials with CAT-RELY will not serve to make you forget that dogs and cats go together.

Perhaps some of the problems that arise when attempts are made to have subjects forget laboratory material in the real world, or vice versa, can be explained by recourse to the response-set interference hypothesis. Presumably, real-world responses can be held in a different response set than laboratory responses, and once the subject is out of the lab, they can easily be regained. It seems, therefore, that in order to get some idea of the role of interference theory in explanations of real-world forgetting, it is necessary to mimic the real world in the laboratory. We have to use the laboratory (whatever that may consist of) in order to control our manipulations, but at the same time, we want to mimic forgetting as it occurs outside of an experimental setting. In addition, we cannot split our experiment between the laboratory and nonlaboratory setting, or we will get the complications of differing response sets.

FORGETTING AND NATURAL LANGUAGE

Some experiments that shed light on our basic problem—what is the nature of forgetting in the real world?—can be found. Often, these experiments look at forgetting outside of the context of paired-associate lists by using natural language as the stimulus material. By natural language, we mean just that—words connected to form natural discourse in one's own language. Presumably, by using this form of stimulus, we will be able to look at forgetting in a more natural way. That is, we really will be imitating the world outside. So let us look at some representative studies.

The first thing we discover is that when forgetting of English text is induced experimentally, it is often in the context of a thinly disguised

A–B, A–C experiment, rather than one that does not resemble the list-learning procedure. For example, if we read to subjects successive prose passages and test their memory with a recognition test for their general meaning (Slamecka, 1960a, b), little evidence of forgetting is obtained. That is a situation far removed from the A–B, A–C lists. However, interference effects can be obtained with English text as the stimulus material under other conditions closer to A–B, A–C learning. For example, Crouse (1971) had subjects learn a biographical passage about some fictional character. Included in the passage were specific facts such as place and date of birth, father's occupation, particulars of parents' deaths, and so on. Next, the subjects were given two related passages. These were also biographical—in fact, their wording was essentially identical to the first passage except for changes in detail, such as a different name and date of birth, slightly different particulars concerning the deaths of parents, and so on. Then, memory for the first passage was tested by questioning the subjects about specific facts that had been changed between the initial and interpolated passages. Subjects in those conditions recalled much less than a control group that had heard two unrelated passages between presentation and recall of the initial biography. Thus, RI had been produced in a natural-language setting (in this case, English prose). Apparently, this kind of demonstration is effective because the to-be-recalled and interpolated passages use identical general wording (like A terms in an A–B list), and only some specific words are different (much like the change to an A–C list). Thus, we find interference effects in situations which resemble the typical PI and RI experiments, but not in other situations.

What does it mean when the demonstration of interference in natural-language settings requires using the natural language in ways similar to A–B and A–C lists? Perhaps forgetting in extralaboratory situations does not resemble forgetting in the traditional interference procedures. We can't really make that strong a statement, however. Instead, let us look more closely at what forgetting in the real world might be like.

One of the best-known experiments on forgetting of natural language was performed by Bartlett (1932). (Actually, Bartlett did not consider his work to be particularly directed to forgetting, but that does not mean we cannot consider its relevance to this discussion.) Bartlett had subjects attempt to reproduce a story they had read. The story is a legend of a tribe of North American Indians and is called "The War of the Ghosts." (See Figure 9.6.) When Bartlett's subjects, who were not Indians, tried to reproduce the tale, they were found to make rather systematic errors.

The War of the Ghosts

One night two young men from Egulac went down to the river to hunt seals, and while they were there it became foggy and calm. Then they heard war-cries, and they thought: "Maybe this is a war party." They escaped to the shore, and hid behind a log. Now canoes came up, and they heard the noise of paddles, and saw one canoe coming up to them. There were five men in the canoe, and they said:

"What do you think? We wish to take you along. We are going up the river to make war on the people."

One of the young men said: "I have no arrows."

"Arrows are in the canoe," they said.

"I will not go along. I might be killed. My relatives do not know where I have gone. But you," he said, turning to the other, "may go with them."

So one of the young men went, but the other returned home.

And the warriors went on up the river to a town on the other side of Kalama. The people came down to the water, and they began to fight, and many were killed. But presently the young man heard one of the warriors say: "Quick, let us go home: that Indian has been hit." Now he thought: "Oh, they are ghosts." He did not feel sick, but they said he had been shot.

So the canoes went back to Egulac, and the young man went ashore to his house, and made a fire. And he told everybody and said: "Behold I accompanied the ghosts, and we went to fight. Many of our fellows were killed, and many of those who attacked us were killed. They said I was hit, and I did not feel sick."

He told it all, and then he became quiet. When the sun rose he fell down. Something black came out of his mouth. His face became contorted. The people jumped up and cried.

He was dead.

Subject's Reproduction

Two youths were standing by a river about to start seal-catching, when a boat appeared with five men in it. They were all armed for war.

The youths were at first frightened, but they were asked by the men to come and help them fight some enemies on the other bank. One youth said he could not come as his relations would be anxious about him; the other said he would go, and entered the boat.

In the evening he returned to his hut, and told his friends that he had been in a battle. A great many had been slain, and he had been wounded by an arrow; he had not felt any pain, he said. They told him that he must have been fighting in a battle of ghosts. Then he remembered that it had been queer and he became very excited.

In the morning, however, he became ill, and his friends gathered round; he fell down and his face became very pale. Then he writhed and shrieked and his friends were filled with terror. At last he became calm. Something hard and black came out of his mouth, and he lay contorted and dead.

FIGURE 9.6

Text of Bartlett's "War of the Ghosts" (1932).

Since the original passage did not necessarily fit into their cultural conceptions of what was logical and conventional, their errors of reproduction were distortions that tended to rearrange the story into what they considered a normal pattern. Bartlett proposed that subjects erred in this way because, in first reading the story, they formed a mental "schema," or abstract representation, of the story's general theme. Such a schema would of necessity be assimilated into the subject's personal system of beliefs, emotions, and so on. That assimilation would result in the systematic changes that were observed. In short, we might conclude that the subjects tried to fit the story into their existing LTM structure. They would "forget" certain aspects of the legend that did not fit in with, or were incompatible with, or actually generated interference with their LTM structure.

Bartlett's demonstration of the distortion of learned material in the direction of "cognitive reality" is not an isolated case. Recent research has tended to support the idea that in remembering natural language, subjects tend to form a mental representation of the general "theme", and then use that representation if asked to recall specific words they heard, answer questions, recall facts, and so on.

A classic demonstration of the memory-for-theme effect is that of Sachs (1967). She had subjects listen to recorded passages. At some time after a sentence in the passage had been heard, a sentence like it was presented. The new sentence could be either identical to the one presented in the passage or slightly changed. If changed, it could be different in wording (syntax) but not meaning, or it could be different in meaning (semantics). For example, if the original sentence had been "The boy hit the girl," a syntactic change might be "The girl was hit by the boy," whereas a semantic change might be "The girl hit the boy." Sachs found that if the changed sentence was presented immediately after the original version, almost any change could readily be recognized. (Presumably, that is because recall at a short interval would utilize information in STM, which would contain the sentence verbatim.) However, as other verbal material intervened between the original presentation of a sentence and its second version, changes in meaning were much more recognizable than purely syntactic changes. That is, the sentence could be distorted in form without the subject's realizing it, but not in semantic content.

Sachs' experiment gives us another illustration of natural-language forgetting. In this case, in contrast to Bartlett's experiment, it is not meaning that is forgotten but the specifics of wording. Yet, the forgetting of Sachs' subjects is like that of Bartlett's in that it is some distortion of the original input. It seems that Sachs' subjects stored a representation of the meaning of the passage in LTM and forgot the wording. This memory for meaning rather than exact form was revealed when the time came to recall the wording. There was, however, no need to distort the meaning (as did Bartlett's subjects) because it did not conflict with LTM structure. Is this interference? Not in the conventional sense. We might be able to consider this type of forgetting as interference, but only to the extent that the subjects' linguistic knowledge might be said to "interfere" with the storage of wording. That is, subjects might know that in general, the wording of a sentence is not important as long as the meaning is retained. Such linguistic knowledge induces them to store meaning, rather than specific wording. There is some support for this notion, for it is readily shown that subjects can store the wording of a sentence if they know it will be advantageous to do so (Anderson and Bower, 1973; Wanner, 1968).

Thus far, we find that natural-language forgetting seems minimally related to the interference-caused forgetting of PI and RI procedures. In the experiments we have discussed, it is possible to consider the forgetting of sentences and paragraphs as due to something akin to interference, but only if we stretch the definition of interference quite a bit. What we end up with bears little resemblance to the unlearning, response-competition, and response-set competition hypotheses. The case for the interference theory of forgetting is further weakened by the finding that, in some cases, forgetting appears to consist of subjects remembering more, not less, than was originally presented. This type of "forgetting" forms the basis for the constructive approach to memory for natural language, an approach of the researchers Bransford, Barclay, Franks, and their associates.

You may recall from Chapter 4 that Franks and Bransford (1971) demonstrated that when subjects were shown a series of complex visual forms, they appeared to abstract the prototype of those forms and use the prototype for subsequent recognition judgments. Thus 'they recognized test forms by their distance from the prototype, rather than by whether they had actually been presented. Bransford and Franks (1971) have demonstrated a similar effect for sentence memory. They started with a set of four simple sentences, like: *(a)* The ants were in the kitchen. *(b)* The jelly was on the table. *(c)* The jelly was sweet. *(d)* The ants ate the jelly. These sentence forms can be combined in twos, threes, or all four together to form new sentences. For example, combining *a* and *d* gives: The ants in the kitchen ate the jelly. Combining *c* and *d* gives: The ants ate the sweet jelly. Combining *b, c,* and *d* gives: The ants ate the sweet jelly that was on the table. All four combined give: The ants in the kitchen ate the sweet jelly that was on the table. That last sentence is the equivalent of the prototypical form in the Franks and Bransford visual-memory experiment, for it is a sentence that contains all the information in the basic ones (*a through d*).

Bransford and Franks then presented subjects with a subset of the total set of sentences that could be derived from the four basic ones. The subset included two sentences out of the four simple ones (*a* through *d*); two from the set made by combining them in twos, and two from the set made by combining them in threes. The sentences selected managed to represent all four of the basic forms in one combination or another, and when presented were interspersed with sentences from other sets unrelated to ants, kitchens, and jelly, but derived in the same fashion. Then the subjects were given a recognition test and were asked to indicate how confident they were of their recognition judgment. The results were analogous to those of the experiment on visual forms: the subjects rated themselves most confident of having seen the sentence that was prototypical—the one that combined the four basic sentences. But that was a sentence that they had never been shown! In addition, subjects tended to rate their recognition of sentences combining three of the basic forms as more confident than that of sentences combining two; and their recognition of sentences combining two as more confident than that of the simple sentences. In short, whether a sentence had actually been seen or not was unimportant for its "recognition." What was important was how many of the simple forms a given sentence combined—the more it combined, the more likely it was to be "recognized."

Bransford and Franks suggested that their results occurred because the subjects abstracted and stored the combined content of the sentences they had been shown. They "constructed" a memory representation from the given raw material, and that representation built on—but was not restricted to—the information initially presented. Again, we have a failure to remember the specifics of the information presented. Again, we have a distortion of that information. In this case, the distortion takes the form of constructing a "prototypical" semantic representation from more isolated facts.

In related experiments, Barclay (1973) and Bransford, Barclay, and Franks (1972) found evidence indicating that subjects could go beyond the information given in a sentence and store information not only about the sentence itself but also about its implications. For example, Bransford et al. found that if subjects were presented with a sentence like THREE TURTLES RESTED ON A FLOATING LOG AND A FISH SWAM BENEATH THEM they would falsely recognize "Three turtles rested on a floating log and a fish swam beneath it." The replacement of "them" by "it" represents an inference from the initial sentence—we know that if the turtles were on the log, then a fish swimming beneath the turtles (them) would also be swimming beneath the log (it). In contrast, if the original sentence is "Three turtles rested *beside* a floating log, and a fish swam beneath them," and the test sentence replaces "them" with "it," a similar recognition error does not occur. That is because the use of "beside" does not permit the same inference. If a fish swam beneath the turtles who were beside the log, there is no guarantee that the fish also swam beneath the log. Again, these results indicate that subjects hearing a sentence put more in memory than just its words. Instead, they appear to store its content (but not the specific wording) and even to store inferences that can be made from that content. In Bartlett's terms, we might say they store a "schema" of the sentence. As a result, the kinds of forgetting that occur in relation to the sentence look little like PI or RI: "forgetting" takes the form of storing the sentence with something added, rather than simply losing part of the information.

INTERFERENCE: SUMMING UP

At this point, it is time to re-examine the interference theory of forgetting. First, we know that the interference theory, in one form or another, can explain most of the phenomena typically observed in the A–B, A–C procedures. We also know that if we "stretch" the theory, using the term "interference" in a very general sense, it can handle some forgetting of natural-language material, although it works best if the natural language comprises a thinly disguised A–B, A–C situation. Finally, we know that some of the phenomena of memory for natural-language inputs present difficulties for the interference theory: for example, interference does not explain why subjects hearing sentences may remember their implications rather than the specific words which were used. In short, we can say that although it has been shown that interference theory can explain certain specific kinds of forgetting, it cannot handle many of the findings of experiments on natural language.

It may be fair to say that the kinds of data best accounted for by traditional interference theories of forgetting are those which fit into the S–R format. For example, the use of paired associates was originally intended as a means of directly studying the S–R association. It is not surprising, then, that work with paired associates forms much of the basis for the interference theories that grew out of the S–R tradition. However, those interference theories are much less able to explain memory for sentences and paragraphs. The kinds of theories that can better explain that kind of memory are those with a linguistic basis—such as the theories of semantic memory we have discussed.

As an example, the HAM model, with its associative-network structure, can provide the basis for a version of interference theory (Anderson and Bower, 1973). Retroactive interference in HAM results from the nature of the Match process (discussed in Chapter 8). The Match process is evoked when LTM is searched for a propositional structure that matches some input—this is a basic component of retrieval. The LTM search begins at the locations corresponding to terminal nodes of the input tree; pathways leading from those locations are given a priority ordering. The search process begins with the highest-priority pathways from each location and continues through the ordering, either until the search succeeds in finding a match or until a certain amount of time has passed and the search is abandoned. Not all pathways can be searched, for that would take too much time. Now, by assuming that the priority ordering reflects the recency with which pathways have been followed, a mechanism for RI is obtained. Pathways corresponding to recently learned information will have a high priority, and searches for those pathways will thus lead to more successful matches than will searches for less recently used pathways (which are "buried" under more recent paths). This means that learning new information will tend to impair memory for previously learned information, producing RI. With this and similar interference mechanisms, the HAM model is compatible with the traditional interference results. Moreover, this model can better accommodate the encoding and retention of natural language, with its emphasis on sentence-like forms.

Thus, corresponding to changes in the kinds of experiments performed (from paired-associate learning to memory for sets of sentences), there have been changes in theories of forgetting. Many of the changes serve to make the theories more "cognitive"—and from the viewpoint of this book, that kind of change results in their being better equipped to account for the many facts of human cognition.

10

REMEMBERING: CODING PROCESSES

So far in our discussion of LTM, we have considered models of its structure and of processes that work with that structure, such as those that underlie the verification of sentences and the forgetting of previously learned information. In this chapter and the next, we are going to discuss a variety of other processes associated with LTM, all of which could be subsumed under the general term "remembering."

From Chapter 1, you may recall that when information is remembered, three things must have occurred: encoding, storage, and retrieval. First, the information must have once been encoded. In general, to encode means to put into a form compatible with internal storage. For example, letters are encoded into the icon by processes that isolate visual features and separate figures from their backgrounds. Encoding verbal information into STM may take the form of labeling (as, for example, when A becomes "ay"), and it may also use the process of chunking. Thus, encoding may be a quite complex operation.

After encoding, the material is stored—put away in memory. Things that may happen while it is in storage may result in its not being remembered later. Often, the word "storage" is used to include the process of putting-into-storage; that is, to refer to encoding as well as storing. Since storage may be considered a rather passive phenomenon—like keeping your winter coat in the closet over the summer—the use of that label to include encoding seems reasonable enough; if we sometimes use it in that way here, the context should make clear what is meant.

Finally, we have the third aspect of remembering—retrieval. It is not unusual for us to encode and store information that we cannot remember later. The information may still be in memory; it's just that we cannot get at it. We are, in this case, the victims of retrieval failure. Retrieval refers to the getting-at process—obtaining access to information in memory.

The term "encoding" is often used to refer to a sensory-registration process or an STM process; "storage" and "retrieval" are most often used in reference to LTM processes. Perhaps that is because information is not stored in either the registers or STM for very long, and retrieval from these stores is either very easy or impossible—the material is either there and immediately available or has been lost from the store. Applied to LTM, however, "encoding," "storage," and "retrieval" are all meaningful terms. Encoding processes, the acts that accompany the storage of information in LTM, will be the focus of the present chapter. We shall include here the processes of natural-language mediation and organization. In Chapter 11, we shall examine theories of the retrieval process.

NATURAL-LANGUAGE MEDIATION

One phenomenon in which encoding plays an important role is that of natural-language mediation. In general, mediation refers to certain processes that intervene between the presentation of a stimulus and the occurrence of overt responses to the stimulus; these processes are not predictable from the stimulus by itself (Hebb, 1958). In S-R theory, the concept of mediation is essential if one is to explain why a given stimulus can elicit responses to which it has not been directly connected in the past. For example, a subject in a free-association task might respond "lakes" to the stimulus word SEVEN. His response becomes explicable if we understand that there has been a mediating link in between the stimulus and response. The word "seven" elicited the internal response "seas," which in turn elicited "lakes," which became the overt response. In short, the internal response was mediational: it served to transform the stimulus in a way that enabled it to elicit indirect associative connections.

Let us consider another example of a mediational process. Suppose you were an S-R theorist trying to discover how subjects build up habit strength for items in memory. Following the lead of Ebbinghaus, you might decide to use items the subject had never seen before—nonsense syllables (of the form consonant-vowel-consonant, or CVC)—to eliminate the possibility that the subject might rely on previously existing associations rather than those he was supposed to learn. You might present to the subject the CVC MOT along with a list of some others. You might instruct the subject to repeat the syllables to himself and to try to memorize the list. Later, when you test the subject, you discover that he can remember MOT better than the other CVCs. Little do you know that the subject thought of "mother" when you presented MOT, and, in that way, has altered the list you presented.

In the example just given, the subject has used a mediational process to learn the CVC. That is, in the process of encoding the information, he has used information in LTM (namely, that MOT is the same as the first three letters in "mother") to modify the presented stimulus. This kind of mediational process is very common. Quite often, when subjects are instructed to learn lists by rote memorization, in a directly repetitive fashion, they mediate instead. Later, they remember by recalling the mediated form of the stimulus and the device they used to transform it. Then they decode the mediated form into the original, and produce the original form. This is essentially the same process we have discussed in the context of chunking in STM. In particular, the example just given illustrates the use of an NLM—natural-language mediator. That label, NLM, simply refers to the fact that the information taken from LTM was information about natural language—spelling patterns, word meanings, and so on (as contrasted, for example, with the number-recoding device discussed in Chapter 5, which does not refer to natural language usage).

Although the use of NLMs can present a problem to the experimenter who wishes subjects to learn by rote memorization, it is a topic of interest in its own right. How does mediation work? Does it aid memory? When is it most effective? What mediational devices are commonly used? These are among the questions we shall discuss.

The first thing to note about NLM usage is that sometimes it truly aids memory. Our subject who used "mother" to remember MOT was right to do so, for he remembered "mother" better than he would have remembered plain old MOT. This claim needs qualification, however— using a NLM in the course of encoding is not going to do much good if you forget that you used it. The mediated items will be recalled correctly only if both their recoded form and the device used in mediation are remembered. What good would it do if we remembered "mother" and reported that the CVC was "Mom"? This point has been illustrated in several experiments.

Use of NLMs in Paired-Associate Learning

Montague, Adams, and Kiess (1966) investigated the use of NLMs in a paired-associate learning task. While learning a list of paired associates, subjects wrote down any NLMs they formed, although they were not required to form them. For example, seeing the pair PAB–LOM, the subject might write down "pablum." At the time of test, the stimulus terms were shown to the subject, and he was to recall, for each stimulus, not only the response but also the NLM he had originally formed with that stimulus (if any). Then the authors analyzed the extent to which the response terms were correctly recalled, separating the paired associates according to whether the subject had originally formed an NLM for a pair or had not, and whether he remembered the NLM or not. They found that on the average for cases where no NLM was reported during the study of the list, the subject recalled only 6% of the response terms correctly. For cases where an NLM was reported, that recall jumped considerably— but only if the subject could remember his NLM. On the average, if he had used an NLM and forgotten it, his recall of the response was at 2%; if he remembered the NLM he used, he recalled 73%.

In addition to the recall findings, Montague et al. found that more NLMs were used in some situations than in others. For one thing, more NLMs were used when the paired associates were presented for study at a slow rate (30 seconds per pair) than at a faster rate (15 seconds). Also, more NLMs were formed when the CVCs were high in "meaningfulness" than when they were low. The meaningfulness of a CVC (Noble, 1961) refers to the number of associations that are typically given to the CVC in a limited time period by a group of subjects. High m (meaningfulness) indicates a large number of associations. A syllable like WIS, for example, might lead to the associations: "whiskey," "Wisconsin," "whisper," "whistle," and so forth. It would be high in meaningfulness. A low-m syllable might be something like GOQ. Thus, it seems that the more readily a CVC elicits associated words, the more likely it is to be used in NLM formation in a paired-associate task. And the more time is available to mediate, the more likely an NLM is to be formed. What these results mean, essentially, is that NLM formation takes time and a certain amount of work. It is not automatic or effortless. The subject must think up an NLM for a CVC, and although this task is made easier if the CVC gives rise to a large number of associations because there will be several candidates for the NLM, it all takes time.

Prytulak's T-Stack Model for the Use of NLMs

One flaw in the experiment just described is that it does not reveal how an NLM is formed. We know that NLMs are related to better recall, and we can see that their formation is not effortless, but we are really in the dark about the mechanism of NLM formation. Prytulak (1971) attempted to clarify such points with an extensive investigation of natural-language mediation. He attempted to take apart the NLM process; to separate it into its phases of encoding (the original formation and application of the NLM) and decoding (the later transformation of the NLM into the originally presented stimulus at the time of retrieval). He did this by forming a very detailed classification scheme for the types of NLMs that subjects formed from CVCs.

To begin with, Prytulak had subjects look at some CVCs and write down, for each one, "whatever meaningful thing came to mind"—their NLM. That might be a word, a phrase, an acronym, or the CVC itself if it were meaningful. Then Prytulak classified the various NLMs the subjects had produced, according to the kinds of "operations" that had to be applied to the CVCs in order to yield the NLMs. For example, one kind of operation is substitution—the CVC FET can be converted to "pet" by substituting "p" for "f." Another operation is internal addition, adding a letter inside a CVC. For example, inserting a "u" in FEL yields "fuel." A deletion gets rid of letters in CVCs, as when GOH becomes "go." Prytulak found that seven major operations characterized his subjects' NLM formation. These seven operations could be used either alone or in combination. For example, combining substitution and suffixing (adding a letter at the end of a word, a form of external addition), we can get from the CVC HOZ to "hose." The sequence of operations used to convert a CVC to an NLM is called a "transformation" by Prytulak. A transformation may consist of one or several operations; Prytulak found 272 different transformations (combinations of operations) that were used by his subjects.

After forming the NLMs, each of Prytulak's subjects was then given his NLMs and asked to decode them, that is, reconstruct the CVCs from which he had produced them. Prytulak used the subjects' reconstructions to order the transformations according to what percentage of the time the NLMs produced by them could be decoded. For example, the transformation consisting of adding a suffix would be ranked above that of deletion if the NLMs resulting from suffixing were more readily decoded into their corresponding CVCs that were NLMs produced by deletion. In this fashion, all the transformations were ordered in what we might think of as a "usefulness ranking." Prytulak called the resulting ordered list a T (for transformation) stack.

Finally, Prytulak used the T-stack concept to propose a model of natural-language mediation. He proposed that a subject learning a CVC will encode it by working his way down the T stack, starting with the most useful T (transformation) and continuing down until he finds a T that will work. That is, he looks for the first T which can be applied to the CVC to produce an English word. The lower in the list is the T he finds, the less successful the resulting NLM should be, because lower Ts are those that are less useful. When the time comes to recall the original CVC, the subject decodes the NLM. To do so, he must remember both the NLM and the T that produced it. Either or both can be forgotten, and it can be assumed that there will be more failures to remember as the subject must go lower and lower in the stack to find a usable T.

Prytulak suggested that remembering the T that was chosen would depend on its complexity, in terms of the number of operations it comprised. Thus, a single-operation T would be easier to remember than those that consisted of several operations. In addition, some T operations are apparently more readily forgotten than others. In particular, an operation will be more likely to be remembered if the resulting NLM in some way gives a clue to what produced it. For example, if the subject recalls the NLM "locomotion," the facts that the NLM is long and has a CVC at its beginning are clues that the operation that produced it may have been suffixing. The subject can thus figure out and report that the CVC was "loc."

Prytulak went on to test the T-stack model in a variety of ways. First, he characterized a large number of CVCs by the distance one would have to go down in the T stack to produce an NLM for them (their "stack depth"). He obtained CVCs that were "high in stack depth," that is, very easily formed into NLMs, and those that were lower in stack depth. He found that the concepts of T stack and of stack depth were good predictors of such varied data as rate of paired-associate learning, short-term retention, and time required to generate an NLM from a CVC.

SENTENCE AND IMAGE MEDIATORS

Although we have been discussing mediation in relation to CVCs, the formation of NLMs from nonsense syllables is certainly not the only form that mediation takes. For example, learning of paired associates can be markedly influenced by the use of sentence mediators (Bobrow and Bower, 1969; Rohwer, 1966). A sentence mediator converts the paired associates into a sentence. For example, given the pair BOY–DOOR, we might mediate by thinking, "The boy is closing the door." If we did so, we would later be able to recall door, given BOY, more readily than if we had not used the sentence mediator. Another example of mediation comes from an experiment of Schwartz (1969). She had subjects learn lists like A–PIE, D–CAT, and so on. When the subjects were told that the pairs could be mediated by common associations to the response terms, they learned better than if they were not given this hint. That, is, A–PIE could be converted to "apple–pie;" D–CAT to "Dog–Cat," and so on. Later, given A–?, the subject would think of "A–apple"–"apple–pie"–and report "pie."

We will mention one last form of mediation here, mediation of a rather different sort. The mediators we have discussed are verbal; that is, they use words, sentences, or phrases. However, mediators can also use mental pictures, or images. We shall have much more to say about imagery in LTM in Chapter 12, so, at this point, we shall just briefly describe an experimental procedure using this kind of mediating process. Bower (1972b) instructed subjects learning to associate pairs of nouns to form a mental picture in which the two nouns in each pair interacted. For example, given the pair DOG–BICYCLE, the subject might picture a dog riding a bicycle. A control group of subjects was not given such a special instruction, but instead was given the standard instruction—just to learn to give the response term when given the stimulus. The results were very clear—the group given imagery instructions remembered about one and one-half times as well as the control group. Thus, the experimental instruction seemed to have a powerful facilitating effect on paired-associate learning. One hypothesis about the effectiveness of imagery is that formation of an image acts to store the two nouns together, as integral parts of an interaction. When the stimulus noun is later presented, it elicits recall of the entire image, and since the image contains the response noun as well as the stimulus noun, the response noun can be reported. For example, the word DOG elicits the image of a dog riding a bicycle, leading to the recall of the response "bicycle." This interpretation of the imagery effect has been called the "conceptual peg" hypothesis (Paivio, 1963), because it assumes that the stimulus word serves as a peg to which the response term is attached during image formation.

We have discussed several encoding processes. They include chunking, natural–language mediation (to CVCs and in other forms in paired-associate learning) and imagery mediation. The next encoding process we shall discuss is organization, as studied in the context of the free-recall task.

ORGANIZATION IN FREE RECALL

First, we must note that under the term "organization" are subsumed all of the encoding processes listed above. Whenever a subject acts on incoming information to modify it systematically, he can be said to be organizing that information. In this sense, organization can occur at the level of perception. When the subject isolates the figure F from the page around it, he is organizing the visual field; when he groups YMCAFBI into "YMCA FBI," a process we discussed under "chunking," he is organizing; when he thinks of "Wisconsin" as an NLM for WIS, he is organizing; and so on. In the free-recall procedure, however, we have one of the most natural situations in which to study organizational processes. In free recall, we have: (a) full access to information in LTM (that is, we are tapping information beyond sensory levels when we recall word lists); (b) freedom to re-arrange list words in accordance with organizational tendencies (because it is *free* recall); and (c) usually, enough words in the list so that there is ample material to organize. With these conditions, then, organization should be most accessible to our inspection. Usually, we define organization in free recall as occurring when there are *consistent* discrepancies between the order of the list items as presented and their order as recalled. The idea is that such discrepancies arise because the subject is internally modifying (organizing) the input, and this systematically affects how the items are recalled.

Experimenter-Imposed Organization

Quite often, when organization has been studied in free recall, the organization has been manipulated by the experimenter's choice of words to use in the list. Consider, for example, some experiments by Jenkins, Russell, and Mink (Jenkins, Mink, and Russell, 1958; Jenkins and Russell, 1952). These experimenters constructed lists by manipulating the association value of pairs of words in the list. (The association value between two words reflects the number of times subjects give one word in a free-association task when the other word is given as a stimulus. For example, BUTTERFLY and MOTH are highly associated; BUTTERFLY and GARDEN are less highly associated, and BUTTERFLY and BOOK are non-associates.) Jenkins and Russell, in one experiment, selected twenty-four pairs of highly associated words, such as MAN–WOMAN, TABLE–CHAIR, and so on. They then separated the pairs, scrambled these words, and presented them in random order as a forty-eight-word free recall list. They found that although the words had been scrambled at presentation, they tended to be unscrambled at recall. That is, words were likely to be reported together if highly associated. Even though we might separate *table* and *chair* by seventeen other words when we construct the list, subjects often report them together at recall. Moreover, Jenkins, Mink, and Russell found that the stronger the association between pairs of words in a free-recall list, the higher the recall score (the percentage of items recalled correctly), and the more likely that associated pairs would be recalled together. Thus, we see that word relationships are reflected both in the recall *score* and in the *manner* of recall. It seems that the subject has organized the list—has modified it in such a way that he can take advantage of associated words. We have strong evidence that the list-as-presented is not the list-as-encoded, just as a CVC presented may not lead to a CVC stored, but to an NLM instead.

We might at this point raise a question. Is it really fair to talk about the organizing of a free-recall list as an encoding process? Conceivably, the subject might not act on the list at the time of its presentation; instead, his recall might reflect the effects of LTM structure in some way other than encoding. For example, he might report highly associated words together because they are *stored* together in LTM and he finds them together at the time of retrieval. This has been a question of some interest to organization theorists, and, as we shall see, it seems that organization does occur, to some extent, during encoding.

We have seen that associations among word pairs interspersed in a free-recall list can be reflected in organized recall of the list. We could carry this further than pairs, certainly. We could include *groups* of associated words in our list. One fruitful example of just such an approach is the use of category instances in list generation. By that is meant the use of several words from each of several classes in the list. For example, we could take several members of the category "animal": DOG, CAT, BIRD, FISH, etc., or several members of some of those subcategories, such as "fish": TROUT, TUNA, CARP, SMELT, SARDINE, etc., and scramble them with members of other categories to make a list. We would find that when used in a free-recall list, categorical structure does have an effect much like the effect of associated word pairs.

Bousfield (1951; 1953) used categorical structure in free recall as follows. In one experiment, he used four categories to make up his list. From each, he took fifteen words, to make a list of sixty words in all. The words were presented in random order for free recall. Bousfield found what he called "categorical clustering." This refers to the tendency of subjects to recall members of the same category together, even when they were not originally presented together. This is, of course, much like the finding of Jenkins and Russell that highly associated pairs of words are recalled together, or clustered.

Presumably, words that are all members of a given category will also tend to be associated with one another. We could therefore ask whether categorical clustering is in any way different from the associative clustering of the Jenkins, Russell, and Mink experiments. The answer seems to be yes: the effects of categorical relationships can be distinguished from the effects of associative relatedness. Evidence for this comes from the finding that when a list is composed of words that have categorical relationships but that are not associated, categorical clustering nevertheless occurs (Bousfield and Puff, 1964; Wood and Underwood, 1967). For example, SPOOL, BARREL, and BASEBALL all come from the category "round objects." They are not associated with one another in terms of association value, but under appropriate conditions, they will be recalled together. Another piece of evidence for the independent contribution of categorical relationships is that clustering is greater when words in a list are both categorically *and* associatively related than when their relationship is only associative (Cofer, 1965). For example, BED *and* CHAIR are both in the same category and are highly associated; BED and DREAM are associated but in distinct categories. And lists made up of pairs of the first type are more highly clustered than lists constructed of the second type of pair.

Bousfield's explanation of the category-clustering effect (Bousfield and Cohen, 1953) is that in learning a categorized list, all the instances of a given category will become associated to a higher-order structure representing the category itself. Later on, the recall of just one of the instances will tend to activate that superordinate structure, which will in turn facilitate the recall of the other instances of the category. Those instances will be recalled together, yielding a cluster. For example, if a list contains several animal names, remembering LION may activate "animal," leading to recall of DOG, ZEBRA, etc.

Work subsequent to Bousfield's original discovery of categorical clustering has helped to clarify this type of organization. It seems that recall of categorized lists reflects at least three basic processes (Bower, 1972a): (1) learning which categories are represented by list words, (2) learning to associate the category name with instances in the list, and (3) recalling category names.

First, the subject must determine what categories are represented in the list. We could make his job easier by presenting all the members of one category, then all the members of another, and so on—in blocks, rather than randomly interspersed. Indeed, presenting category instances in blocks increases both clustering and recall (Cofer, Bruce, and Reicher, 1966).

Second, the subject must learn, for each category, which members are present in the list. He must somehow store the occurrence of category members in the list, and associate those members with the category name, so that later, in recalling the category name, he will be able to recall the members that were in the list. We would expect factors that represent increased association between members of the category and the category name to improve this second stage and therefore facilitate recall. And we do find this. For example, the frequency with which subjects report various instances when asked for examples of a category has been studied (Battig and Montague, 1969). It has been found that "iron" is a high-frequency response to the category "metal," whereas "lead" is relatively low-frequency; that "dog" is a frequent instance of "four-footed animal" whereas "mouse" is low, and so on. What is relevant to the free-recall task is that if a categorized list is constructed from high-frequency category instances, it is recalled better than a list constructed from low-frequency category instances (Bousfield, Cohen, and Whitmarsh, 1958; Cofer et al., 1966).

Finally, we assume that recall leads off with retrieval of category names, which, in turn, cue retrieval of the category members that were in the list. The category members are then reported in recall. We therefore expect factors that improve retrieval of category names to lead to better recall of the list. For example, when Tulving and Pearlstone (1966) and Lewis (1972) told subjects, at the time of the recall test, which categories had been represented in the list; the recall scores of the subjects substantially improved.

Experiments on the recall of categorized lists help us to understand how organization works. It seems that learning categorized lists is a complex process, in which units are organized into larger units that can later be decoded into the original inputs. All of the phenomena we have discussed under the general label of "organizational processes" fit into this pattern. Although specific properties of the larger units produced by organization may differ from one case to another (for example, the organization of categories may produce structures that differ from those that simply associate related words), the building up of higher-order units, followed by a retrieval process that leads from retrieval of those units to recall of their components, seems to be the nature of organization in general. Organization thus encompasses chunking, the use of NLMs, the clustering of associatively related and categorized lists, and, as we shall see, "subjective organization."

Subjective Organization

Subjective organization stands in contrast to the kind of organization we have just been discussing, in which the experimenter builds some structure into the list. In subjective organization, the subject himself builds structure into a list that the experimenter may have thought was truly disorganized. This is something like what happens when the subject thinks of "mother" given the stimulus MOT. Although subjective organization may differ from organization of a categorized list in this sense, similar processes are going on in the two situations.

Subjective organization, a term proposed by Tulving (1962), is more difficult to assess than deliberately induced organization of the type imposed on categorized lists. How can we tell that a subject is organizing a free-recall list? One way to tell is by observing the order in which words are recalled. We already know that if highly associated words are included in a list, they will tend to be recalled together, and that members of the same category will be recalled together from categorized lists. Thus, it would seem that the same sort of effect should be present in subjective organization—that words organized into the same structure should be recalled together, or clustered. This should occur no matter what order they were presented in, so that, if we observed recall over a series of trials with the same list, the words that are organized together should be recalled together each time. In short, we would suspect that organization would reveal itself by the subject's recalling words in some consistent order, even though the input order of the words varied over trials. It is just this reasoning that leads to measures of subjective organization.

Two notable measures of subjective organization are Tulving's SO measure and Bousfield and Bousfield's (1966) ITR measure (SO stands for subjective organization; ITR stands for intertrial repetitions). These measures are based on consistency of recall order—the more consistent the subject's recall order is from trial to trial, the more he tends to recall pairs of words in the same order from one trial to the next, the higher these measures will be. And the measures are assumed to indicate the amount of organizing the subject is doing. Thus, we think that the more he organizes, the more consistent his ordering of words in recall should be, and the higher his measure of subjective organization will be as a result.

Do the measures work? If so, what do they do? For one thing, we would expect that subjective organization of a list would lead to better recall, on the basis of what we know about the effect of organization on categorized lists. Thus, we would expect that SO would correlate with recall—that is, the higher the SO score, the higher would be the recall score. By and large, experimental results have supported this view (e.g., Tulving, 1962; 1964). On the other hand, some theorists have claimed there is no great consistency in the correlation. In reply, supporters of the view have suggested that it is not the idea that organization leads to recall that is at fault—it is merely that we could use better measures of organization (Postman, 1972; Wood, 1972).

Other evidence for the existence of subjective organization, and for its effect on recall, comes from experiments in which a manipulation is found to affect both organization and recall similarly. For example, subjects learning a list in a free-recall task may be instructed to group certain items together. Such instructions tend to increase measures of both organization and recall (Mayhew, 1967). In contrast, instructions that emphasize encoding of each item as a separate unit tend to impair both organization and recall (Allen, 1968). This pattern of results supports the idea of subjective organization.

The subjective organization that occurs in free recall appears to share many characteristics with experimenter-imposed organization. The SO score is an index of the subjective counterpart of category clustering; thus, the data on SO scores indicate that subjects produce subjectively determined clusters in recall. Another similarity between subjective and experimenter-imposed organization is found in their positive effects on recall. Both categorical clustering and SO scores correlate positively with recall. All of this indicates that both types of organization, the subject's own and that controlled by the experimenter, operate in essentially the same way.

Further support for the essential similarity of categorical and subjective organization comes from a study by Mandler and Pearlstone (1966). In their experiment, subjects were given a set of fifty-two cards, each having a word printed on it. They were told to sort the cards into two to seven categories. The cards were scrambled and then sorted by the subject repeatedly, until he had sorted the cards in the same way twice in succession. An important manipulation in this experiment was that one group of subjects was free to sort the cards in whatever way they wished. A second group, in contrast, was constrained by the experimenter, who told them how the cards were to be sorted. (As a control for differences in the various categorization schemes, each subject in the constrained group was told to sort in a way that had been adopted by a subject in the other, free group.) After the sorting task, each subject was asked to recall as many of the words as he could.

Mandler and Pearlstone found, not surprisingly, that it took the constrained group of subjects many more trials to sort the cards in the same way twice in a row than it did the free subjects. However, the two groups did about as well as on the recall test. This means that it was not the amount of experience with the words that mattered (for the constrained group had more sorting trials); it was the organization which was achieved that determined recall. Another important result was a strong positive correlation between the number of categories subjects used in sorting and their recall scores. Subjects recalled about five words for each category sorted, so the more categories they used, the more words they recalled. This is very similar to a finding for categorized lists (Cohen, 1966; Tulving and Pearlstone, 1966). Namely, if subjects manage to recall any members of a category, then they tend to recall the words from that category fairly well. Thus, in the categorized-list situation, the more categories from which any items are recalled, the higher the overall recall score. This general similarity between subjective and experimenter-determined organization supports the idea that the two types of organization work in a similar manner.

Having established to some degree that subjective organization, categorical clustering, associative clustering, NLM formation, and chunking all operate in a similar fashion, a point of clarification seems in order concerning the relationship between *chunking,* which we discussed in connection with STM (in Chapter 5), and *organization,* discussed here in connection with LTM. The nature of that relationship should be clear, but let's consider it for a moment. We have already noted that chunking is a form of organization. In fact, chunking and organization are fundamentally the same process. In some situations, the different terms simply correspond to different methods of testing that process. For example, if a subject organizes the set CAT, DOG, FISH into "pet" when the situation calls for immediate recall and the list of items is fairly short, then we can assume we are studying chunking. That is because we have described an STM situation, and chunking is a label for organization in STM. On the other hand, if a longer list were used, and there was a fairly lengthy retention interval between presentation and test, then LTM would presumably be tapped. Then, the subject's combining CAT, DOG, FISH into "pet" would be called organization. Where does organization occur? To the extent that it takes place at the time of encoding, we can conveniently place it in the "working memory" of STM, as discussed in Chapters 5, 6, and 7. Since we assume that STM encoding can affect both what is stored in STM and what is transferred to LTM, it seems that the same organizational processes apply to both. The point to note is that the labels organization and chunking refer primarily to the research procedure used to study them—and, correspondingly, to the memory store we think might be predominant in that paradigm.

Organization: At Encoding or Retrieval?

We have, at this point, a fairly general idea of what organization is: the formation of superordinate units from collections of input items. Later, the superordinate units can be "decoded" to yield individual input items. This seems to hold whether the information is held for a short term (as in chunking) or for longer intervals, and whether the input has some formal structure (as in categorized lists) or a structure that is perceived only by the person doing the organizing (subjective organization). We have been referring to organization as an encoding process, and the description of organization just given would seem to fit with that idea. That is, organization could be an event that occurs at the time of storage, and that acts to bind up several items into one unit. That view of organization can be called the encoding, or storage view; it says that organization facilitates the encoding and storage of information. It is also called the dependent view, because it claims that the various items that are stored together are mutually dependent. As such, they make fewer demands on the capacity to store items in a free-recall list. Thus, organization will facilitate recall. It will also lead to the recall of items in clusters, because when the superordinate unit is decoded, all the items in it are retrieved and recalled at the same time.

The dependent–encoding view of organization has been challenged by the independent–retrieval view (Slamecka, 1968; 1969) that holds that when a subject studies a list of items, he first notices the general structure of the list when it is presented. He then stores that general structure. At the same time, he stores the items in the list separately, keeping them independent of one another. The effects of the organization actually occur at the time of retrieval, according to this view. When it comes time to recall the list, the subject activates a retrieval plan that then guides his search through memory for the list items. The plan is based on the general structure of the list, which the subject stored when it was presented. Because he is using a planned search, the subject is likely to find items that are related to one another at about the same time. He will recall them together, resulting in output clusters. The use of a plan will also increase the number of items recalled, for it will be superior to a random search.

The two views of organization just proposed differ in where they see organizational effects as occurring. The former says at the time of encoding; the latter at retrieval (although the latter view includes encoding and storage effects—the general structure of the list is said to be stored).

They also differ in that the first says organized items are stored together, and the second says they are stored independently. However, the entire distinction between dependent–independent, encoding–retrieval views has come up against criticism (Postman, 1972). In fact, there is ample reason to consider organization as a process that encompasses both encoding and retrieval. That evidence comes from work on the principle of "encoding specificity" (Thomson and Tulving, 1970).

Encoding Specificity

The principle of encoding specificity says that "What is stored is determined by what is perceived and how it is encoded, and what is stored determines what retrieval cues are effective in providing access to what is stored (Tulving and Thomson, 1973, p. 353)." In other words, recall is the result of a rather complex interaction between encoding (or storage) processes and retrieval. In order to best get at information stored in memory, the retrieval operation should have available the same information that was present at the time of encoding. That means that the encoding of the input should match the cues for retrieval.

We have already mentioned an instance of encoding specificity in the context of the Tulving and Pearlstone (1966) study. They presented subjects with a categorized list in which all the instances of a given category were grouped together and preceded by the category name. Then, at the time of the test, one group of subjects was given the category names as cues for recall, while a control group was given no cues. The group given the recall cues remembered more words from the list than the control group. This indicates that making the information that had been available at the time of storage (in this case, the category names) also available at the time of testing had a facilitative effect on recall. Thus, this finding is consistent with the encoding specificity principle—recall was best when the encoding situation matched the testing, or retrieval situation.

In related experiments, Tulving and Osler (1968) and Thomson and Tulving (1970) expanded on this finding. Their general method was in part as follows. The subjects were given a list of words for free recall. For some subjects, each to-be-remembered word was accompanied by an associate; for example the word EAGLE might be accompanied by its associate, SOAR (the lists were set up so that the subject knew which of the two words was to be remembered, and was instructed that the other was a word that might be helpful in remembering it). Other subjects got no associates with their list words. At the time of the test, some subjects in each group were given the associate of the list word as a recall cue; others got no cue. Thus, there were four groups: (1) associate at both input and at test, (2) associate at input only, (3) associate at test only, (4) no associates given. The results were clear. The first group, which got the associate at both the presentation of the list and the test, out-performed the other groups on recall. The second and third groups, which were given associates only at presentation or only at the time of the test, performed worse than the fourth group, which was given no associates at all. These results provide strong support for encoding spec-ificity. When the conditions of encoding and recall are most similar, then recall will be best.

The principle of encoding specificity has been studied primarily in the context of using cues for recalling individual items. However, it can help us to round out our picture of free recall and organization, for the same principle seems readily applicable to recall of organized clusters of words. We can attempt now to describe organization: When a subject is given a list of words, he will tend to organize them as he encodes them. This means that he will form higher-order units of information that combine several single items. Later on, at the time of recall, retrieval of part of the list will lead to recalling the rest. The retrieval process involves decoding the higher-order units of information that were formed during organization, and this will result in clustering of organized groups at output, and will facilitate recall as well. All this will occur as long as the conditions of retrieval are compatible with the organizing that was done at the time of encoding and storage. Moreover, supplying cues at the time of retrieval that help to bring back the conditions of encoding will facilitate retrieval. Finally, we should note that retrieval itself deserves much more discussion than we have given it so far. Ac-cordingly, in the next chapter we shall focus on retrieval from LTM.

11

REMEMBERING:
RETRIEVAL PROCESSES

In the preceding chapter, remembering was discussed in the context of coding processes—operations that work on input information to facilitate the ability to remember it. It became clear that retrieval processes must also be considered in a discussion of remembering. In the present chapter, we shall focus on retrieval. In doing so, we shall find it necessary to look at the experimental procedure called recognition, as well as to add a bit to our knowledge of free recall. As a result, we shall find ourselves constructing models that describe how information is retrieved from memory.

RECOGNITION

Let us begin by reviewing the procedure used to test recognition. In a typical experiment, a subject first studies—looks at, or hears—a list of items. Then, he is tested on them; he is presented with some of the list items along with some others that were not on the list. The latter are called distractors. The subject's job is to pick out those items that were on his list and reject those that were not. The specifics of the testing procedure can vary, although recognition tests generally fit this description. For example, a yes/no test or a forced-choice test can be used. (See Chapter 1 for details of these variations.)

Recognition Performance Versus Recall

One of the important facts about recognition testing is that, in general, a subject can recognize list items much better than he can recall them. In fact, if we first give the subject a chance to recall the list, and then give him a recognition test, we will usually find that he can recognize many items he was unable to recall.

Shepard (1967) provided a dramatic demonstration of the ability of subjects to recognize large numbers of items. He used three kinds of items in a series of experiments—words, sentences, and pictures. In one experiment, subjects were presented with 540 words, each printed on a card. The subjects looked through the cards in order; then were given a series of sixty two-alternative, forced-choice tests on the words. Shepard found that they could perform on the tests with a mean accuracy rate of 88%! Subjects who saw 612 colored pictures performed even better: their recognition accuracy was 97%. In a third experiment, subjects shown 612 sentences scored 89% on a subsequent recognition test. Shepard was also able to persuade a couple of friends to look at 1,224 sentences—and they scored 88% in a subsequent recognition test.

Shepard's results emphasize the fact that recognition performance is extremely high, relative to recall. We might well ask if this is always true. It is not—it is possible to design recognition-testing situations in which performance is rather poor. For example, we can use as distractors items that are strongly associated with or very similar to list items. We might present CAT as a list word and use DOG as a distractor. This sort of manipulation leads to decrements in recognition-test performance (e.g., Underwood, 1965; Underwood and Freund, 1968). Or, we can use a large number of distractors. For example, we can present the list words on the test together with ninety alternatives. It is difficult to recognize list words in this situation (Davis, Sutherland, and Judd, 1961).

Another fact about recognition testing is that performance remains high even with long retention intervals. That is, forgetting of items appears to be very slow when it is evaluated with the recognition method. Postman and Rau (1957) found that performance on a test of recognition for short lists of CVCs or words stayed near 100% over a two-day retention interval. Shepard (1967), in one of the experiments mentioned above, tested retention of picture stimuli over a period of 120 days. He tested groups of subjects at retention intervals of no delay, 2 hours, 3 days, a week, and 120 days. As you can see in Figure 11.1, he found that although forgetting took place, it did so very slowly.

The type of test administered also affects the measurement of forgetting over shorter intervals. Forgetting is notably slower when recognition tests are used than when testing uses recall as a measure. Short-term recognition was studied by Shepard and Teghtsoonian (1961). In their experiment, subjects were given a large deck of cards, with a three-digit number written on each. The subjects were instructed to go through the

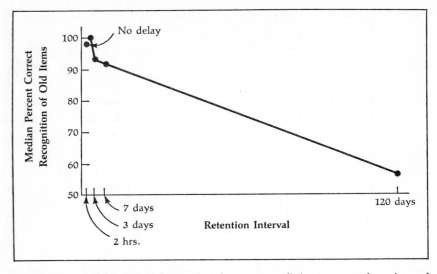

FIGURE
11.1

Correct recognition of old (previously presented) items, as a function of retention interval. [After Shepard, 1967.]

cards, indicating for each one whether or not they had seen it before. Of course, the first few cards all contained numbers that were new to the subject. But the deck was so arranged that after the first few cards, old cards (those containing a number the subject had already seen) and new cards (those containing a number not seen previously) occurred equally often in a random sequence. Except for a few cards at the bottom of the deck that occurred only once (to maintain the equal probability of old and new), each number in the deck occurred just twice.

Shepard and Teghtsoonian were particularly interested in how recognition would vary as a function of the distance between the first and second occurrence of a number. They defined this distance, which they called "lag," as the number of cards that intervened between the first and second appearance of a given number. For example, if the series of cards seen during some period was: 147, 351, 362, 215, 111, 147, we can expect the subject to say "new" to the first appearance of 147 and "old" to the second. We can define the lag here as four, because four items intervene between the two 147s. Now, if we plot the percentage of correct responses to old items as a function of lag, the results are as shown in Figure 11.2 below. We see that the subjects' performance is better than chance for lags of as many as sixty items, with chance meaning the level of correct responses a subject could get if he were merely guessing.

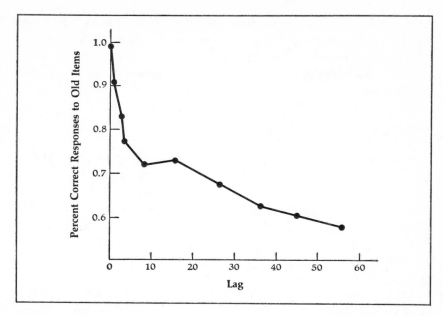

FIGURE
11.2

Percent correct responses to old items as a function of lag—number of stimuli intervening between the first and second presentations of the item. [After Shepard and Teghtsoonian, 1961. Copyright 1961 by the American Psychological Association.]

Since each time he responds he has a 50:50 chance of being correct (the item is either old or new), his guessing level is 50%. When he does better than 50%, we suspect that he is doing more than just guessing—he is working with information in memory, and this information helps him to do better than he would by chance. Thus, we see that the lag during which forgetting occurs in this situation is about sixty items.

We can contrast these results with results obtained in a similar experiment that measured recall rather than recognition: An approximate parallel in recall is found in the Waugh and Norman (1965) probe-digit task discussed in Chapter 6. There we had a lag, defined as the number of digits intervening between the first and second appearance of the probe. And there, too, we had a recall measure—recall of the digit adjacent to the probe. Waugh and Norman found that performance decayed to guessing levels when about twelve digits intervened. Thus we see that although the forgetting curves look the same, with gradual decreases in memory as more and more items intervene, the number of intervening items necessary for what appears to be complete forgetting is quite different. In recognition there is still memory of an item after sixty subsequent items, whereas in recall, memory has vanished with twelve. Thus, over the short term, to the extent that these experiments are comparable, forgetting measured with recognition methods seems to be less than forgetting measured by recall, just as it is over longer intervals.

Signal-Detection Theory and Recognition

With some of the basic facts about recognition at hand, it is time to look at a theoretical model of the recognition of an item in memory. This is, in fact, the first retrieval model we shall discuss. It is the signal-detection model for recognition memory. The model enables us to derive an estimate of the amount of information in memory on which a subject bases his recognition judgments. In addition, the model provides a means of dealing with a very important problem in recognition testing: the problem of response bias, or guessing effects.

To illustrate the problem, consider a hypothetical experiment in which we give two groups of subjects a list of items, followed by a yes/no recognition test. That is, the subject is tested with a mixed sequence of list items and distractors and instructed to say "yes" if he thinks a given item was on the list; "no" if he thinks it is a distractor. Now suppose that to one group of subjects (the "free" group), we indicate that performance on the recognition test will be scored on the basis of overall accuracy, and that there will be no penalty for guessing. To a second group of subjects (the "conservative" group), we give somewhat different instructions. We indicate that performance on the recognition test will be scored on the basis of accurate use of the "yes" response, and that there will be a heavy penalty whenever they incorrectly identify a distractor as having been on the list. Clearly, the two groups of subjects would be well advised to use different strategies. Since the first group is not penalized for guessing, they should do so. Whenever they are unsure whether an item is old or new, they should attempt to guess. The second group, in contrast, must be very conservative in their use of the "yes" responses. This means that if they are not absolutely certain whether an item is from the list or a distractor, they should indicate that it is a distractor.

In view of their different strategies for responding, our two groups of subjects should perform differently. First, considering the correct recognition of list items—that is, the percentage of the time the subject said "yes" to a list item on the test—we will probably find better performance by the free group. That is because subjects in that group were free to guess "yes," and some proportion of those guesses were probably correct. On the other hand, conservative subjects used their "yes" response more cautiously. Although a large proportion of their "yes" responses may be correct, they were forced to say "no" to many list items during the test. Thus, they have lower scores on recognition of list items. In addition, the overall accuracy of the free group may be better, for they were permitted their "best guess." To the extent that subjects in the conservative group were forced to say "no" to items that they felt were probably on the list but did not want to take a chance on, they were forced into error.

Now the point of this exercise can be seen. Although there is no reason to suppose that the two groups of subjects have different amounts of information about the list in memory, their recognition scores differ. If we were to use recognition performance to make inferences about their memory for list items, we would be in error. For it is our instructions that have biased the responses of the two groups and have caused them to perform differently. This means that in order to use recognition performance to assess what subjects actually remember, we must have some way to account for the effects of response bias and guessing.

Actually, there are several methods available for "correcting for guessing," to obtain a good estimate of memory performance. One is to use yes/no or two-alternative, forced-choice tests and to give the subject a "corrected" score of number right minus number wrong. This assumes that the subject's guesses are random, with a 50:50 chance of being correct, and that every time he gets an item wrong, he was guessing. In that case, we would expect the number wrong to represent only *half* of his guesses—because the other half of his guesses could be right purely by chance. Thus, we must subtract the number of correct guesses from his recognition score. For a two-choice test, the number of correct guesses would be equal to the number of incorrect guesses, so we would give him a corrected score of the total number correct minus the number wrong. For example, if he guessed ten times in answering one hundred questions, he should average five right answers and five wrong answers. Thus, we must take five away from his score of ninety-five correct because he was guessing—not remembering—when he gave five of the correct answers.

However, this particular method of correction is considered an inaccurate one by some psychologists. A problem is that in assuming that the subject has a 50:50 chance of being correct when he guesses, it ignores the possibilities that the subject may be biased toward making a particular response, or that he may be better at recognizing old items than at recognizing distractors. As we shall see, the signal-detection approach provides a more reasonable correction for guessing. It is this approach we will discuss in some detail, because it is used as much more than a correction for guessing. It can also be considered a theory of recognition memory.

The theory of signal detection actually originated with the study of auditory-detection tasks (Green and Swets, 1966). Typically, in such a task, a subject listens for some signal (for example, a tone) to occur against a background of white noise (a hissing, or static-like sound). He presses a button if the signal occurs within a certain period. In this situation, there are essentially four things that can happen within any given period; they are called hits, misses, correct rejections, and false alarms. If the signal occurs and the subject presses the button, a *hit* is recorded. If the signal occurs and the subject misses it and fails to press the button, a *miss* is recorded. If the signal does not occur, and the subject does not press the button, a *correct rejection* is recorded. If the signal does not occur, but the subject nevertheless presses the button, a *false alarm* is recorded. Thus, in the event of a hit or a correct rejection, the subject's response is correct, whereas in the event of a miss or false alarm, the subject has made an error.

The auditory signal-detection task has a direct parallel in the yes/no recognition situation. Consider an experiment in which a subject has first seen a list of items and then is performing on a yes/no test. That means he is shown a sequence of items, and to each item he says "yes" (or "old") if he thinks it was on the original list, and "no" (or "new") if he thinks it is a distractor item. In this case, the occurrence of an old item (one that was actually on the list) is like the occurrence of the signal in the auditory-detection task, and the occurrence of a new item (a distractor) is like the absence of the signal. Another similarity to the auditory task is that as each item comes up on the test, there are four situations that can occur. These are shown in Figure 11.3. First, the item can be an old item (that is, previously on the list), and the subject can say "old"; he is giving the correct response, and as in the auditory task, this is called a *hit*. Second, the item can be old but the subject may incorrectly say "new"; this is called a *miss*. Third, the item can actually be new, and the subject can say "new"; again, as in the auditory task, this is a *correct rejection*. And last, the subject can say "old" when the item is really new; this is a *false alarm*. Thus, signal detection and recognition testing are analogous, and it is for this reason that the theory originally developed for signal detection has been applied to recognition memory.

Note that the four cells (compartments) in Figure 11.3 are not independent. This means that knowing the rate of occurrence of only some

		Subject has seen an old item.	Subject has seen a new item.
Subject says?	"Old"	Hit (——%)	False Alarm (——%)
	"New"	Miss (——%)	Correct Rejection (——%)

TOTALS: Old items (100%)　　　　New items (100%)

FIGURE 11.3

Types of trials that can occur in a yes/no recognition test.

of the events, we can figure out the rate of occurrence of the others. Suppose, for example, that we give the subject a yes/no test on twenty list items. There are forty items on the test, twenty old and twenty new. Now, suppose we know that the subject is correct on fifteen old items; that is, fifteen out of the twenty times an old item was presented on the test, he said "old." He is said to have a *hit rate* of 75% (which represents the fifteen hits he made out of the twenty that were possible). Now, we can fill in the cell marked "miss," because we know he missed five of the twenty old items. That is, we know there were twenty old items, and we know his hit rate was 75%; that he hit fifteen out of those old items. He must have been wrong with the other five; that is, he must have said they were "new," and this is what defines a miss. His *miss rate* is 25%, equal to the five out of twenty items he missed. (In general, the hit rate and miss rate must add to 100%.) By similar reasoning, if we know his *correct-rejection rate* is 40%, we know he said "new" to 40% or eight of the new items. Then he must have said "old" to the other twelve new items, so we know his *false-alarm rate*—it is twelve out of twenty items, or 60%. Thus, we know all the cells of our table if we know one cell in each column. Most commonly, therefore, only two cells, one in each column, are ever referred to. These are usually the hit cell and the false-alarm cell. (Because they are used so frequently, the terms "hit rate" and "false-alarm rate" are often abbreviated HR and FAR.)

With the classificatory scheme of Figure 11.3 for the outcomes of yes/no recognition tests, we shall now consider the basic assumptions of the model that is applied to them. Its first assumption is that any information in LTM has a certain strength. This is similar to the assumption that information in STM has a certain strength, as discussed in Chapter 6. At this point, we won't attempt to stipulate just what "information" means. Instead, we can focus on single items in LTM, items that may be presented in a list. We can think of the strength of an item as the amount of excitation of a location in LTM that corresponds to the item. Strength can also mean the degree of familiarity—the stronger is the item in memory, the more familiar it will seem.

Our second assumption is that measurements of the strengths of items presented in a list will be distributed normally. Let us briefly expand on that assumption: Each item in the list, after its presentation, has a particular strength in the subject's LTM. The distribution of those values among items is normal—many items have medium strength, a few have very high strength, and a few have very low strength. (You may wish to refer to an introductory psychology text for a review of normal distributions.) On the other hand, consider the items that were not presented, but that will be used as new, or distractor items at the time of the test. We shall assume that each of those new items also has its own strength and that the distribution of their strengths is also normal. (See Figure 11.4.) Moreover, we assume that the variability in the strengths of old items is as great as that of the distractors. Thus, we have two normal distributions to consider—one represents the strengths of the list items; the other represents the strengths of the distractors.

Third, we assume that presenting some item on a list has the effect of increasing its strength in the subject's LTM. That means that presenting the item moves its initial strength, or familiarity, from some starting value to some new, higher value. That also means that items that are not presented to the subject will stay at their initial level of strength, or familiarity. This third assumption is important, because it implies that the distributions for old items and distractors will have different mean strength values. Usually, the mean strength of the old items will be higher, because they have just been presented, and that has moved their strength values up. The new items will be lower in strength, at the level the old items were at before they were presented on the list. If we were to plot the strength distributions along some dimension of familiarity, the presentation of the list would serve to move the distribution of old items a jump along the dimension, tending to separate it from the distribution of distractor items.

The resulting arrangement of the two distributions, one for presented items and one for distractors, would vary according to their initial strength values. (Various possibilities are presented in Figure 11.4.) For example, if the items chosen for presentation in the list had initial high strength values (they were very familiar, or had been presented several times before), then presenting them might push their strength far beyond that of the distractors. More usually, we could expect some overlap of

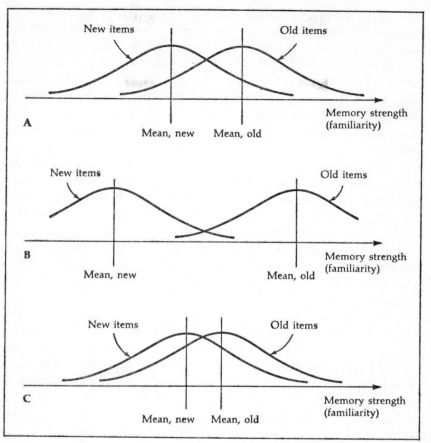

FIGURE
11.4

Possible relationships between the distributions of strengths for old (previously presented) and new (distractor) items in memory: (A) Moderate overlap, (B) old items stronger than new items, (C) old and new items similar in strength.

the two distributions. Although the mean strength of the old items would be greater than that of the new items, there would still be some new items which would be stronger than some old items.

From Figure 11.4, it is clear that the difference between the means of the distributions is a measure of their distance on the familiarity or strength continuum. The further apart the means are, the stronger the old items are relative to the new. In the signal-detection model this distance becomes a measure known as d-prime (d'), which is an indicator of how far apart the old and new items are. More precisely, d' is the distance between the means of the two distributions in standard-deviation units (that is, the difference between the two means, divided by the common standard deviation of the distributions). In addition to the d' value, there is a second theoretical value to consider, called *beta* (β). In terms of the model, β is used by the subject in making a decision. Beta is the criterion strength upon which the subject bases his decision. In order to see how this works, let us review what happens in the experiment.

When a subject is presented with a list of items, we assume: (1) Each item increases in strength. It had a starting strength that has now increased. (2) All items, regardless of their starting strengths, increase by this same amount; this has the effect of shifting the distribution of items presented on the list—now called "old" items—up along the strength continuum by some constant amount. Meanwhile, the items to be used as distractors on the test—called "new" items—remain at their old strength. Presumably, the mean strength of these new items will be less than the mean of the old items.

Now, consider what happens when the subject is tested on the list. A series of items is presented; half are old and half are new. As he considers each item, the subject decides whether it is old or new. In order to make this decision, he adopts a particular strength value (β) and uses it as a criterion. As each test item is presented, the subject evaluates its LTM strength (or decides how familiar it is). Suppose, for example, he determines that a given item's strength is 100, on his scale of strength. Whether he calls the item "old" or "new" depends not only on its strength but also on β. If the item's strength is greater than β, he says "old." If it is less than β, he says "new." So, for example, if β were 90, our item with strength 100 would be called "old." To summarize, we now have a decision rule that says: calculate the strength of the current item, and say "old" if that strength is greater than β; otherwise, say "new."

Now is the time for us to put these ideas about strength distributions, d', and β, together with the outcome labels "hit," "miss," "false alarm," and "correct rejection." This is done in Figure 11.5. Here the two strength distributions are presented, with d' and β drawn in. In the total area under the two distributions, four subareas that are of interest can be identified. What each represents is determined by whether it is under the old or new distribution and whether it is to the left or right of β. For example, consider the area under the old distribution and to the right of β. This area represents the times when an old item is presented on

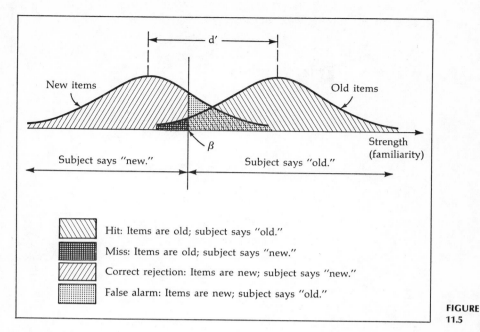

FIGURE
11.5

Concepts in the theory of signal detection as applied to recognition memory.

the test and the subject says "old"—in short, the times when hits occur. The size of the area indicates the proportion of hits—the hit rate. Similarly, the area under the old-item distribution and to the left of β indicates the miss rate. Taken together, these two areas comprise the total area under the old-item distribution, just as they add to 100% in our previous four-celled table (Figure 11.3). Under the new-item distribution, we can find the false-alarm and correct-rejection areas. The false alarms are to the right of β (where the subject says "old" to a new item by mistake) and the correct rejections are to the left of β. The total area under the two distributions contains four regions, and these regions correspond to the four possible outcomes of the yes/no test.

So far, our partly complete model of the recognition process includes the ideas of memory strength, distributions, and decision rules. In order to understand how this enables us to measure recognition performance independently of guessing, we must next consider what happens as d' and β vary. There are various possibilities, shown in Figure 11.6. In Figure 11.6A, we see what happens to the subject's performance as d' changes. An increase in d' corresponds to an increase in the difference

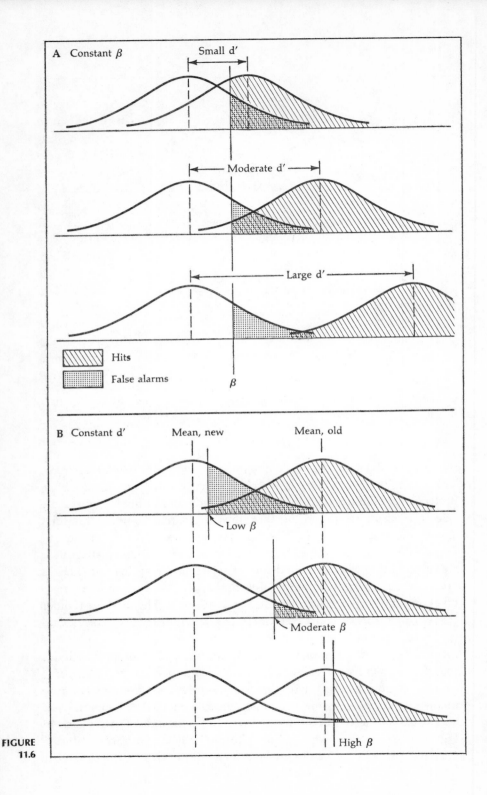

FIGURE
11.6

206

between the strengths of old and new items. For very large d', the strengths are very different, and the subject should find it very easy to tell old items from new. However, if d' is small, it should be difficult to tell the two sets of items apart. Thus, we see that d' is essentially a measure of how sensitive we are to the difference between old and new items—in fact, d' is often referred to as "true" sensitivity. It represents the information that is in memory; it tells us the difference in LTM strength between presented items and distractors. It is d' that we want to get a pure estimate of by ruling out guessing. Note in Figure 11.6A that if β remains constant and d' increases (which corresponds to a true increase in what is available in memory, that is, a true increase in sensitivity), then the hit rate will increase but the false-alarm rate will not. That is because as the subject becomes more sensitive, he is better able to tell an old item when it occurs, relative to the new items.

Now consider Figure 11.6B. It shows what happens if β changes while d' remains the same. This means that the subject is changing his decision criterion, although there is no change in the amount of information in memory—no change in his true sensitivity to old items. In effect, what is changing is the subject's guessing strategy. When β is very low, an item needs little strength for him to say "old." Consequently he will say "old" very often, being correct on most of the items that are actually old but committing many errors on new items. He will, in short, have a high hit rate, but also a high false-alarm rate. If β is high, the situation is reversed. The subject is very cautious, and seldom says "old" unless he is quite sure—which he will be only for items with high familiarity. He will have a relatively low hit rate, for he will often say "new" to old items, simply because he is cautious. On the other hand, he will also have a low false-alarm rate, because he will not often say "old" to new items. Thus, we see that if d' remains constant, shifts in β will cause both the hit and false alarm rates to change, and in the same direction. As β goes up, both hit rate and false-alarm rate go down.

The pattern of changes in hits and false alarms with changes in d' and β enables us to use the signal-detection model to correct for guess-

---

Effects of variations in β and d' on recognition: **(A)** Effects of changes in d' when β remains constant. As d' increases, the hit rate increases without a corresponding change in false alarms. Estimates of d' will therefore increase. **(B)** Effects of variations in β when d' remains constant. As β increases, both the hit and false alarm rates will decrease, and estimates of d' will remain constant.

ing. For each pair of values of hit and false-alarm rates, there is a corresponding value of d'. It is that fact that allows the model to be used to eliminate guessing effects. For given a change in β, the hit and false-alarm rates will both change—but their new values will be associated with exactly the same d' as before. That is, the subject may change his guessing strategy (as he might if we begin to penalize him for false alarms), and that may result in a new hit rate and a new false-alarm rate—but that new pair of values will correspond to the same d'. In contrast, if there is a change in the subject's true sensitivity to old items (as there might be, for example, if the list were presented a second time, causing the strengths of old items to be incremented), then there will be a change in hit rate without a concomitant change in false alarms. The resulting changed hit and false-alarm rates will correspond to a new value of d'. In short, it is the *pair* of values, hit rate and false-alarm rate, which determines the estimate of memory strength, not just the hit rate or false-alarm rate alone. And the manner in which those paired values change determines whether a change in true sensitivity (d') or response criterion (β) can be inferred.

Experimenters who use the signal-detection analysis have available special tables that list values of d' for each pair of values for the hit rate and false-alarm rate. From the table, the experimenter can tell if an experimental manipulation that might have changed both the hit and false-alarm rates has actually changed d'. If what has changed is merely the subject's guessing strategy, then the hits and false alarms will have changed together, and d' will be the same for the new values as for the old. In this way, the use of d' rather than a simple percentage of correct responses enables the experimenter to correct for guessing in a theoretically meaningful way.

Moreover, the representation of the recognition task that this theory provides can actually be considered a theory of memory. Essentially, it says that presenting an item has the effect of increasing its strength, or exciting its location, or boosting the familiarity value for that item. (Which of these terms you use is not too important—all have been used at one time or another.) It also says that the subject is able to assess the familiarity of any item he is given, and then use his assessment to decide if the item was on the list. If it is familiar enough to have been there, he will identify it as a list item. Various circumstances may alter his criterion for "familiar enough."

Let us use this theory to account for some of the data from recognition experiments. Consider, for example, what happens if we use as distractors words that are similar to the list words. That is, we might present DOG as a distractor when CAT was on the list. We know this tends to reduce recognition scores. An explanation in terms of our model is not hard to come by—we simply assume that when the list words are presented, similar and associated items also receive a boost in strength, somewhat indirectly. At the time of the test, their strength will therefore be higher than most other items that could be used as "new" items on the test, and the overlap of the distributions will be that much greater. Higher overlap means lower d'; thus, using similar or associated distractors will yield poorer recognition performance.

Consider another finding; namely, that recognition is usually better for infrequent words than frequent words (Shepard, 1967; Underwood and Freund, 1970). Here, the frequency of a word refers to how often it is used in natural language, for example, in literature. Tables of word frequency are readily available (e.g., Thorndike and Lorge, 1944), and frequency is often deliberately varied in experiments using words. The word-frequency effect on recognition performance can be explained in terms of signal-detection theory much as the effect of associated distractors was explained (Underwood and Freund, 1970). We assume that when a word is presented, its high associates are somewhat increased in strength by virtue of their association with the presented word. For high-frequency list words, there will be quite a few associated words receiving the strength increase, and most of the associated words will also be of high frequency. Some of the words that receive the indirect increase in strength will be list words themselves, whereas others will be among those presented as distractors. If we assume that the indirect strength increase has a greater effect on the relatively low-strength distractor items than it has on the already high-strength list items, then it follows that the magnitude of the increase of the distractors' strengths (which shifts the distribution of new items up on the strength continuum) will outweigh any effects on other list items. The net result will be considerable overlap between the old and new distributions when high-frequency words are presented, owing to the indirect increases in strength of those list words' associates.

Now consider a list of low-frequency words. These words will elicit relatively few associates, and thus induce increases in strength of relatively few words. There will be very little shift in the strength of the distractor items, in general, and thus no great overlap in the distributions of old and new items. As a result, the d' measured will be greater for low-frequency words than for high-frequency words, and this accounts for frequency effects on recognition.

The signal-detection model can also be applied to forgetting, if we assume that the strength increment due to presentation declines in the course of time, and the distribution of old items slowly sinks back down the continuum into the distribution of new items. Thus d' decreases, and if we wait long enough, may eventually reach zero.

We see that this theory accounts for certain recognition phenomena, and at the same time provides a means of separating the subject's memory (d') from his decision process (β). Admittedly, some of the explanations seem a bit after-the-fact, but they do fit with the theory. On the whole, then, let us be satisfied—at least temporarily—with the signal detection model as a retrieval theory. It describes how information is reported from memory; the decision process is assumed to include a strength analysis of a presented item and internal comparison to a standard. Thus, it is a model of retrieval to the extent that it describes the processes that occur when information is obtained from memory.

It may seem at this point that a detailed theory of retrieval is not really required for a model of recognition. That is, it may seem that there is little to retrieve when the thing to be retrieved is given to the subject at the time of the remembering. We shall see that information *is* retrieved when an item is recognized. However, it is in recall that retrieval, in the sense of looking for something in memory, is most clearly important. For that reason, it is time to examine recall a bit more and to try to construct a retrieval theory that includes recall.

RETRIEVAL AND RECALL

We already know quite a bit about recall. We know, for example, about interpretations of the serial-position curve, about modality differences, about the effects of categorized lists, and about subjective organization. Before we proceed further with the discussion of free-recall phenomena, let us first try to characterize the basic nature of the task. It seems, intuitively, that recall is the experimental procedure that comes closest to tapping what we think of as "remembering," in the term's commonly used sense.

Bower (1972a) has noted the similarity between free recall of a list of words and recall in situations outside of the laboratory. He points out that most generally, free recall corresponds to reproducing all the items that are members of a designated set. For example, you may be asked to recall all the words on a list you just saw, you may be asked to name the Presidents of the United States, or the people you met at a party, or you may be asked to recall the retention intervals in the experiment of Peterson and Peterson (See Chapter 6). In the laboratory, of course, free recall is usually like the first example—remembering all the items in some previously presented list.

In general, we could describe recall as a procedure in which a subject is first given a set of to-be-remembered (TBR) information and then given some cue to retrieve and report that information. In a recall experiment, the experimenter may use a temporal cue—such as "Recall the list you learned last Monday"—or an ordinal cue—such as "Recall the list you learned before this one." In everyday remembering as well, a cue usually directs recall. It might be a direct request, as when you are asked a question on a test. Or it might be a smell that triggers a memory. Retrieval cues can also be internal, as when you begin to feel hungry and remember that you forgot to eat breakfast. In these cases, the cues are analogous to that given by an experimenter when he says, "Recall the previous list."

The fact that recall generally occurs in the presence of a retrieval cue also points to a similarity between the free-recall and paired-associate procedures. In a sense, free recall is like remembering a paired associate: the stimulus term is the retrieval cue and the response is actually a set of responses—all the items in the TBR set. For example, if there are two recall lists to be learned, each consisting of several items, then what is learned may be something like a pairing of the stimulus "first list" with one set of items and "second list" with the other set.

A Model of Recall

How might the recall process work? One fairly detailed theory of recall has been presented by Anderson and Bower (1972; 1973) in the context of their associative-network view of memory (as presented in the discussion of their HAM model in Chapter 8). In their model, when a subject studies the words in a list for subsequent recall, several events occur. (See Figure 11.7.) First of all, given a list word (such as CAT), the subject marks its location in LTM by associating it with a "list marker." (For example, he may associate with that location a proposition indicating "on the list I studied 'cat'.") He also follows associative pathways from that word, searching for other words that are marked to indicate they were on the list. For example, following a pathway in LTM connecting "cat" to "dog" (such as the proposition "Cats chase dogs"), he might find that "dog" is also associated with the list marker. If a pathway is found that connects the current list word (CAT) to another (DOG) also on the list, the pathway itself is marked by an association with the list marker. (For example, the proposition connecting the two words "cat" and "dog" can be embedded in a proposition indicating its connection with the list.) In summary: when a given word is studied, it is marked as belonging on the list, and any pathways that are followed in a brief

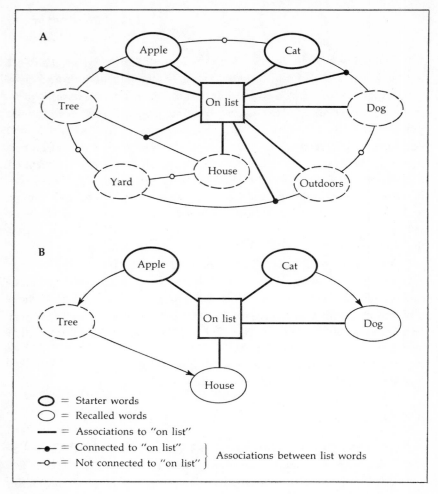

FIGURE
11.7

The recall model of Anderson and Bower. **(A)** When the list is studied, locations of list words in memory are connected to a list marker ("On list"). Pathways connecting list words are also marked, and a small set of starter words is formed. **(B)** When the list is recalled, a search process follows associative pathways from each starter word, and marked words that are found in that search are reported. Note that a word can be marked but not recalled, because it is not found in the search (an example is "Outdoors"); also, a word can be found in the search and not recalled, because it is not appropriately marked (an example is "Tree"). [After Bower, 1972a.]

search from the word are similarly marked if they lead to other list words. Essentially, this means that the subject *organizes* the list as he studies it. He is also assumed to select some small set of words that are particularly rich in connections with other list words. This "starter set" is given a special status in associating it with the list, for words in the set will be used as starting points in the retrieval process.

Retrieval in the Anderson-Bower model commences (after an initial recall of any words that may be in STM) with the words in the starter set. Picking one word from the set, the associative pathways from that word's location in LTM are followed in a search for other words connected to the list marker. Only those pathways that were previously marked as leading to list words will be followed, for it would not be possible to follow every single path from a given word. When words are found to be marked to indicate they were on the list, they are reported. If the process ends at a word that has no marked pathways leading from it, then the process returns to the starter set, again picks up a word there, and begins following pathways. The recall process ends when there are no more words in the starter set—all have been used.

Errors occur in the recall process, according to this model, because the process of marking word locations and associative pathways is probabilistic. That is, it is not certain that a word that is studied will be marked as belonging to the list, and it is not certain that a pathway connecting two list words will be marked. Nor is it certain that the starter set will contain connections rich enough so that every word in the list can be reached from one starter word or another. All these factors lead to errors in recall.

In general, the Anderson-Bower model of recall might be described as follows. First, study of the TBR items serves to organize them; to associate them with some common label and with one another. Then, recall is initiated by a retrieval cue (such as an instruction to recall the list). This cue signals the LTM location from which recall is to begin. The recall process then consists of following associative pathways from various words connected with the cue. This might be called the search process, for it is a search for marked items from the TBR set. When such items are found, they are reported. We might note that finding and reporting requires another step. As the search proceeds along pathways in LTM, sooner or later it is bound to run into items that are not in the TBR set. For example, if asked to recall the Presidents, you might retrieve Eisenhower, and then Stevenson. But just because Stevenson is associated with Eisenhower, he is not necessarily one of the Presidents. Thus there must be some decisions about the items found during the course of the search. Are they in the TBR set or are they not? (In the Anderson-Bower model, the question is phrased, "Are they appropriately marked or are they not?") Thus, we can think of recall as comprising a search for items and decisions about those which are found.

This characterization of recall will lead us to some problems; our description of the process is not as comprehensive as it might seem. However, we can learn a great deal about recall from Anderson and

Bower's associative-network model: it helps, for example, to explain the effects of organization discussed in the previous chapter. It seems that a good general rule about recall is: anything that facilitates associations among the items in the TBR set will facilitate later recall. That is because it will make the study and search processes—the marking of items and following of pathways—a bit easier. There should be more and better pathways connecting items on a list when the list has an associative structure than when it does not.

COMPARING RECOGNITION AND RECALL

At this point, we have two hypotheses or theories of "remembering." We can think of them as retrieval theories, for they address the question of how information that is in memory is regained. However, the two theories are quite different. Our theory of recognition is based on the notion of strength and a rather complex decision process. Our theory of recall relies on such concepts as associative pathways and searches. Retrieval seems to employ different processes, depending on whether we study recognition or recall. But do the retrieval processes of recognition and recall differ? If so, how do they differ?

The Threshold Hypothesis

The question of how recognition differs from recall is not a new one. The problem has interested psychologists ever since recognition and recall were first defined, and the superiority of performance with recognition testing was noted (McDougall, 1904). One of the first attempts to account for the difference was the "threshold" hypothesis. It states, quite simply, that both recognition and recall performance depend on the strength of items in memory. It suggests that an item must have a certain amount of strength before it will be recognized; this criterion value is called the *recognition threshold*. There is also a certain amount of strength necessary in order for an item to be recalled; this amount is the *recall threshold*. The threshold for recall is assumed to be higher than the threshold for recognition. That, essentially, is the threshold hypothesis.

Consider what this means. It means that some items, with very high strength, will be both recalled and recognized. Others, with very low strength, will not be remembered in either fashion. A third set of items, with intermediate strength (above the recognition threshold but below the threshold for recall) will be recognized but not recalled. This accounts for the fact that recognition testing produces results superior to recall testing.

Kintsch (1970) has reviewed the evidence for and against the threshold hypothesis in a detailed comparison of recognition and recall. He points out that it is evidence for the hypothesis when a variable is found to affect both recognition and recall in the same way. But if even a single variable were found that affected recognition and recall differently the validity of the hypothesis would be in doubt. An example of evidence supporting the hypothesis is the finding, noted in this chapter, that although the time-course of forgetting differs, forgetting is a function of the number of items that intervene between presentation and test, for recognition as for recall, and the form of the forgetting function is similar in the two situations. Variables such as the presentation rate of the list and the number of presentations also have similar effects in both tasks, and both recognition and recall give rise to a serial-position function having primacy and recency effects (Schiffrin, 1970; and see Chapter 2). All these results can easily be explained by a threshold hypothesis (and thus support it), if one assumes that such manipulations push the strengths of items up or down the strength continuum, and that recognition and recall go up or down together.

On the other hand, suppose we found a manipulation that improves recognition performance and impairs recall. The better recognition performance implies that the manipulation has improved the strength of items in memory, but the impaired recall implies just the reverse. Thus, because the threshold hypothesis attempts to explain both measures by the same idea, it may be possible to show that it is wrong. For if there is only one mechanism underlying both recognition and recall, then a given manipulation can only produce changes in performance in one direction: performance for both recognition and recall can go up, or down, but the directions of change cannot differ.

Are there such variables that affect recognition and recall differently? In fact, there are several (Kintsch, 1970). The most important is word frequency. You may recall that the frequency rating of a word is determined by how often it appears in English text. It is a very common finding that frequent words are recalled better than infrequent words. Other things being equal, if we give subjects a list of words and ask them to recall the words, they will do much better if those words are frequent words than if they are not. But in recognition, the outcome is just the reverse. Frequent words, when used in a list and tested with recognition tests, lead to worse performance than do infrequent words.

It is easier to recognize infrequent words. With this variable (and others that affect recognition and recall differently), the threshold hypothesis is shown to be inadequate as an explanation of the difference between recognition and recall.

The Dual-Trace Hypothesis

Another hypothesis (Adams, 1967) is one we might call the dual-trace hypothesis. Unlike the threshold hypothesis, it claims that recognition and recall performances depend on different mechanisms; in fact, that they depend on different sets of information in memory. The theory says that when an item is presented, two sets of information are placed in memory. (A set of information is often called a *trace*; in general, the memory trace of an event is the residue that remains in memory after the event has vanished.) There is a linguistic (verbal) memory trace, and a pictorial (perceptual) memory trace. The former represents the event in verbal form; the latter represents it in a form closer to its sensory occurrence. For example, when presented visually, the word BIG might be stored as a meaningful verbal item or as a pictorial form. The hypothesis states that recognition relies on the perceptual trace, whereas recall uses only the verbal trace. We will have more to say about pictorial traces in the next chapter; however, one inadequacy of this dual-trace hypothesis is easily seen if we consider the effects of using high associates of list words as distractors on recognition tests. Here, we have a detrimental effect of semantic similarity. That is, performance suffers when the distractor items are highly associated with the list items. The dual-trace hypothesis, relying as it does on perceptual rather than linguistic events for recognition, cannot readily explain such a finding.

The Dual-Process Hypothesis

A third hypothesis about the difference between recognition and recall is the dual-process hypothesis (Anderson and Bower, 1972; Kintsch, 1970). This hypothesis has in recent years received much attention. It has the advantage of unifying theories of recognition and recall, as well as accounting for differences in the data resulting from the two procedures. That is, the dual-process hypothesis reconciles our discrepant notions of strength (as applied to recognition) and search processes (as applied to recall). It does so by assuming that recall includes recognition as a subprocess. You should remember that our previously described theory of recall includes the processes of search (following pathways in

216

LTM and finding items), and decision (deciding whether or not those items are appropriate to report). The dual-process model accepts this sequence of events as a model for recall, and further suggests that recognition corresponds to the decision process. That is, it suggests that recall includes search and recognition. The decision stage of recall is assumed to involve the same processes as are involved in recognition; the processes described by the signal-detection theory. Thus, we see that recognition is essentially recall with the search processes removed.

Obviously, the dual-process interpretation has a lot to recommend it. By assuming that both recognition and recall draw on the same kinds of memorial information, it avoids the complications of adding yet another kind of memory to our list (unlike the dual-trace hypothesis). By assuming that there are separable processes involved in recall and recognition, it allows for variables that affect the two situations differently. In addition, by retaining the concept of strength for recognition memory, it can explain all the findings that the signal-detection model explains. And it still allows for the search processes of recall, which account for the effects on recall performance of the organizational manipulations we have previously discussed. Thus, it would seem that the dual-process hypothesis, by integrating our separate theories for recognition and recall, combines the advantages of both.

What kind of evidence is there for the dual-process model, aside from the after-the-fact explanatory power it appears to have? We could claim evidence for it if we found manipulations that separately affected the search and decision components of the process. Such a finding would indicate at least that the search and decision stages could be separated, which is certainly an essential aspect of the theory. One such experiment has been conducted by Kintsch (1968). He measured memory for categorized lists using both recognition and recall tests. Two kinds of lists were used. There were high-association lists, in which each of the list words was highly associated with the name of its category, and low-association lists, which used category members only weakly associated to the category name. By manipulating category membership in this way, Kintsch was essentially manipulating the extent to which the list was structured. He found that low structure led to worse free recall than did high structure, as expected, but there was no difference in recognition performance with the same lists. This finding is consistent with the idea that list structure affects the search portion of recall and does not affect the decision phase of recall or recognition. Others too have found that manipulating the organization of a list affects recall, without affecting recognition performance (for example, Bruce and Fagan, 1970).

Although the dual-process model, as described so far, appears to account for many of the important phenomena of recall and recognition, Anderson and Bower (1972) have pointed out one modification that is needed. They suggest that the notion of "strength," as used in the signal-detection model for recognition (and therefore in the decision stage of the dual-process model for recall) is inadequate. The authors point out that a simple strength theory cannot explain what is called "list differentiation." This refers to subjects' ability to distinguish among items on the basis of which of a series of lists contained them. This ability is very good; in fact, subjects can tell whether a given item appeared in the first and fourth of a series of lists, or whether it was in the second and third (Bower and Anderson; reported in Anderson and Bower, 1972). Or, for another example, if List 1 is presented ten times and List 2 is presented once, we would predict that items in the first list should have greater strength than that of items in List 2 on a test following List 2. List 1 items should therefore be falsely recognized when used as distractors in a test of List 2. On the contrary, discrimination of List 1 items from List 2 items is even better in this case than in the usual recognition procedure (Winograd, 1968). In short, a simple strength theory cannot explain how a subject can tell an item was from some list not being tested at present, even though its strength should be as great or greater than the items from the currently tested list. Thus, list differentiation poses a problem for strength theories.

Anderson and Bower (1972) suggest that list differentiation and recognition involve essentially the same processes; that is, recognizing that an item occurred in a certain list is essentially the same as recognizing that it occurred in the only list that was presented. Since simple strength is not adequate for list differentiation, according to this reasoning, it is not adequate for models of recognition and recall. As an alternative, they propose what we might call "contextual strength." To see what this is, first consider the fact that when a list of words is presented, its presentation occurs in a context. The context includes such things as the temperature, the time of day, the state of the subject's stomach, the color of the experimenter's hair, and so on. All these contextual "elements"—stimuli associated with the context—add up to a totality of context. It is assumed that as the subject learns the list, these contextual cues become associated with the marker for "the list" in LTM. That in turn will become associated with the words in the list (just as in the model for free recall previously discussed).

Now, consider what happens at the time of the test, according to Anderson and Bower. The subject searches for and finds words in memory (or just goes right to them if it is a recognition test) and must decide whether each word he finds is on the list being called for. He does so by evaluating the item, not with respect to some simple strength or excitation, but instead with respect to the degree of association between that word and the context elements of the called-for list. For example, asked to recall items from List 2, the subject will retrieve some items. For each item, he checks to see whether it is sufficiently associated to the context elements of List 2. If so, he reports the item; if not, he rejects the item. It is easy to see how the ability to differentiate lists is predicted by this theory—each list will have occurred in a different context, even if the differences are slight. We could even expect subjects to be able to describe the context in which an item was presented, and they often can. And the theory can also be applied to straightforward recognition—that is, list "differentiation" with just one list.

To support their revised dual-process model, Anderson and Bower manipulated list context, and this resulted in separable effects on recognition and recall. They had subjects learn a series of lists. Each list contained sixteen words, and those words were pulled from a master list of thirty-two words. Thus, the lists overlapped considerably, since each was taken from the same thirty-two-word pool. In one of their experiments, after each list was presented, the subject first tried to recall as many of the words from the master list as he could. That is, he recalled all of the words he had previously seen, from any list. Next, the subject was instructed to indicate which of the recalled words came from the most recently presented list. Of course, for the very first list, those words were the same as the ones recalled. However, as the subject received more and more lists, the situation changed. Recall of the master list improved steadily as more lists were presented. This is not surprising, for the retrievability of the total set of words (the master list) is expected to improve as the words are studied more and more often. However, the ability of the subject to recognize which of the recalled words had been most recently presented deteriorated with the number of lists. The authors explained this by assuming that presenting more and more of the overlapping lists results in attaching the same words to more and more contexts. This makes it increasingly difficult to use contextual elements to differentiate words on the most recent list from the others, causing "recognition" of those words to decline. Moreover, their experiment dissociates this decline in recognition from the improvement in recall, supporting the dual-process model.

A brief review is in order. We now have a dual-process hypothesis for retrieval. It says that recall works as follows: Given a retrieval cue, LTM is entered at an appropriate point. From this point, a search process moves out, following previously studied pathways of associations from one item to another. Whenever an item is found, a recognition process occurs—is this item in the set to be recalled? If so, it is reported; if not, the search goes on. From this retrieval theory follows the general rule that any factor that tends to facilitate the associations between the retrieval cue and TBR items or among TBR items, such as categorical structure or mediation, will facilitate initial organization and search—and therefore recall.

Tulving and Thomson (1973) have reported results that require further modification of our retrieval model. They pointed out that the dual-process model will predict that recognition performance should never be worse than recall—because recall includes recognition, plus another process (search). Since recall depends on recognition, it can never be performed any better than recognition—it can only be the same or worse. However, Tulving and Thomson have demonstrated, rather ingeniously, that recall can be better than recognition. They had subjects learn lists of twenty-four items. Each list item was presented with a weak associate; for example, the item COLD was presented in the form "ground COLD." After the list had been presented, the subject was given a recall test in which the associates appeared as cues; thus, the subjects learned that the associates were useful when the time came to recall. However, after two such lists, Tulving and Thomson surprised the subjects. They did not offer the usual cued recall test, but instead used a variety of tests. These included giving subjects strong associates of list items and asking them to freely associate to those words.

For example, consider the subject who was given COLD on the list, with "ground" as an associate. Later, he is given the word HOT (a strong associate of COLD) and asked to freely associate to it. He has not seen HOT when given the list; it is called an extra-list cue. Under these conditions, subjects often produced list words as free associates to the extra-list cues. For example, the subject would be likely to report "cold" as an associate of HOT. After the free association task had been completed, the subjects were asked to indicate which of the associates had been on the previously presented list. In our example, if the subject gave "cold, warm, sun, and fire" to the stimulus word HOT, he should indicate that "cold" was on his list. In short, he should recognize "cold." Here is where the surprise occurs—subjects did very poorly at recognizing which of their free associates had been on the list. In one experiment in this series, subjects produced eighteen out of the twenty-four list words on the free-association task, but then recognized only about four of them as having been on the list. But in another task, they were able to recall fifteen of the words, given as a cue the weak associates that had been on the original list. Thus, their ability to recall (with the appropriate cue) exceeded their recognition performance.

Tulving and Thomson's example of recall exceeding recognition provides another illustration of encoding specificity (discussed in Chapter 10). It seems that their subjects encoded the list words in the context of the weak associates presented with them. Thus they could not take advantage of another kind of cue—a strong associate. This is contrary to what we would expect from the dual-process hypothesis, which would cause us to expect that any cue, especially a strong associate, should facilitate recall by improving the search process. It seems that the situation in which items are encoded and tested can greatly influence the relationship between recognition and recall of those items. Encoding can include very specific information about the conditions of initial storage, to the point that retrieval will be virtually impossible if the encoding context is not reproduced at the time of retrieval.

Search Processes in Recognition

In a more recent version of their dual-process model, Anderson and Bower (1974) emphasized the importance of the encoding context by describing its role in recall in terms of their HAM model (discussed in Chapter 8). The propositional structure of HAM provides a means for explicit description of what we termed "contextual cues" in discussing the previous version of the Anderson and Bower model. A contextual cue can be formulated as a proposition that describes specific conditions in which the list occurred. Anderson and Bower made an additional modification of the model in postulating that recognition, like recall, has a search component. The proposed search process of recognition involves gaining access to an appropriate location in memory, given a to-be-recognized item. This assumption is important, for it helps to account for the effects of encoding specificity. In traditional recognition experiments, when a word is tested, the retrieval operation of finding its location in memory is usually immediately successful. However, the encoding specificity results show that this operation can be made difficult, and that access to the location of the desired meaning of a word is not guaranteed when the word is tested.

There is other evidence that recognition is not purely a decision process, but involves a search component as well. This view has been espoused by Mandler and his associates (Mandler, 1972; Mandler, Pearlstone, and Koopmans, 1969). One important line of evidence for this claim is that in some experiments, the degree to which a list is organized affects recognition of list items. It is important to note that this result is in direct contrast with previously described experiments in which organization of a list was found to affect recall, but not recognition (for example, Kintsch, 1968). However, list organization can affect recognition, as has been found with some consistency, particularly for highly structured lists (Bower, Clark, Lesgold, and Winzenz, 1969; D'Agostino, 1969; Lachman and Tuttle, 1965). Since organization is usually assumed to affect search and not decision processes, this implies that recognition must include some search processes.

Mandler et al. (1969) have suggested one way in which recognition could be affected by list structure. They propose that during recognition, some items will be judged as "old" with great confidence; some will be judged as "new" with great confidence. In between these two classes are some old and some new items that cannot be judged unequivocally. These items will be subjected to a "retrieval check." That check asks whether the item could be recalled; that is, whether the item would be found by the search process if the task involved recall. If the answer is positive, then the item will be called old; if not, it will be called new. It is the retrieval check, which is subject to organizational effects in the same way as search processes in recall, that produces the effects of organization in recognition situations.

A related model has been proposed by Atkinson and Juola (1973). They propose that when a recognition test is given after presentation of a list, some of the test items can be immediately designated as either list items or distractors. However, when other items are presented, the subject must make an extensive search of LTM before he can respond. Their model suggests that the LTM search is analogous to that proposed in Sternberg's STM scanning experiments (discussed in Chapter 7).

The evidence for search processes in recognition has necessitated some fundamental changes in the dual-process hypothesis. Anderson and Bower (1974) have described the relationship between recognition and recall with what we might call a "four-process model." They distinguish among four subprocesses involved in retrieval—(a) searching associative pathways for the locations of TBR items, (b) examining contextual information to see whether a retrieved item is actually to-be-recalled, (c) generating a word after retrieving its meaning (finding its location in LTM), (d) and arriving at a meaning (location in LTM) when given a word. Whereas the first three processes are components of recall, the second and fourth appear to operate in recognition. Thus, recognition and recall have overlapping subprocesses, as proposed in the dual-process model. However, the four-process modification implies that the interrelationships between recognition and recall are more intricate than previously described.

In the last two chapters, we have come full circle. First, we concentrated on the process of encoding, and we were led to consider the complexities of retrieval. Having looked at retrieval, we were led back to the importance of encoding. And, on the whole, this discussion of remembering has reinforced our impression that the human information-processing system is a remarkable and versatile entity.

12

VISUAL REPRESENTATIONS IN LTM

The role of visual information in LTM, which is the focus of the present chapter, has been discussed to a certain extent in previous chapters. When we discussed pattern recognition, we found that in order to understand how humans recognize incoming visual stimuli as members of meaningful categories, we had to assume that LTM contains information about the visual characteristics of stimuli. We considered various ways in which this visual information might be represented—such as feature lists, prototypes, or rules for constructing patterns. When we discussed visual representations in STM, we postulated that there could exist in STM visual images of well-known patterns, such as letters of the alphabet, generated from information in LTM. We found that such visual representations could be rotated and used for comparisons with other stimuli. When we discussed mediation, we discovered that subjects who were instructed to use "mental pictures" in learning pairs of words did better than other subjects who received neutral instructions. And when we discussed Shepard's (1967) study of recognition, we saw that subjects could recognize a large number of pictures they had seen just once.

Visual memory is the central concern of the present chapter. In particular, we will find it necessary to clarify our concept of the visual image. What is an image? What is it good for? Are there really pictures stored in LTM? If so, what are they like? All these questions will come up here, and in the space we have, we will barely do justice to the complexity of imagery as a psychological topic.

Are there images in memory? If you use your subjective judgment, you are quite likely to say, "yes." Consider, for example, your answer to the following question. In the house you live in (or some house you know well), how many windows are in the kitchen? Shepard (1966) points out that in answering such a question, it seems that we construct a mental picture or image of the kitchen. Then, we go around the room looking at the windows and counting them. For another example (discussed in Chapter 7), consider what happens when you compare this ⅄ to the letter R. Ask yourself: are they the same, except for a rotation, or are they mirror images of one another? In answering, you may feel that you mentally rotate the tilted figure into upright position. Since the figure itself does not move, what moves must be a mental image. However, such demonstrations of the compelling *subjective impression* of image formation do not necessarily mean that there are pictures in your brain—or do they?

MEMORY FOR PICTORIAL INFORMATION

Do we have visual images in memory? Although this question is debatable, there is no doubt that memory contains information about visual events. Just consider our ability to recognize faces in a variety of orientations and conditions—even in caricatures. And consider our ability to remember scenes. These capacities have been investigated experimentally, for example, in Shepard's (1967) demonstration of our ability to remember pictures of common objects. Standing, Conezio, and Haber (1970) carried this sort of demonstration even further. They showed subjects 2,560 slides for 10 seconds each. Later, on a recognition test of a subset of those slides, subjects scored 90%. With such high recognition levels, it seems that the subjects must have had something other than verbal descriptions of the slides in memory; instead, there must have been some kind of picture-like information available. After all, think of all the words they would need to describe 2,560 pictures. (If a picture is really worth a thousand words, that would mean 2,560,000 words would be needed!)

Other evidence for pictorial memory has been provided by Shepard and Chipman (1970). They asked subjects to go through a deck of 105 cards. On each card were the names of two states of the United States, selected from a group of fifteen states. (The 105 cards exhausted all paired combinations of the fifteen states.) The subjects were asked to rank order the 105 cards according to the similarity of the shape of the two states represented on them. Thus, the two states most similar in shape would be ranked first; the two next-most similar ranked second, and so on. The rank ordering is essentially an estimate of the similarity of shape, with lower ranks corresponding to higher similarity. The rank ordering can also be thought of as a distance measure, with low rank order (and therefore high similarity) corresponding to minimal distance between the two states with respect to shape.

Given such similarity measures for the 105 pairs of states, Shepard and Chipman fed that data into a multidimensional scaling program. You may recall from Chapter 8 that multidimensional scaling takes similarity measures among pairs of items and describes an arrangement of the items in a multidimensional space, with distance in the space inversely related to item similarity. Moreover, the dimensions of the resulting space can be used to make inferences about the basis of subjects' similarity ratings. For the fifteen states of the Shepard and Chipman experiment, the two-dimensional solution to the scaling routine based on estimates of shape similarity is shown in Figure 12.1. There seem to be four groupings of states: small, irregular, and wiggly-bordered (*spread across the bottom*); rectangular and straight-bordered (*grouped at the top*); vertically elongated states with irregular shapes (*far left*); and states with a handle, or elbow (*on the right*). Thus, the multidimensional solution reflects the visual properties of the states, even though the subjects were given only their names when they made the ratings of similarity. In fact, as the figure shows, essentially the same solution was obtained when the subjects were shown outlines of the states rather than state names. This finding suggests that subjects had information about the shapes of the states in LTM, and that given the names, they could use that information in judging shape similarity.

Shepard (1968; Shepard and Chipman, 1970) has suggested that visual information in memory may bear a relationship of "second-order isomorphism" to the corresponding information in the real world. Isomorphism is a mathematical term for the relationship of two entities that are essentially identical. Second-order isomorphism, as used by Shepard, implies something more like similarity. He proposed that two sets of items will be second-order isomorphic if the relationships between items in one set correspond to their relationships in the other. Thus, some items in the real world would be second-order isomorphic to the corresponding items in memory if the relationships among the real-world items were also relationships among the items as represented in memory. It seems to be so for the shapes of states. The real-world relationship between Oklahoma and Idaho (both have "handles") was represented

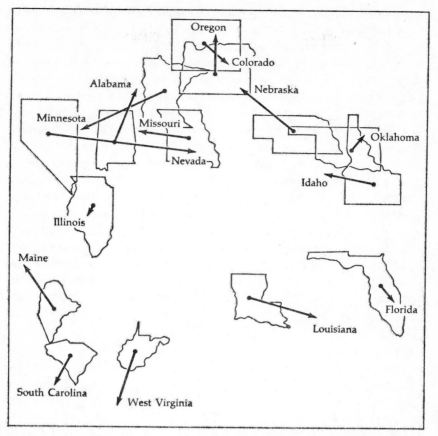

FIGURE
12.1

Two-dimensional spaces derived from subjects ratings of states on the basis of similarity of shapes. Two conditions are represented: in one, the subjects were presented with state names (*heads of arrows*); in the other, subjects were presented with state outlines (*tails of arrows*). The outline drawing of each state has been centered on the tail of the corresponding arrow. [After Shepard and Chipman, 1970.]

in their relationship in the memories of Shepard and Chipman's subjects (at least, as inferred from the scaling solution). Shepard suggests that visual information in memory is generally second-order isomorphic to the corresponding real-world data—that "mental images" resemble real images in the sense that the relations among mental images are the same as the corresponding relations among the visual images.

The idea of picture-like codes in LTM receives more support from the work of Frost (1972). She first selected a set of sixteen drawings of common objects; some are shown in Figure 12.2. The drawings could be categorized on a semantic basis, for there were four categories represented by them—animals, articles of clothing, vehicles, and furniture. However, the drawings could also be categorized on a visual basis, for they were in one of four orientations—the long axis could be vertical, horizontal, tilted right, or tilted left. The sixteen drawings were shown to groups of subjects. One group was led to expect a recognition test, and another to expect a free-recall test on the object names. Then, both types of subjects were given a free-recall task. Frost found that the free recall of the group of subjects who expected to recall showed clustering on the basis of semantic category. That is, the objects from a common semantic category tended to be recalled together. In contrast, the group expecting a recognition test recalled in clusters based on both semantic and visual characteristics. Frost's results suggest that subjects who expected the recognition task stored a visual representation of the objects in LTM. They used this representation as well as a semantic representation when the time came to recall. Just as in recall of categorized lists, the subjects' output reflected the organization of the list. For those subjects who expected the recognition test and encoded on the basis of visual

FIGURE 12.2

Stimuli that can be categorized by semantic category (*columns*) or orientation (*rows*), as used by Frost (1972). [After Hunt and Love, 1972.]

characteristics, the organization included visually based categories. In contrast, subjects expecting free recall only organized on the basis of semantic categories and therefore did not produce visually determined clusters. This hypothesis also receives support from Frost's other results. For one thing, she found that subjects who expected recognition were efficient on a visual-recognition task, whereas those who expected recall were more efficient in name recognition.

The import of the foregoing discussion seems to be that we can store information in LTM about the visual characteristics of experiences we have had. These experiences include faces we have seen, maps we have studied, scenes we have witnessed, and so on. Moreover, there is evidence that this visual information in LTM to some extent resembles a picture. Such picture-like codes are to be contrasted with verbal descriptions of the corresponding experience. In short, one sense in which the term "visual imagery" can be used is as a label for memorial representations of specific visual experiences.

MENTAL IMAGES AND MEMORY

The history of the concept of visual imagery is related to another problem, however. The idea is that images may serve as an alternative to verbal codes as a means of representing information. For example, you may form an image of a dog riding a bicycle in order to remember the paired associate DOG–BICYCLE. In this way, imagery may serve much the same function as the label "dog riding a bicycle." Thus, imagery may be a medium for representing information that could readily be described by words. And, imaginal representations may be as useful or even more useful than verbal representations in LTM when they are used in tasks involving learning and memory.

One of the foremost proponents of the view just described is Paivio. The theory that he advocates is called dual-system, or dual-coding, theory (Paivio, 1969; 1971); it represents what may seem to be a significant departure from the theory of memory we have been advocating so far in this book. Essentially, dual-system theory assumes that there are really two basic ways of representing information in memory—two coding systems, we might call them. One is the word, or verbal, or linguistic representation we have for the most part been discussing, especially in the last two chapters. The other is nonverbal; it may be called imaginal, and it includes (although it is not restricted to) the visual images we have just been discussing. The two systems are strongly connected, to be sure, so that we can derive an image from a verbal label, or vice versa. However, the two systems of representation also differ in some fundamental ways.

For one thing, the imaginal system can deal better with picturable, *concrete* entities, like "dog" or "bicycle." How could we picture something abstract like "truth"? What this means is that we can think of certain psychological entities as best represented by words, whereas others can be represented either verbally or nonverbally. In the latter category would be such things as concrete nouns, like "house" or "basket," but not abstract nouns, like "justice" or "thought." Another way in which the two systems differ is in the way they process information. In the verbal system, it seems serial order is of primary importance. When words are perceived in speech, for example, the sounds come in a sequence, and what meaning is assigned to those sounds largely depends on their order. However, we can contrast this with the way we deal with visual inputs—it seems that visual information is handled in a "spatially parallel" manner. That is, we process all the information in an area of space at once. In viewing the letter A, for example, we can simultaneously process the whole thing, rather then viewing it as / \ —.

One of the implications of the dual-coding view of memory is that information that can be held in both the verbal and imaginal systems should be more accessible than information held in just one system. That is because we should be able to get at the information by either a verbal or nonverbal retrieval process. In a sense, there is twice as much information about a twice-coded item than about an item that exists in only one form. Thus, it should be easier to remember concrete words than abstract words. Concrete words can be represented either imaginally or verbally; abstract words can be represented only verbally. And we will find, in fact, that this prediction is supported.

The amount of psychological data that can be interpreted in terms of the dual-system theory is considerable. We will restrict ourselves in this discussion to the high points—general findings that are fairly representative of the kinds of evidence that work for the theory. This evidence includes the effects on verbal-learning tasks of a measure of noun imaginability (I); the effects of stimulus type—word or picture—in various experimental procedures; and the effects of using imagery in mediation (something we have already referred to in Chapter 10).

As we have just indicated, one of the ways in which the dual-coding hypothesis has been useful is in dealing with the effects on various learning situations of "noun imaginability." We have already mentioned one measure that can be associated with a noun—the measure of meaningfulness (m, as defined by Noble, 1961). The m-value of a word is directly based on the number of associations given to that word in a free-association task within a fixed amount of time. Thus, the meaningfulness of the word reflects the extent to which it is interconnected with other words. Now, let us define a measure corresponding to how readily an image can be conjured up when a word is given. Subjects were asked by Paivio (1965) to indicate when they had an image for a given word; the image could be a mental picture or even a sound. The speed with which they indicated that an image had been produced was used to formulate an imagery measure, I, for the word. The higher the I value, the more readily a word could be used to produce an image. In general, we might note also that I is highly related to concreteness; that is, the more the word refers to some concrete entity, the higher its I value tends to be. This is certainly not surprising, since we might expect words like DOG that refer to concrete objects to produce images of those objects, whereas words like THOUGHT have no readily available referent (thing referred to by the word), and therefore no readily available image.

The imagery value for nouns has proved to be a potent predictor of performance in a variety of tasks. In fact, the I-value of a noun has proved to have greater effects on performance in many tasks than has the m-value for the same noun. One of the situations where I correlates with performance is recognition testing. When lists of items are presented and subsequently tested with recognition tests, concrete nouns (high I) lead to better performance than do abstract nouns (low I). Moreover, pictures are recognized even better than concrete nouns, as we might expect from the high accuracy of picture recognition described previously (also reviewed in Paivio, 1971). Similar effects are found in free recall, that is, the recall of lists of abstract words is not as great as the recall of lists of concrete words. And when pictures are used with the lists (with instructions to recall labels given along with the pictures), recall is better than it is for concrete words. These effects hold over retention intervals as short as five minutes as well as for longer intervals, like a week. Similar orderings of performance for pictures, concrete words, and abstract words are found in the realm of serial learning (Herman, Broussard, and Todd, 1951; Paivio and Csapo, 1969). And it should also be noted that these effects appear to depend only on I values, and to be independent of the m values of the words used on the lists (for example, Paivio, Yuille, and Rogers, 1969).

The general conclusion to be drawn from such findings is that imaginability (the reported ease with which an image is produced) and concreteness do affect memory for verbal information. This result has been interpreted as evidence supporting the dual-coding theory by the following reasoning. We assume that words which are high in *I* value are represented in LTM in two different systems, each with its own code. There is a verbal code, and some sort of imaginal, or pictorial, code. When words that are low in *I* value are presented, however, only one code is available—the verbal code. And if pictures are presented, a very strong imaginal code is maintained in memory, as well as a verbal description or label. When the time comes to remember these items— by either recognition or recall—the performance will depend on how much information is in memory. If two codes are present, performance will be better than if there is just one. In a sense, we can think that the strength of an item is the total of its verbal and imagery strength.

The Role of Imagery in Mediation

Further support for the dual-code hypothesis comes from work on the role of imagery in mediation. The basic results on imaginal mediators are described in Bower's work, previously discussed (Bower, 1972b). He found that when subjects were given imagery instructions for learning pairs of nouns in a paired-associate task, they did extremely well. The imagery instructions told them to imagine the two nouns in each pair interacting in a mental picture. For example, the pair DOG–BICYCLE might be represented as a mental image of a dog riding a bicycle. Other subjects, given standard instructions with no mention of images, did only about 2/3 as well on the paired-associate task. Thus, it seems that images served as good mediators in the task. The idea is that at the time of recall, the subject uses the stimulus word, DOG, to retrieve the image he formed earlier; the dog on the bicycle. From it, he retrieves the image of the bicycle, and reports "bicycle."

Bower examined the role of images in paired-associate mediation in even more detail. He found, for example, that several response terms could be associated with a single stimulus term in the same way that just one could be. For example, we might ask a subject to remember the five words: DOG, HAT, BICYCLE, POLICEMAN, FENCE, given the stimulus word CIGAR. The subject might conjure up an image of a policeman smoking a cigar, stopping a bicycle-riding dog (wearing a hat, of course) by a fence. Can he retrieve the five nouns from this image, given the single noun CIGAR? He can, according to the results of the experiment. Bower found that recall did not depend on the number of items which were to be associated with a stimulus term in an image. Subjects recalled as well after associating twenty list words to a single stimulus term as when they used twenty stimulus terms, one for each word in the list. A stimulus term, in this case, is called a peg-word, because it acts as a peg on which the various responses may be hung.

Bower also found that imagery works to enhance recall only when the peg-word and response items are combined in a composite image. If we ask subjects to imagine a dog, and then separately to imagine a bicycle, in order to remember "dog–bicycle" as a pair, they will not do nearly as well as if we tell them to imagine a dog and bicycle interacting in some scene. This is not surprising, because a separate image of a bicycle is not much good when the image of a dog, all by itself, is retrieved. To get to "bicycle," given DOG, we must have some picture that can be produced from one word but includes both objects. That is, the image must serve to unite the two items so that we can retrieve one from the other.

Mediation through imagery is useful outside of the paired-associate task as well. For example, Delin (1969) used imagery instructions in a serial-learning task. He told subjects that to learn which item followed another, they should picture each consecutive pair interacting. He gave them plenty of time to do so, by presenting the words slowly (eleven seconds each). For example, in a list including the series DOG, BICYCLE, HAT, the subject might first picture a dog on the bicycle, and then (in a separate picture) a hat hanging over a bicycle's handlebar, and so on. This instruction facilitated serial recall—subjects given the imagery instructions did better than those who had standard, nonimaginal, instructions.

Imagery and Natural Language

Another way in which the imagery idea has been useful is in the study of memory for natural language. We have seen previously (in Chapter 9) that the forgetting of natural-language material often takes the form of the forgetting of specific wording but not of meaning. In a study by Sachs (1967), for example, subjects did not notice whether a sentence had been changed from active to passive as much as they noticed a change in the meaning, such as from a positive sentence to its negative. Begg and Paivio (1969) carried this experiment even further. They used both abstract and concrete sentences in the Sachs situation. An example of a concrete sentence, one that involves concrete nouns, is "The loving mother served an excellent family." An abstract sentence is "The absolute faith aroused an enduring interest." Sentences like these were presented in a short text, and then a recognition test was given. Each distractor item on the test resembled one of the original sentences, but was changed either in wording alone or in meaning. For example, a wording-only change in the concrete sentence above might result in "The loving mother served an excellent household," and a semantic change might be "The loving family served an excellent mother."

The results of the Begg and Paivio (1969) experiment are shown below in Figure 12.3. We see that the Sachs results hold for the concrete material, but not for the abstract. The subjects recognized changes in meaning better than wording alone if the sentence was concrete, but wording changes were recognized better than semantic changes when the sentence was abstract. In order to understand why this might be so, let us turn to Paivio for an interpretation in terms of imagery. He theorizes that in a concrete sentence, the meaning is stored more by images than words. Thus, changes in wording that do not change meaning will be consistent with the image and will not be noticed. On the other hand, an image is not an effective way to store the meaning of an abstract sentence. For abstract material, meaning must be stored by words. For this reason, changes in wording *are* noticed.

From this last experiment and its interpretation, it seems that imagery is being advocated as a theory of linguistic comprehension. A proponent of this view is Paivio (1971), who suggests that imagery plays a vital

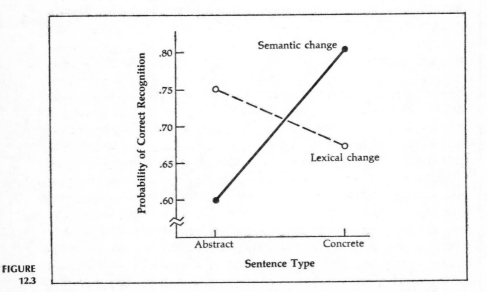

FIGURE
12.3

Probability of correct recognition of semantic versus lexical (wording only) changes, for abstract and concrete sentences [After Begg and Paivio, 1969.]

role in understanding and remembering information conveyed by language. That is, he suggests that we understand linguistic inputs by the images they convey, particularly when their messages are concrete. Of course, there are alternative theories of language comprehension and meaning—so many that to discuss them would be beyond the scope of this book. However, we should point out here that the theories of semantic memory discussed in Chapter 8 are concerned with the knowledge that is conveyed through language; thus, they provide descriptions of language comprehension that do not depend on the concept of imagery.

It might seem, at this point, that we have overwhelming evidence in favor of the existence of picture-like representations in LTM. This is therefore a good time to look at the other side of the coin—to examine opposing ideas. In fact, the image/no-image controversy is an old one in psychology (see Paivio, 1971, for a review). It has recently gained renewed interest because of new, more detailed theories that relate imagery to contemporary cognitive psychology.

REBUTTAL OF THE IMAGERY HYPOTHESIS

Common sense might make us question a theory that says there are pictures stored in LTM, especially if we claim those pictures look just like the world outside. Pylyshyn (1973) has pointed out many of the important problems with such a concept. First of all, we might ask what these mental images look like. If they do look just like the information we perceive, it would seem that there must be a great many such pictures. Since we can perceive an essentially unlimited number of different visual scenes, it would require an unlimited amount of space in LTM to store detailed copies of all those scenes. Another point to consider is how we would use those stored scenes. They would somehow have to be retrieved, which would require reperceiving and analyzing them to "see" what was there. But if the stored pictures have to be reperceived before they are used, they might as well be stored as already-perceived entities rather than as perfect copies of visual events. Still another problem is how we would get access to a picture from a word—there is any number of images that can correspond to a single word—how do we know which one to retrieve? Pylyshyn argues with points like these that the images, or whatever we may call them, must exist in memory as analyzed entities rather than as raw sensory material. As such, they cannot look just like the world outside the sensory register, but more like a description of what has been perceived. This does not mean people do not have the subjective impression of forming picture-like images; it just means that their impressions are misleading.

Anderson and Bower (1973) argue in favor of Pylyshyn's point of view. They feel that the representations we might think of as images do not differ from those we might think of as "purely verbal." In their HAM model, all knowledge in LTM can be represented by propositions; abstract structures composed of related concepts. The propositional framework can account for the representation of both verbal and imaginal (as we have been calling them) codes. The substance of propositions (the nodes and associations) is sufficiently abstract so that it transcends such labels as "verbal" or "imaginal." Propositional configurations can describe knowledge about both words and pictures.

In addition to the logical arguments against the existence of pictures in memory, there is experimental evidence favoring a unitary theory of imagery and verbal processes (that is, that both processes are essentially the same, rather than distinctly different forms of representing information). Although Bower's original work on paired-associate learning and imagery was more consistent with the dual-coding theory, his later experiments led him to favor the unitary view.

In one experiment (Bower and Winzenz, 1970), it was found that instructing subjects to use sentences as paired-associate mediators worked about as well as instructing them to use images. Sentence mediation instructions tell the subject to construct sentences relating the paired items—for example, given the pair DOG–BICYCLE, to construct a sentence like "The dog is riding a bicycle." What is more surprising than the finding that sentences and images work about equally well is the finding that when subjects are sometimes instructed to use one and sometimes the other, they cannot remember very well which they used (Bower, Munoz, and Arnold, 1972). It seems that if imagery instructions led to the formation of pictures, and sentence instructions led to the formation of sentences, then subjects would be able to tell which they had used to mediate the associated words. But they cannot differentiate very well at all. This suggests the "images" are not any different from what is formed with sentence mediation. Bower suggests that with both image- and sentence-mediation instructions, the subject is induced to seek out and encode meaningful relationships between the word pairs. According to Bower, it is the formation of semantic relationships that facilitates paired-associate memory rather than some mental picture; that is why the two types of mediation work equally well.

Wiseman and Neisser (1971) offered other experimental evidence for the unitary view of imagery and verbal coding. They showed subjects a series of "Mooney pictures," which are formed when the contours are deleted from scenes. The pictures are difficult to interpret, but it is sometimes possible to figure out what the scene is despite the distortion. Viewing the pictures, the subjects tried to decipher what they represented. They then were given a recognition test on the pictures, with other such pictures serving as distractors. Wiseman and Neisser found that recognition performance was accurate only when the subjects assigned some interpretation to a picture when it was first presented; then assigned it the same interpretation during the recognition test. Otherwise (if the picture could not be interpreted either at presentation or at test), recognition accuracy was poor. This finding suggests that recognition does not consist of comparing pictures presented on the test to pictorial traces stored in memory. What was important to these subjects was having interpreted the picture when it was tested in the same way as when it was presented. Simply seeing a picture identical to one presented before was not sufficient for accurate recognition. During the recognition test, subjects apparently did not compare the pictures with raw, uninterpreted scenes stored in LTM. Rather, they were comparing what they had previously decided was in the scenes to their current interpretation. Thus, this favors the idea that the subjects stored information about their analysis of the stimulus rather than a copy of it.

An experiment by Nelson, Metzler, and Reed (1974) also provides evidence against the idea that detailed copies of pictures are stored in LTM. They noted that such an idea has often been advanced as a possible explanation of the amazing ability of subjects to recognize previously presented pictures (as in Shepard, 1967). That is, it has been proposed that the superiority of picture memory over verbal memory is due to more detailed storage of the pictures. If pictures are stored in great detail, then recognition of any of the details should lead to recognition of the picture, which would give pictures the advantage over relatively barren words. To test this hypothesis, Nelson et al. constructed four types of stimuli for the same scenes. (See Figure 12.4.) A given scene was represented by a photograph, a one-phrase description of the photo, a detailed drawing of the photo, and a nondetailed drawing of it. Each subject viewed stimuli of one of the four types and was then given a recognition test on the stimuli. Nelson et al. found that recognition performance for any of the types of pictorial stimuli (photos, detailed drawings, or nondetailed drawings) was better than that of the verbal

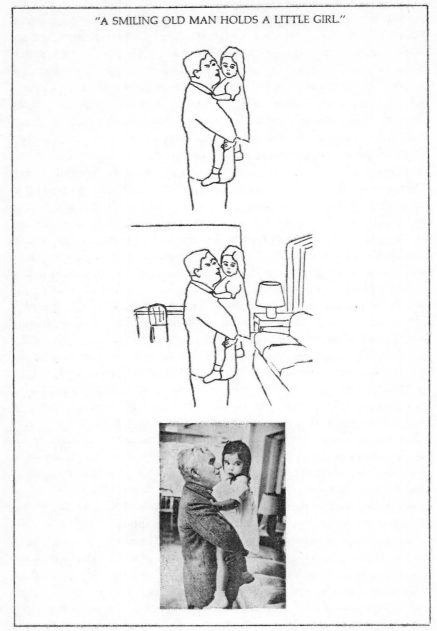

FIGURE
12.4

Example of an item that can be represented by (*from top to bottom*) a phrase, a drawing with little detail, a detailed drawing, and a photograph. [From Nelson et al. 1974. Copyright 1974 by the American Psychological Association.]

descriptions. However, the recognition scores for the various types of pictorial stimuli did not differ from each other; that is, greater detail did not facilitate recognition. This indicates that the superior memory for pictures is not due to the fact that they were stored in LTM as detailed copies. Instead, it raises the question of whether pictorial stimuli are stored in LTM as pictures at all. The fact that recognition was as good for nondetailed as detailed pictures is consistent with the idea that subjects store their interpretations of the stimuli. In this case, those interpretations seem to be sufficiently abstract so that they can describe nondetailed and detailed pictures equally well.

The idea that imagery is the basis of language comprehension has also come up against experimental rebuttal. Specifically, the hypothesis of Begg and Paivio (1969)—that concrete sentences might be represented in memory by imagery, and abstract sentences by words—has been attacked. For one thing, the Begg and Paivio results have proven difficult to replicate (for example, Tieman, 1971), and there is a possibility that the abstract and concrete sentences used in the study may have differed in factors like comprehensibility as well as imagery (Johnson, Bransford, Nyberb, and Cleary, 1972). In another vein, Franks and Bransford (1972) cast doubt on the imagery hypothesis. They performed an experiment similar to their earlier study of linguistic abstraction, discussed in Chapter 9 (Bransford and Franks, 1971). Recall that in the earlier experiment subjects were shown groups of sentences formed by combining four simple sentences in various ways. Later, they tended to recognize test sentences on the basis of how many of the four simple ideas they combined rather than on whether or not they had actually been presented. From this, Franks and Bransford concluded that when they were given the initial group of sentences, the subjects integrated the information contained in them and stored an integrated version. Their recognition judgments were then based on that integration, so that the more simple forms a sentence contained (and therefore the more it resembled the integrated form), the more it was "recognized" as old.

In their early study, Bransford and Franks (1971) used concrete sentences. The idea of Begg and Paivio would suggest that their results should not extend to abstract sentences. That is because Begg and Paivio claim that abstract sentences are stored verbally, making changes in wording more recognizable and changes in meaning less so. This would imply that in the Franks-and-Bransford experiment, subjects should be more accurate with recognition judgments when the sentences are abstract. Contrary to the imagery thesis, however, Franks and Bransford (1972) showed that their initial results were replicated when the sentences were abstract. Moreover, this implies that concrete and abstract sentences are processed similarly in memory, for both produce the same results in the Franks-Bransford situation. On the whole, it is a negative outcome for the imagery hypothesis of sentence memory.

IMAGERY VERSUS NO IMAGERY: A POSSIBLE RESOLUTION OF THE CONFLICT

If the imagery hypothesis is inadequate, as the above logical and experimental arguments would seem to indicate, what is left? How can we explain such phenomena as the effects of imagery on memory tasks and the strong subjective impression we often have of forming images? One answer to the question of how such things as imagery instructions and *I* values work to facilitate memory has been proposed by Anderson and Bower (1973). Essentially, what they suggest is that under imagery-evoking conditions, a richer, more conceptually detailed body of information is encoded and stored in LTM. Thus, the difference between imaginal and nonimaginal storage is one of details of encoding rather than a qualitative difference, as between pictures and words. The semantically richer "imaginal" codes are more efficiently retrieved, giving rise to the imagery effects in verbal learning tasks.

For an explanation of our subjective impression of having picture-like images, we can return to the concept of the "work space" portion of STM. In Chapter 7, a case was made for the existence of visual codes in STM. These could follow the presentation of a visual stimulus, or alternatively, be generated from information in LTM. If what is stored in LTM is not a visual image but some more abstract description of a visual event, it might still be possible to construct a more picture-like code in STM. (A related argument has been advanced by Pylyshyn, 1973.) This constructed "image" could be the basis of our subjective feelings of having some sort of mental picture. However, it should be noted that since such an image is constructed from information in LTM, it can be no more detailed than that LTM information. Thus, it is at best an abstract copy of a visual event. In Shepard's terms, we might say it is second-order isomorphic to the visual event. However, Shepard's mental-rotation experiments (discussed in Chapter 7) also indicate that images can in some cases resemble their real-world counterparts very closely.

From the foregoing, it seems clear that a strong case can be made for the existence of images—and a strong case can be made for their nonexistence. That is really not surprising—as we noted, the imagery controversy is one of the oldest in psychology, and it looks as if it will continue to go on for some time. Despite the controversy, some basic points can be made about visual memory. One is that the world is not represented in LTM in full pictorial detail; that seems to be ruled out on both logical and experimental grounds. Another point is that there must be stored in LTM information about visual events, for such information is needed in order to recognize patterns and remember things previously seen. What is uncertain is just how much the visual information in LTM, or the images generated from that information, resemble mental "pictures." On that point it is certainly still possible to argue.

13

MNEMONISTS,
CHESS PLAYERS,
AND MEMORY

In the last twelve chapters, we have come a long way. Our discussion of human memory has included a variety of topics, such as the identification of input from the world, memory over short intervals, and the most complex aspects of long-term memory. In this concluding chapter, we shall consider two related topics. One is mnemonics; the other is the relation of memorial abilities to expertise. As an example of expertise, we shall consider a topic psychologists have studied in some detail: the abilities of chess players. Each of these topics is of interest in its own right; however, the purpose of discussing them here lies not so much in their intrinsic interest as in their capacity to help us integrate much of the material we have discussed. For in considering mnemonics and chess, we will find it necessary to consider the roles of perceptual, short-term, and long-term memory processes.

MNEMONICS AND MNEMONISTS

As was mentioned in Chapter 5, the term "mnemonics" refers to the use of learned devices and strategies to aid in remembering. We have touched on many mnemonic devices in previous discussions. For example, two such devices are: using a visual image or a sentence to mediate memory for paired associates; using NLMs to encode nonsense syllables. Some other mnemonic tricks are familiar to almost everyone, such as rhymes that define rules of spelling ("i before e, except after c . . .") or days in a month ("Thirty days hath September . . ."). Several devices can be used to remember lists of items. One is the method of loci, an ancient means of remembering a list by imagining each item in turn in one of a previously learned sequence of locations. Another device for remembering a list is to weave a story around the items.

Yet another way to remember a list is called the "peg-word" system. This system enables the mnemonist to remember lists of up to ten items, and it can easily be expanded to include more. First, the mnemonist must learn the following rhyme: "One is a bun; two is a shoe; three is a tree; four is a door; five is a hive; six are sticks; seven is heaven; eight is a gate; nine is a line; ten is a hen." Once you have the rhyme, the mnemonic device is much like that used in the method of loci. Suppose you are to learn the following list of items: BREAD, EGGS, MUSTARD, CHEESE, FLOUR, MILK, TOMATOES, BANANAS, BUTTER, ONIONS. To remember the list, think of each item in its sequence as interacting with the corresponding item in the peg-word sequence. Think of a bun as growing out of the side of a loaf of bread; some broken eggs in a shoe, dripping out of the sole; a Christmas tree with cans of mustard hanging on it; and so on. Later, to recall the list of items, you just recall the peg-word rhyme. "One is a bun" leads to retrievel of the bun growing out of the loaf of bread. Thus, you recall bread. "Two is a shoe" brings to mind the eggs, and so on. With the pegword mnemonic, the entire list of items can easily be remembered.

Many mnemonic devices are easy to learn. Other mnemonics are not so easy; in fact, some mnemonic devices are used only by especially skilled mnemonists—people who, for one reason or another, specialize in rote memorization. Bower (1973) has reported his experiences with a group of such mnemonic experts. He attended a convention of mnemonists, where each tried to impress his fellows with mnemonic twists and tricks. And their skills were impressive, Bower reported. One man could take four words called out by his audience and with great speed, write down the letters from one of the words upside down, those from another, backwards, those from another both upside down and backwards, and those from the fourth in normal fashion. But that's not all—while writing them down, he regularly interspersed the letters from one word with those from the others, at the same time retaining their proper sequence within each word. And if that were not enough, at the same time he recited "The Shooting of Dan McGrew!" Another mnemonist could scan through a shuffled deck of cards and then recite their order.

It is not difficult to document the skills of these amazing mnemonists. Nor is it difficult to be impressed by them. But what is difficult is to discover just how they do what they do. Bower asked the mnemonist who could scramble the words how he performed his feat. His answer was that he had practiced it so much that his hands just knew what to do while he thought about the words. It is not surprising that his answer was so lacking in insight. We might have just as much difficulty verbally describing how we play a piece on the piano, or how we arrive at the answer to "What is three times two?," or how we balance while riding a bicycle. Skills like these are not very amenable to introspective investigation.

Yet, it is possible to study mnemonists in more rigorous ways. There are two highly skilled mnemonists whose skills have been investigated in detail. One was the subject of Luria (1968); the other was studied by Hunt and Love (1972). These two men were similar in several respects, including the fact that the places where they spent their early lives were only thirty-five miles apart. On the other hand, their mnemonic skills were somewhat different—for example, Luria's mnemonist reported much greater use of imagery than did Hunt and Love's.

Let us consider Hunt and Love's mnemonist in detail, for there is a great deal of experimental data available in his case. He is referred to as VP. The life of VP would not make an exciting book. He was born in Latvia in 1935, the only child in his family. He showed early promise of intelligence, reading by the age of three-and-a-half. He also showed some early indication of his memory skills—by age five he had memorized a street map of a city of half a million, and at the age of ten he memorized 150 poems as part of a contest. He also began to play chess at eight years of age. We might think that all these things indicate a person of high intelligence, and VP's scores on recently taken intelligence tests bear this out. His high scores on the IQ tests were primarily obtained on those tests relating to memory. He scored in the ninety-fifth percentile on a test in which short-term retention plays an important part. He also scored extremely well on a test of perceptual speed, the ability to perceive details quickly. On the whole, Hunt and Love point out, his test scores indicate an intelligent person, but they certainly do not predict an exceptional memorizer.

There is no doubt, however, that VP has exceptional memory skills. Hunt and Love were able to document this in a variety of experiments, many of which should by now be familiar to the reader. (Where appropriate, the number of the chapter in which an experimental procedure has been discussed will be noted.) Let us consider first VP's performance on tasks related to STM. One of the most basic tasks is the memory-span task, usually used to assess the chunk capacity of STM (Chapter 5). We know that the span is usually in the range of five to nine items. At first, VP's span for a series of rapidly presented digits did not appear to be exceptional. However, he soon developed a way to increase his span.

When digits were presented at a rate of one each second, he reported grouping them in sets of three to five, then associating with each set some verbal code (for example, 1492 is an obviously codable group). In this fashion, he increased his span to seventeen digits with little effort. Control subjects who were told about VP's coding device were able to improve their memory spans too, but not nearly as much.

The short-term forgetting data of the Peterson-Peterson task (Chapter 6) are also of interest. In that task, the subject tries to remember three consonants while counting backward by threes. In contrast to the usual rapid decay found over an 18-second retention interval in this task, VP showed little or no forgetting over 18 seconds. This held not only for the first trial (when PI is at a minimum and maximum recall is found) but for the remaining trials as well. One possible explanation of these results was offered by VP. He said that given a set of three consonants to remember, his knowledge of several languages enabled him to associate some word with it in almost every case. Thus, he converted it to a single chunk. His lack of forgetting is in that case predictable on the basis of what is known about the effect of the number of chunks in the Peterson task—forgetting is much greater for three chunks than for one. Moreover, the use of several languages might act, in effect, to produce a release from PI (as in the work of Wickens, Chapter 7), which would tend to decrease forgetting in this task. That is because each different language would act as a new class of to-be-remembered items, and switching to a new class generally produces a release from PI.

Hunt and Love also investigated VP's memory-scanning capacity in the Sternberg procedure (Chapter 7). You should recall that in that task, the subject indicates whether or not a given test stimulus was a member of a recently presented set of items. The measured variable is RT, and it is commonly found that RT increases linearly with the number of items in the initially presented set. However, VP's data showed no such increase. He was able to process a memorized set of six items about as fast as he processed one, and his rate for one item was comparable to that of other subjects in the task. This suggests that, unlike most subjects, VP's search among items in STM was an unlimited-capacity parallel process.

The STM results suggest that VP's memory span is not markedly different from that of normal individuals. However, his STM is remarkable in other respects. He can scan information in STM in parallel; he is able to remember items in STM in circumstances in which others forget; he can chunk more efficiently than other subjects. To some extent at least, these effects appear to derive from an ability to mediate and recode incoming information with incredible speed. This enables VP to chunk rapidly, which in turn underlies his ability to increase the memory span and to withstand the effects of interference in STM. In view of the related effects of mediation and organization on long-term storage, we might expect VP's long-term retention to be as exceptional as his short-term retention. In fact, this is the case.

Hunt and Love tested VP on several LTM tasks. One was with Bartlett's story, "War of the Ghosts," which most listeners tend to distort in recall (Chapter 9). The story was read to VP; then he counted backwards by sevens from the number 253 until he reached zero. He then reconstructed designated parts of the story at intervals ranging from one minute later to six weeks later. On each occasion, his retention of the story was remarkable. He could not recall it verbatim, but he did recall it with great fidelity. And his retention was as good after six weeks as after a one-hour retention interval.

How does VP perform so well on such tests of memory? One finding is that he does not appear to use visual imagery to do so. To be sure, VP is sensitive to imagery variables, remembering high-imagery items better than low (Chapter 12). He reports occasional use of imaginal mnemonics, but he is primarily a verbal mnemonist. One indication that VP does not use imagery very often comes from his performance on Frost's visual-clustering task (Chapter 12). Both VP and control subjects first viewed Frost's picture stimuli (which can be categorized semantically or by visual orientation), and then, after a delay, they were given a surprise free-recall test. The control subjects showed strong clustering by visual orientation, but VP showed only semantic clustering. Thus, it appeared that he did not store the stimuli in visual form. In still another case, VP was asked to memorize two matrices consisting of eight rows of six numbers each. One matrix had regular rows, but in the other the rows were staggered and irregularly spaced. After studying the matrices briefly, VP could recall both perfectly. Moreover, he recalled them both at the same rate. Since the staggered matrix takes longer to read, this outcome suggests that VP was not "reading" the matrix from an image in memory. In fact, VP reported using verbal mnemonics, such as storing a row by thinking of it as a date and remembering what he had done on that day.

Thus, it seems that VP is an exceptional verbal mnemonist. He is able to quickly derive mnemonic schemes, given unrelated stimuli, and use such schemes to chunk and organize the material. This gives rise to his incredible performance in tests of short- and long-term memory. In this he is also aided by an excellent ability to perceive details rapidly—this ability helps him to find quickly a basis for using some mnemonic technique. There is also another factor that may underlie VP's ability, and that is early training. Both VP and the mnemonist studied by Luria grew up in similar school systems (even in the same geographical area), which emphasized rote learning rather than using knowledge in social interactions. In such a situation, it behooves the student to improve his rote-memorization ability. It is extremely speculative, to be sure, but it is tempting to conclude that this early training may have provided VP with the impetus to hone his mnemonic skills.

MEMORY AND CHESS

It is interesting to note about VP that he is a superior chess player. He has played in exhibitions where he simultaneously undertook seven blindfold games of chess! He also carries on large numbers of games in correspondence with others, in which he does not need to keep a written record to keep track of what is happening. Such feats are impressive exhibitions of memory, and as such they are consistent with what we know of VP as an outstanding memorizer. But it is somewhat surprising to consider that in the realm of chess, such feats are not uncommon. Most chess players at the level of master or grand master are able to reproduce almost perfectly a configuration of chess pieces after viewing it for only 5 seconds (de Groot, 1965; 1966). This holds true when the configuration is meaningful in the context of the game. However, for randomly placed pieces, the ability of masters to reproduce a chess board is no better then that of weak players. The latter result indicates that it is not some exceptional STM capacity of masters that underlies their ability to reproduce the board; instead, it must have something to do with their knowledge of the game.

The capacity of chess masters to reproduce playing configurations has been studied in a series of papers by Simon and others (Simon and Barenfeld, 1969; Chase and Simon, 1973; Simon and Gilmartin, 1973). One outcome of this research is a computer simulation of chessboard memory. This computer program is of special interest because it illustrates how the capacities and processes of perception, short-term storage, and long-term memory combine to form the basis for a memorial skill.

Simon and Barenfeld (1969) first concentrated on the perceptual aspects of chessboard reproduction. In particular, they were concerned with the ways in which chess players looked at the chessboard in the first few seconds after being presented with a novel configuration of pieces. The data on memory for such configurations indicates that good players can pick up a remarkable amount of information in just those first few seconds. Moreover, when eye movements of chess players are recorded, it is found that vision is concentrated on the pieces on the board that are strategically most important.

Simon and Barenfeld proposed a model of chessboard perception that they implemented as a computer program. Essentially, their program assumes that the chess player first fixates on an important piece on the board. When fixated on a particular piece, the player at the same time gathers information about its neighbors, through peripheral vision. In particular, he takes note of neighboring pieces bearing a meaningful relation to the piece—attacking it, defending it, attacked by it, or defended by it. Then the player shifts his vision to one of the related pieces, fixates on that, and so the process continues. What this means is that the subject's visual attention is pushed around the board from one important piece to another, directed by the meaningful relations among the pieces. With these assumptions, the simulation program produced much the same eye movements as those produced by human chess players.

Efficient visual encoding of the chess board is but one aspect of reproducing a chess configuration. How does the player retain the configuration, having perceived it? Somehow, the player is able to reproduce the board immediately after a 5-second viewing. With such a short retention interval, we would suspect that it is STM capacity that is tapped in the performance. But if STM has a limited capacity, the chess information must be stored as no more than several chunks. Thus, it seems that the reproduction task requires chunking the information from the board and storing it in STM, once it has been perceived.

The role of STM in chess-board reproduction was studied by Simon, Chase, and Gilmartin. Their starting point was the hypothesis that chess masters were adept at reproducing chessboards because they could use their knowledge to chunk configurations on the board. According to this hypothesis, a skilled chess player looking at the board will recognize certain combinations of pieces as familiar. To these clusters he is able to assign some label or code which enables it to be chunked (much as YMCA, consisting of four letters, can be a single chunk). By combining various clusters of pieces into chunks, the player can reduce the demands on STM. He is then able to store the information on the board and use it to reproduce the pattern. Less experienced players would undoubtedly be far less able to recognize and encode clusters of pieces as chunks, and this would mean that their reproductive capacity would suffer. Moreover, masters and weak players would be equally unprepared to encode random configurations, for in these cases the clusters of pieces would not be recognizable as meaningful. This would explain why masters do no better than lesser players at reproducing random boards.

Chase and Simon tested this hypothesis by having players at levels from master to novice take part in two tasks. (See Figure 13.1.) One was a test of memory; the board reproduction task we have been discussing, in which the player tries to reconstruct a chessboard after seeing it for only 5 seconds. The other was a perception task, in which the player tried to reproduce a board that was in plain sight. A videotape machine allowed the player's glances back and forth between the stimulus board and his reproduction to be recorded.

For the perception task, Chase and Simon defined as a "chunk" any set of pieces that were placed on the reproduction board between successive glances at the to-be-reproduced board. For the memory task, a "chunk" was defined as all the pieces placed on the board with very short intervals (2 seconds or less) between them. If a longer interval occurred between placement of two pieces, they were assumed to be in different chunks. This definition is plausible if we assume that the subject should place all the chess pieces contained in a single chunk quickly, then pause while he attempts to decode the next chunk, quickly place the pieces in that chunk, pause, and so on. (The same sort of reasoning was adopted for Johnson's transitional-error probabilities discussed in Chapter 5.) That these definitions of "chunk" were reasonable was indicated by the fact that the relationships among pieces assumed to be placed within a chunk

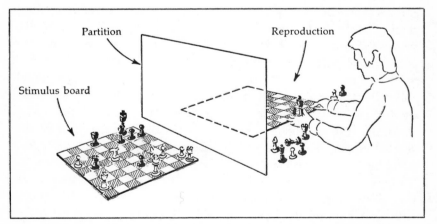

FIGURE 13.1

Diagram of the chessboard reproduction tasks used by Chase and Simon (1973). For the *memory task,* the partition is removed and replaced five seconds later; the subject then tries to reproduce the stimulus board. For the *perception task,* the partition is removed but not replaced. The subject then reproduces the stimulus board as quickly as possible.

were similar in the perception and memory tasks. Moreover, the inferred chunk sizes (in pieces) were about the same for both tasks, with an average chunk containing 2.3 pieces in the perception task and 2.2 in the memory task.

Having defined chunks in this way, Chase and Simon recorded the average number of chunks and the number of pieces per chunk for a master, a class-A player, and a beginner (listed in a decreasing order of expertise). They found that for the memory task, chunk size was related to the skill of the player. The number of pieces per chunk decreased from the master to the class-A player, and from the class-A player to the novice. This is consistent with the hypothesis that experienced players can reproduce chessboards better than weak players because they can pack more pieces into a chunk. Another difference between the players was found in the perception task. Although chunk size in that task was about the same as in the memory task, unlike the memory task, chunk size did not vary with level of player—the number of pieces per glance at the to-be-reproduced board was about the same for the novice as for the master. However, the better the player, the less time he took to glance at the board. This indicates that in the perceptual task, the master took much less time but picked up as much information as did the novice. Thus, we find that masters can perceive and encode the board faster, and they can chunk more of what they have perceived.

A final point noted by Chase and Simon concerns the nature of the chunks that master players form. The configurations corresponding to single chunks in the memory task fell into a rather restricted set of patterns. These patterns represented meaningful relations in the context of the game. In fact, over 75% of all of the master's chunks fell into only three categories of chessboard patterns, and those were all highly familiar and regular. This means the master could accomplish chunk formation by using a relatively small number of configurations stored in LTM. Thus, the results support the hypothesis that chess masters use stored subpatterns in LTM to recode chessboard configurations rapidly, facilitating their short-term memory for chessboards.

Simon and Gilmartin (1973) extended the chess studies by constructing a simulation program that combined the original perception program with a learning-memory program. They showed that this more complex program could reproduce chessboards about as well or better than a class-A player, once it had about 1,000 configurations stored in LTM. They estimated that with about 50,000 or possibly even fewer patterns, it might equal the performance of a master player. And it seems quite plausible that a master could acquire a pattern repertory of that size in his years of playing the game (Simon and Barenfeld, 1969).

It seems that looking in some detail at two situations in which memory plays a crucial role provides a retrospective glance at some of the topics covered in this book. Considering the abilities that underlie the performances of spectacular mnemonists and chess masters has brought us to consider all of memory, from the initial inputs to their final analysis and storage. The knowledge of encoding, storage and retrieval processes, contained in the last twelve chapters, has proven fruitful for the analysis of these two special cases. Cognitive psychologists hope that it will also prove fruitful for a more general understanding of human memory and its role in intellectual functioning.

REFERENCES

Adams, J. A. *Human Memory*. New York: McGraw-Hill, 1967.

Allen, M. Rehearsal strategies and response cueing as determinants of organization in free recall. *Journal of Verbal Learning and Verbal Behavior*, 1968, 7, 58–63.

Anderson, J. R., and Bower, G. H. Recognition and retrieval processes in free recall. *Psychological Review*, 1972, 79, 97–123.

Anderson, J. R., and Bower, G. H. *Human Associative Memory*. Washington, D.C.: V. H. Winston & Sons, 1973.

Anderson, J. R., and Bower, G. H. A propositional theory of recognition memory. *Memory & Cognition*, 1974, 2, 406–412.

Atkinson, R. C., and Juola, J. F. Factors influencing speed and accuracy of word recognition. In S. Kornblum (Ed.), *Attention and Performance IV*. New York: Academic Press, 1973.

Atkinson, R. C., and Shiffrin, R. M. Human memory: A proposed system and its control processes. In K. W. Spence and J. T. Spence (Eds.), *The Psychology of Learning and Motivation: Advances in Research and Theory* (Vol. 2). New York: Academic Press, 1968.

Averbach, E., and Coriell, A. S. Short-term memory in vision. *Bell System Technical Journal*, 1961, 40, 309–328.

Averbach, E., and Sperling, G. Short-term storage of information in vision. In C. Cherry (Ed.), *Fourth London Symposium on Information Theory*. London and Washington, D.C.: Butterworth, 1961.

Baddeley, A. D. Retrieval rules and semantic coding in short-term memory. *Psychological Bulletin*, 1972, 78, 379–385.

Baddeley, A. D., and Dale, H. C. A. The effect of semantic similarity on retroactive interference in long- and short-term memory. *Journal of Verbal Learning and Verbal Behavior*, 1966, 5, 417–420.

Barclay, J. R. The role of comprehension in remembering sentences. *Cognitive Psychology*, 1973, 4, 229–254.

Barnes, J. M., and Underwood, B. J. "Fate" of first-list associations in transfer theory. *Journal of Experimental Psychology*, 1959, 58, 97–105.

Bartlett, F. C. *Remembering: A Study in Experimental and Social Psychology*. Cambridge: Cambridge University Press, 1932.

Battig, W. F., and Montague, W. E. Category norms for verbal items in 56 categories: A replication and extension of the Connecticut category norms. *Journal of Experimental Psychology Monograph*, 1969, 80 (3, Pt. 2).

Begg, I., and Paivio, A. Concreteness and imagery in sentence meaning. *Journal of Verbal Learning and Verbal Behavior*, 1969, 8, 821–827.

Bobrow, S. A., and Bower, G. H. Comprehension and recall of sentences. *Journal of Experimental Psychology*, 1969, 80, 455–461.

Bousfield, A. K., and Bousfield, W. A. Measurement of clustering and of sequential constancies in repeated free recall. *Psychological Reports*, 1966, 19, 935–942.

Bousfield, W. A. Frequency and availability measures in language behavior. Paper presented at annual meeting, American Psychological Association, Chicago, 1951.

Bousfield, W. A. The occurrence of clustering in the recall of randomly arranged associates. *Journal of General Psychology*, 1953, 49, 229–240.

Bousfield, W. A., and Cohen, B. H. The effects of reinforcement on the occurrence of clustering in the recall of randomly arranged associates. *Journal of Psychology*, 1953, 36, 67–81.

Bousfield, W. A., Cohen, B. H., and Whitmarsh, G. A. Associative clustering in the recall of words of different taxonomic frequencies of occurrence. *Psychological Reports*, 1958, 4, 39–44.

Bousfield, W. A., and Puff, C. R. Clustering as a function of response dominance. *Journal of Experimental Psychology*, 1964, 67, 76–79.

Bower, G. H. Organizational factors in memory. *Cognitive Psychology*, 1970, 1, 18–46.

Bower, G. H. A selective review of organizational factors in memory. In E. Tulving and W. Donaldson (Eds.), *Organization of Memory*. New York: Academic Press, 1972. (a)

Bower, G. H. Mental imagery and associative learning. In L. Gregg (Ed.), *Cognition in Learning and Memory*. New York: Wiley, 1972. (b)

Bower, G. H. Memory freaks I have known. *Psychology Today*, 1973, 7, 64–65.

Bower, G. H., Clark, M. C., Lesgold, A. M., and Winzenz, D. Hierarchical retrieval schemes in recall of categorized word lists. *Journal of Verbal Learning and Verbal Behavior*, 1969, 8, 323–343.

Bower, G. H., Munoz, R., and Arnold, P. G. On distinguishing semantic and imaginal mnemonics. Unpublished manuscript, 1972.

Bower, G. H., and Springston, F. Pauses as recoding points in letter series. *Journal of Experimental Psychology*, 1970, 83, 421–430.

Bower, G. H., and Winzenz, D. Comparison of associative learning strategies. *Psychonomic Science*, 1970, 20, 119–120.

Bransford, J. D., Barclay, J. R., and Franks, J. J. Sentence memory: A constructive versus interpretive approach. *Cognitive Psychology*, 1972, 3, 193–209.

Bransford, J. D., and Franks, J. J. The abstraction of linguistic ideas. *Cognitive Psychology*, 1971, 2, 331–350.

Briggs, G. E. Acquisition, extinction, and recovery functions in retroactive inhibition. *Journal of Experimental Psychology*, 1954, 47, 285–293.

Briggs, G. E. Retroactive inhibition as a function of the degree of original and interpolated learning. *Journal of Experimental Psychology*, 1957, 53, 60–67.

Broadbent, D. E. *Perception and Communication.* London: Pergamon Press, 1958.

Brown, J. A. Some tests of the decay theory of immediate memory. *Quarterly Journal of Experimental Psychology*, 1958, 10, 12–21.

Brown, R. W., and McNeill, D. The "tip of the tongue" phenomenon. *Journal of Verbal Learning and Verbal Behavior*, 1966, 5, 325–337.

Bruce, D., and Fagan, R. L. More on the recognition and free recall of organized lists. *Journal of Experimental Psychology*, 1970, 85, 153–154.

Ceraso, J., and Henderson, A. Unavailability and associative loss in RI and PI. *Journal of Experimental Psychology*, 1965, 70, 300–303.

Chase, W. G., and Simon, H. A. Perception in chess. *Cognitive Psychology*, 1973, 4, 55–81.

Cherry, E. C. Some experiments on the recognition of speech with one and two ears. *Journal of the Acoustical Society of America*, 1953, 25, 975–979.

Clifton, C., Jr., and Tash, J. Effect of syllabic word length on memory-search rate. *Journal of Experimental Psychology*, 1973, 99, 231–235.

Cofer, C. N. On some factors in the organizational characteristics of free recall. *American Psychologist*, 1965, 20, 261–272.

Cofer, C. N., Bruce, D. R., and Reicher, G. M. Clustering in free recall as a function of certain methodological variations. *Journal of Experimental Psychology,* 1966, *71,* 858–866.

Cohen, B. H. Some-or-none characteristics of coding behavior. *Journal of Verbal Learning and Verbal Behavior,* 1966, *5,* 182–187.

Collins, A. M., and Quillian, M. R. Retrieval time from semantic memory. *Journal of Verbal Learning and Verbal Behavior,* 1969, *8,* 240–247.

Collins, A. M., and Quillian, M. R. Does category size affect categorization time? *Journal of Verbal Learnin and Verbal Behavior,* 1970, *9,* 432–438.

Conrad, R. Acoustic confusions and memory span for words. *Nature,* 1963, *197,* 1029–1030.

Conrad, R. Acoustic confusions in immediate memory. *British Journal of Psychology,* 1964, *55,* 75–84.

Cooper, L. A., and Shepard, R. N. Chronometric studies of the rotation of mental images. In W. G. Chase (Ed.), *Visual Information Processing.* New York: Academic Press, 1973.

Craik, F. I. M., and Lockhart, R. S. Levels of processing: A framework for memory research. *Journal of Verbal Learning and Verbal Behavior,* 1972, *11,* 671–684.

Craik, F. I. M., and Watkins, M. J. The role of rehearsal in short-term memory. *Journal of Verbal Learning and Verbal Behavior,* 1973, *12,* 599–607.

Crossman, E. R. F. W. Discussion of Paper 7 in National Physical Laboratory Symposium. In *Mechanisation of Thought Processes* (Vol. 2). London: H. M. Stationery Office, 1958.

Crouse, J. H. Retroactive interference in reading prose materials. *Journal of Educational Psychology,* 1971, *62,* 39–44.

Crowder, R. G., and Morton, J. Precategorical acoustic storage (PAS). *Perception & Psychophysics,* 1969, *5,* 365–373.

D'Agostino, P. R. The blocked-random effect in recall and recognition. *Journal of Verbal Learning and Verbal Behavior,* 1969, *8,* 815–820.

Darwin, C. T., Turvey, M. T., and Crowder, R. G. An auditory analogue of the Sperling partial report procedure: Evidence for brief auditory storage. *Cognitive Psychology,* 1972, *3,* 255–267.

Davis, R., Sutherland, N. S., and Judd, B. R. Information content in recognition and recall. *Journal of Experimental Psychology,* 1961, *61,* 422–429.

de Groot, A. D. *Thought and Choice in Chess.* The Hague: Mouton, 1965.

de Groot, A. D. Perception and memory versus thinking. In B. Kleinmuntz (Ed.) *Problem Solving.* New York: Wiley, 1966.

Delin, P. S. The learning to criterion of a serial list with and without mnemonic instructions. *Psychonomic Science*, 1969, *16*, 169–170.

Deutsch, D. Tones and numbers: Specificity of interference in immediate memory. *Science*, 1970, *168*, 1604–1605.

Deutsch, J. A., and Deutsch, D. Attention: Some theoretical considerations. *Psychological Review*, 1963, *70*, 80–90.

Donders, F. C. Die Schnelligkeit psychischer Processe. *Arch. Anat. Physiol.*, 1862, 657–681.

Ebbinghaus, H. *Über das Gedächtnis*. Leipzig: Duncker & Humblot, 1885.

Franks, J. J., and Bransford, J. D. Abstraction of visual patterns. *Journal of Experimental Psychology*, 1971, *90*, 65–74.

Franks, J. J., and Bransford, J. D. The acquisition of abstract ideas. *Journal of Verbal Learning and Verbal Behavior*, 1972, *11*, 311–315.

Freud, S. [A note upon the "Mystic writing-pad."] (J. Strachey, trans.) *International Journal of Psycho-Analysis*, 1940, *21*, 469.

Friedman, M. J., and Reynolds, J. H. Retroactive inhibition as a function of response-class similarity. *Journal of Experimental Psychology*, 1967, *74*, 351–355.

Frost, N. Encoding and retrieval in visual memory tasks. *Journal of Experimental Psychology*, 1972, *95*, 317–326.

Gardiner, J. M., Craik, F. I. M., and Birtwistle, J. Retrieval cues and release from proactive inhibition. *Journal of Verbal Learning and Verbal Behavior*, 1972, *11*, 778–783.

Gray, J. A., and Wedderburn, A. A. I. Grouping strategies with simultaneous stimuli. *Quarterly Journal of Experimental Psychology*, 1960, *12*, 180–184.

Green, D. M., and Swets, J. A. *Signal Detection Theory and Psychophysics*. New York: Wiley, 1966.

Guttman, N., and Julesz, B. Lower limits of auditory periodicity analysis. *Journal of the Acoustical Society of America*, 1963, *35*, 610.

Haber, R. N. Introduction. In R. N. Haber (Ed.), *Information-processing Approaches to Visual Perception*. New York: Holt, 1969.

Halle, M., and Stevens, K. N. Analysis by synthesis. In W. Wathen-Dunn and L. E. Woods (Eds.), *Proceedings of the Seminar on Speech Comprehension and Processing*. Bedford, Mass.: Air Force Cambridge Research Laboratories, 1959.

Halle, M., and Stevens, K. N. Speech recognition: A model and a program for research. In J. A. Fodor, and J. J. Katz (Eds.), *The Structure of Language: Readings in the Psychology of Language*. Englewood Cliffs, New Jersey: Prentice-Hall, 1964.

Hebb, D. O. *The Organization of Behavior.* New York: Wiley, 1949.

Hebb, D. O. *A Textbook of Psychology.* Philadelphia: W. B. Saunders, 1958.

Herman, T., Broussard, I. G., and Todd, H. R. Intertrial interval and the rate of learning serial order picture stimuli. *Journal of General Psychology,* 1951, *45,* 245–254.

Houston, J. P. First-list retention and time and method of recall. *Journal of Experimental Psychology,* 1966, *71,* 839–843.

Hubel, D. H., and Wiesel, T. N. Receptive fields, binocular interaction, and functional architecture in the cat's visual cortex. *Journal of Physiology,* 1962, *160,* 106–154.

Hunt, E., and Love, T. How good can memory be? In A. W. Melton and E. Martin (Eds.), *Coding Processes in Human Memory.* Washington, D.C.: V. H. Winston & Sons, 1972.

Jakobson, R., Fant, G. G. M., and Halle, M. *Preliminaries to Speech Analysis: The Distinctive Features and their Correlates.* Cambridge: M.I.T. Press, 1961.

James, W. *The Principles of Psychology* (Vol. 1). New York: Henry Holt and Co., 1890.

Jenkins, J. J., Mink, W. D., and Russell, W. A. Associative clustering as a function of verbal association strength. *Psychological Reports,* 1958, *4,* 127–136.

Jenkins, J. J., and Russell, W. A. Associative clustering during recall. *Journal of Abnormal and Social Psychology,* 1952, *47,* 818–821.

Johnson, M. K., Bransford, J. D., Nyberb, S. E., and Cleary, J. J. Comprehension factors in interpreting memory for abstract and concrete sentences. *Journal of Verbal Learning and Verbal Behavior,* 1972, *11,* 451–454.

Johnson, N. F. Sequential verbal behavior. In T. R. Dixon and D. L. Horton (Eds.), *Verbal Behavior and General Behavior Theory.* Englewood Cliffs, New Jersey: Prentice-Hall, 1968.

Kahneman, D. *Attention and Effort.* Englewood Cliffs, New Jersey: Prentice-Hall, 1973.

Katz, J. J., and Fodor, J. A. The structure of a semantic theory. *Language,* 1963, *39,* 170–210.

Keppel, G., and Underwood, B. J. Proactive inhibition in short-term retention of single items. *Journal of Verbal Learning and Verbal Behavior,* 1962, *1,* 153–161.

Kinney, G. C., Marsetta, M., and Showman, D. J. *Studies in Display Symbol Legibility, Part XII. The Legibility of Alphanumeric Symbols for Digitalized Television.* Bedford, Mass.: The Mitre Corp., November 1966, ESD-TR-66-117.

Kintsch, W. Memory and decision aspects of recognition learning. *Psychological Review*, 1967, 74, 496–504.

Kintsch, W. Recognition and free recall of organized lists. *Journal of Experimental Psychology*, 1968, 78, 481–487.

Kintsch, W. Models for free recall and recognition. In D. A. Norman (Ed.), *Models of Human Memory*. New York: Academic Press, 1970.

Klatzky, R. L., and Atkinson, R. C. Specialization of the cerebral hemispheres in scanning for information in short-term memory. *Perception & Psychophysics*, 1971, 10, 335–338.

Koppenall, R. J. Time changes in the strengths of A-B, A-C lists; spontaneous recovery? *Journal of Verbal Learning and Verbal Behavior*, 1963, 2, 310–319.

Lachman, R., and Tuttle, A. V. Approximation to English and short-term memory: Construction or storage? *Journal of Experimental Psychology*, 1965, 70, 386–393.

Landauer, T. K. Rate of implicit speech. *Perceptual and Motor Skills*, 1962, 15, 646.

Landauer, T. K., and Freedman, J. L. Information-retrieval from long-term memory: Category size and recognition time. *Journal of Verbal Learning and Verbal Behavior*, 1968, 7, 291–295.

Landauer, T. K., and Meyer, D. E. Category size and semantic-memory retrieval. *Journal of Verbal Learning and Verbal Behavior*, 1972, 11, 539–549.

Lettvin, J. Y., Matturana, H. R., McCulloch, W. S., and Pitts, W. H. What the frog's eye tells the frog's brain. *Proceedings of the IRE*, 1959, 47, 1940–1951.

Lewis, M. Q. Cue effectiveness in cued recall. Paper presented at the annual meeting of the Psychonomic Society, St. Louis, 1972.

Lindsay, P. H., and Norman, D. A. *Human Information Processing*. New York: Academic Press, 1972.

Luria, A. R. *The Mind of a Mnemonist*. New York: Basic Books, 1968.

Mandler, G. Organization and recognition. In E. Tulving and W. Donaldson (Eds.), *Organization of Memory*. New York: Academic Press, 1972.

Mandler, G., and Pearlstone, Z. Free and constrained concept learning and subsequent recall. *Journal of Verbal Learning and Verbal Behavior*, 1966, 5, 126–131.

Mandler, G., Pearlstone, Z., and Koopmans, H. S. Effects of organization and semantic similarity on recall and recognition. *Journal of Verbal Learning and Verbal Behavior*, 1969, 8, 410–423.

Massaro, D. W. Preperceptual images, processing time, and perceptual units in auditory perception. *Psychological Review*, 1972, 79, 124–145.

Mayhew, A. J. Interlist changes in subjective organization during free-recall learning. *Journal of Experimental Psychology*, 1967, *74*, 425–430.

McDougall, R. Recognition and recall. *Journal of Philosophical and Scientific Methods*, 1904, *1*, 229–233.

McGeoch, J. A. *The Psychology of Human Learning*. New York: Longmans, Green, & Co., 1942.

Melton, A. W., and Irwin, J. M. The influence of degree of interpolated learning on retroactive inhibition and the overt transfer of specific responses. *American Journal of Psychology*, 1940, *53*, 173–203.

Meyer, D. E. On the representation and retrieval of stored semantic information. *Cognitive Psychology*, 1970, *1*, 242–300.

Miller, G. A. The magical number seven, plus or minus two: Some limits on our capacity for processing information. *Psychological Review*, 1956, *63*, 81–97.

Miller, G. A. Some psychological studies of grammar. *American Psychologist*, 1962, *17*, 748–762.

Miller, G. A. English verbs of motion: A case study in semantics and lexical memory. In A. W. Melton and E. Martin (Eds.), *Coding Processes in Human Memory*. Washington, D.C.: V. H. Winston & Sons, 1972.

Miller, G. A., Heise, G. A., and Lichten, W. The intelligibility of speech as a function of the context of the test materials. *Journal of Experimental Psychology*, 1951, *41*, 329–335.

Miller, G. A., and Selfridge, J. A. Verbal context and the recall of meaningful material. *American Journal of Psychology*, 1950, *63*, 176–187.

Milner, B. The memory defect in bilateral hippocampal lesions. *Psychiatric Research Reports*, 1959, *11*, 43–58.

Montague, W. E., Adams, J. A., and Kiess, H. O. Forgetting and natural language mediation. *Journal of Experimental Psychology*, 1966, *72*, 829–833.

Moray, N. Attention in dichotic listening: Affective cues and the influence of instructions. *Quarterly Journal of Experimental Psychology*, 1959, *11*, 56–60.

Moray, N., Bates, A., and Barnett, T. Experiments on the four-eared man. *Journal of the Acoustical Society of America*, 1965, *38*, 196–201.

Morton, J. A functional model for memory. In D. A. Norman (Ed.), *Models of Human Memory*. New York: Academic Press, 1970.

Morton, J., Crowder, R. G., and Prussin, H. A. Experiments with the stimulus suffix effect. *Journal of Experimental Psychology Monograph*, 1971, *91*, 169–190.

Murdock, B. B., Jr. The retention of individual items. *Journal of Experimental Psychology*, 1961, *62*, 618–625.

Murdock, B. B., Jr. The serial position effect of free recall. *Journal of Experimental Psychology*, 1962, *64*, 482–488.

Murdock, B. B., Jr., and Walker, K. D. Modality effects in free recall. *Journal of Verbal Learning and Verbal Behavior*, 1969, *8*, 665–676.

Neisser, U. Visual search. *Scientific American*, 1964, *210*, 94–102.

Neisser, U. *Cognitive Psychology*. New York: Appleton-Century-Crofts, 1967.

Neisser, U., Novick, R., and Lazar, R. Searching for ten targets simultaneously. *Perceptual and Motor Skills*, 1963, *17*, 955–961.

Nelson, T. O., Metzler, J., and Reed, D. A. Role of details in the long-term recognition of pictures and verbal descriptions. *Journal of Experimental Psychology*, 1974, *102*, 184–186.

Nickerson, R. S. Binary-classification reaction time: A review of some studies of human information-processing capabilities. *Psychonomic Monograph Supplements*, 1972, *4*, 275–318.

Noble, C. E. Measurements of association value (*a*), rated associations (*a'*), and scaled meaningfulness (*m'*) for the 2100 CVC combinations of the English alphabet. *Psychological Reports*, 1961, *8*, 487–521.

Norman, D. A. *Memory and Attention*. New York: John Wiley & Sons, 1969.

Osgood, C. E. The nature and measurement of meaning. *Psychological Bulletin*, 1952, *49*, 197–237.

Paivio, A. Learning of adjective-noun paired-associates as a function of adjective-noun word order and noun abstractness. *Canadian Journal of Psychology*, 1963, *17*, 370–379.

Paivio, A. Abstractness, imagery, and meaningfulness in paired-associate learning. *Journal of Verbal Learning and Verbal Behavior*, 1965, *4*, 32–38.

Paivio, A. Mental imagery in associative learning and memory. *Psychological Review*, 1969, *76*, 241–263.

Paivio, A. *Imagery and Verbal Processes*. New York: Holt, Rinehart & Winston, 1971.

Paivio, A., and Csapo, K. Concrete-image and verbal memory codes. *Journal of Experimental Psychology*, 1969, *80*, 279–285.

Paivio, A., Yuille, J. C., and Rogers, T. B. Noun imagery and meaningfulness in free and serial recall. *Journal of Experimental Psychology*, 1969, *79*, 509–514.

Penfield, W. The interpretive cortex. *Science*, 1959, *129*, 1719–1725.

Peterson, L. R., and Peterson, M. J. Short-term retention of individual verbal items. *Journal of Experimental Psychology*, 1959, *58*, 193–198.

Pollack, I. Message uncertainty and message reception. *Journal of the Acoustical Society of America*, 1959, *31*, 1500–1508.

Posner, M. I. Abstraction and the process of recognition. In J. T. Spence and G. H. Bower (Eds.), *Advances in Learning and Motivation* (Vol. 3). New York: Academic Press, 1969.

Posner, M. I., Boies, S. J., Eichelman, W. H., and Taylor, R. L. Retention of visual and name codes of single letters. *Journal of Experimental Psychology*, 1969, *79* (1, Pt. 2).

Posner, M. I., Goldsmith, R., and Welton, K. E., Jr. Perceived distance and the classification of distorted patterns. *Journal of Experimental Psychology*, 1967, *73*, 28–38.

Posner, M. I., and Keele, S. W. On the genesis of abstract ideas. *Journal of Experimental Psychology*, 1968, *77*, 353–363.

Posner, M. I., and Konick, A. F. On the role of interference in short-term retention. *Journal of Experimental Psychology*, 1966, *72*, 221–231.

Posner, M. I., and Mitchell, R. F. Chronometric analysis of classification. *Psychological Review*, 1967, *74*, 392–409.

Posner, M. I., and Rossman, E. Effect of size and location of informational transforms upon short-term retention. *Journal of Experimental Psychology*, 1965, *70*, 496–505

Postman, L. A pragmatic view of organization theory. In E. Tulving and W. Donaldson (Eds.), *Organization of Memory*. New York: Academic Press, 1972.

Postman, L., Keppel, G., and Stark, K. Unlearning as a function of the relationship between successive response classes. *Journal of Experimental Psychology*, 1965, *69*, 111–118.

Postman, L., and Phillips, L. Short-term temporal changes in free recall. *Quarterly Journal of Experimental Psychology*, 1965, *17*, 132–138.

Postman, L., and Rau, L. Retention as a function of the method of measurement. *University of California Publications in Psychology*, Berkeley, 1957, *8*, 217–270.

Postman, L., and Stark, K. Role of response availability in transfer and interference. *Journal of Experimental Psychology*, 1969, *79*, 168–177.

Postman, L., Stark, K., and Fraser, J. Temporal changes in interference. *Journal of Verbal Learning and Verbal Behavior*, 1968, *7*, 672–694.

Postman, L., Stark, K., and Henschel, D. Conditions of recovery after unlearning. *Journal of Experimental Psychology Monograph*, 1969, *82* (1, Pt. 2).

Postman, L., and Underwood, B. J. Critical issues in interference theory. *Memory & Cognition*, 1973, *1*, 19–40.

Prytulak, L. S. Natural language mediation. *Cognitive Psychology*, 1971, 2, 1–56.

Pylyshyn, Z. W. What the mind's eye tells the mind's brain: A critique of mental imagery. *Psychological Bulletin*, 1973, 80, 1–24.

Quillian, M. R. The teachable language comprehender: A simulation program and theory of language. *Communications of the Association for Computing Machinery*, 1969, 12, 459–476.

Reicher, G. M. Perceptual recognition as a function of meaningfulness of stimulus material. *Journal of Experimental Psychology*, 1969, 81, 275–280.

Reitman, J. S. Mechanisms of forgetting in short-term memory. *Cognitive Psychology*, 1971, 2, 185–195.

Reitman, J. S. Without surreptitious rehearsal, information in short-term memory decays. *Journal of Verbal Learning and Verbal Behavior*, 1974, 13, 365–377.

Rips, L. J., Shoben, E. J., and Smith, E. E. Semantic distance and the verification of semantic relations. *Journal of Verbal Learning and Verbal Behavior*, 1973, 12, 1–20.

Rohwer, W. D., Jr. Verbal and visual elaboration in paired associate learning. *Project Literacy Reports*, Cornell University, 1966, No. 7, 18–28.

Rosch, E. On the internal structure of perceptual and semantic categories. In T. E. Moore (Ed.), *Cognitive Development and Acquisition of Language*. New York: Academic Press, 1973.

Rumelhart, D. E. A multicomponent theory of perception of briefly exposed visual displays. *Journal of Mathematical Psychology*, 1971, 91, 326–332.

Rumelhart, D. E., Lindsay, P. H., and Norman, D. A. A process model for long-term memory. In E. Tulving and W. Donaldson (Eds.), *Organization and Memory*. New York: Academic Press, 1972.

Rundus, D. Analysis of rehearsal processes in free recall. *Journal of Experimental Psychology*, 1971, 89, 63–77.

Rundus, D., and Atkinson, R. C. Rehearsal processes in free recall: A procedure for direct observation. *Journal of Verbal Learning and Verbal Behavior*, 1970, 9, 99–105.

Sachs, J. D. S. Recognition memory for syntactic and semantic aspects of connected discourse. *Perception & Psychophysics*, 1967, 2, 437–442.

Salzinger, K., Portnoy, S., and Feldman, R. S. The effect of order of approximation to the statistical structure of English on the emission of verbal responses. *Journal of Experimental Psychology*, 1962, 64, 52–57.

Schwartz, M. Instructions to use verbal mediators in paired-associate learning. *Journal of Experimental Psychology,* 1969, *79,* 1–5.

Selfridge, O. G. Pandemonium: A paradigm for learning. In *The Mechanisation of Thought Processes.* London: H. M. Stationery Office, 1959.

Shepard, R. N. Learning and recall as organization and search. *Journal of Verbal Learning and Verbal Behavior,* 1966, *5,* 201–204.

Shepard, R. N. Recognition memory for words, sentences, and pictures. *Journal of Verbal Learning and Verbal Behavior,* 1967, *6,* 156–163.

Shepard, R. N. Cognitive psychology: A review of the book by U. Neisser. *American Journal of Psychology,* 1968, *81,* 285–289.

Shepard, R. N., and Chipman, S. Second-order isomorphism of internal representations: Shapes of states. *Cognitive Psychology,* 1970, *1,* 1–17.

Shepard, R. N., and Metzler, J. Mental rotation of three-dimensional objects. *Science,* 1971, *171,* 701–703.

Shepard, R. N., and Teghtsoonian, M. Retention of information under conditions approaching a steady state. *Journal of Experimental Psychology,* 1961, *62,* 302–309.

Shiffrin, R. M. Memory search. In D. A. Norman (Ed.), *Models of Human Memory.* New York: Academic Press, 1970.

Shiffrin, R. M. Information persistence in short-term memory. *Journal of Experimental Psychology,* 1973, *100,* 39–49.

Shulman, H. G. Similarity effects in short-term memory. *Psychological Bulletin,* 1971, *75,* 399–415.

Shulman, H. G. Semantic confusion errors in short-term memory. *Journal of Verbal Learning and Verbal Behavior,* 1972, *11,* 221–227.

Simon, H. A. How big is a chunk? *Science,* 1974, *183,* 482–488.

Simon, H. A., and Barenfeld, M. Information-processing analysis of perceptual processes in problem solving. *Psychological Review,* 1969, *76,* 473–483.

Simon, H. A., and Gilmartin, K. A simulation of memory for chess positions. *Cognitive Psychology,* 1973, *5,* 29–46.

Slamecka, N. J. Retroactive inhibition of connected discourse as a function of practice level. *Journal of Experimental Psychology,* 1960, *59,* 104–108. (a)

Slamecka, N. J. Retroactive inhibition of connected discourse as a function of similarity of topic. *Journal of Experimental Psychology,* 1960, *60,* 245–249. (b)

Slamecka, N. J. Differentiation versus unlearning of verbal associations. *Journal of Experimental Psychology,* 1966, *71,* 822–828.

Slamecka, N. J. An examination of trace storage in free recall. *Journal of Experimental Psychology,* 1968, *76,* 504–513.

Slamecka, N. J. Testing for associative storage in multitrial free recall. *Journal of Experimental Psychology*, 1969, *81*, 557–560.

Smith, E. E. Effects of familiarity on stimulus recognition and categorization. *Journal of Experimental Psychology*, 1967, *74*, 324–332.

Smith, E. E., Shoben, E. J., and Rips, L. J. Structure and process in semantic memory: A featural model for semantic decision. *Psychological Review*, 1974, *81*, 214–241.

Smith, E. E., and Spoehr, K. R. The perception of printed English: A theoretical perspective. In B. H. Kantowitz (Ed.), *Human Information Processing: Tutorials in Performance and Cognition*. Potomac, Md.: Erlbaum Press, 1974.

Sperling, G. The information available in brief visual presentations. *Psychological Monographs*, 1960, *74* (Whole No. 498).

Sperling, G. Successive approximations to a model for short-term memory. *Acta Psychologica*, 1967, *27*, 285–292.

Sperling, G., and Speelman, R. G. Acoustic similarity and auditory short-term memory: Experiments and a model. In D. A. Norman (Ed.), *Models of Human Memory*. New York: Academic Press, 1970.

Standing, L., Conezio, J., and Haber, R. N. Perception and memory for pictures: Single-trial learning of 2560 visual stimuli. *Psychonomic Science*, 1970, *19*, 73–74.

Sternberg, S. High-speed scanning in human memory. *Science*, 1966, *153*, 652–654.

Sternberg, S. Two operations in character recognition: Some evidence from RT measurement. *Perception & Psychophysics*, 1967, *2*, 45–53.

Sternberg, S. Memory-scanning: Mental processes revealed by reaction-time experiments. *American Scientist*, 1969, *57*, 421–457.

Tejirian, E. Syntactic and semantic structure in the recall of orders of approximation to English. *Journal of Verbal Learning and Verbal Behavior*, 1968, *7*, 1010–1015.

Theios, J., Smith, P. G., Haviland, S. E., Traupmann, J., and Moy, M. C. Memory scanning as a serial self-terminating process. *Journal of Experimental Psychology*, 1973, *97*, 323–336.

Thomson, D. M., and Tulving, E. Associative encoding and retrieval: Weak and strong cues. *Journal of Experimental Psychology*, 1970, *86*, 255–262.

Thorndike, E. L., and Lorge, I. *The Teacher's Word Book of 30,000 Words*. New York: Teachers College Press, Columbia University, 1944.

Tieman, D. G. Recognition memory for comparative sentences. Unpublished doctoral dissertation, Stanford University, 1971.

Townsend, J. T. Some results concerning the identifiability of parallel and serial processes. *British Journal of Mathematical and Statistical Psychology*, 1972, *25*, 168–199.

Treisman, A. M. Contextual cues in selective listening. *Quarterly Journal of Experimental Psychology*, 1960, *12*, 242–248.

Treisman, A. M. Verbal cues, language and meaning in selective attention. *American Journal of Psychology*, 1964, *77*, 206–219.

Tulving, E. Subjective organization in free recall of "unrelated" words. *Psychological Review*, 1962, *69*, 344–354.

Tulving, E. Intratrial and intertrial retention: Notes towards a theory of free recall verbal learning. *Psychological Review*, 1964, *71*, 219–237.

Tulving, E. Episodic and semantic memory. In E. Tulving and W. Donaldson (Eds.), *Organization and Memory*. New York: Academic Press, 1972.

Tulving, E., and Osler, S. Effectiveness of retrieval cues in memory for words. *Journal of Experimental Psychology*, 1968, *77*, 593–601.

Tulving, E., and Patkau, J. E. Concurrent effects of contextual constraint and word frequency on immediate recall and learning of verbal material. *Canadian Journal of Psychology*, 1962, *16*, 83–95.

Tulving, E., and Pearlstone, Z. Availability versus accessibility of information in memory for words. *Journal of Verbal Learning and Verbal Behavior*, 1966, *5*, 381–391.

Tulving, E., and Thompson, D. M. Encoding specificity and retrieval processes in episodic memory. *Psychological Review*, 1973, *80*, 352–373.

Underwood, B. J. Retroactive and proactive inhibition after five and forty-eight hours. *Journal of Experimental Psychology*, 1948, *38*, 29–38. (a)

Underwood, B. J. "Spontaneous" recovery of verbal associations. *Journal of Experimental Psychology*, 1948, *38*, 429–439. (b)

Underwood, B. J. Proactive inhibition as a function of time and degree of prior learning. *Journal of Experimental Psychology*, 1949, *39*, 24–34.

Underwood, B. J. False recognition produced by implicit verbal responses. *Journal of Experimental Psychology*, 1965, *70*, 122–129.

Underwood, B. J., and Ekstrand, B. R. An analysis of some shortcomings in the interference theory of forgetting. *Psychological Review*, 1966, *73*, 540–549.

Underwood, B. J., and Freund, J. S. Errors in recognition learning and retention. *Journal of Experimental Psychology*, 1968, *78*, 55–63.

Underwood, B. J., and Freund, J. S. Word frequency and short-term recognition memory. *American Journal of Psychology*, 1970, *83*, 343–351.

Underwood, B. J., and Postman, L. Extraexperimental sources of interference in forgetting. *Psychological Review*, 1960, *67*, 73–95.

Wanner, H. E. On remembering, forgetting, and understanding sentences: A study of the deep structure hypothesis. Unpublished doctoral dissertation, Harvard University, 1968.

Watkins, M. J., and Watkins, O. C. The postcategorical status of the modality effect in serial recall. *Journal of Experimental Psychology*, 1973, *99*, 226–230.

Watkins, M. J., Watkins, O. C., Craik, F. I. M., and Mazuryk, G. Effect of nonverbal distraction on short-term storage. *Journal of Experimental Psychology*, 1973, *101*, 296–300.

Waugh, N. C., and Norman, D. A. Primary memory. *Psychological Review*, 1965, *72*, 89–104.

Waugh, N. C., and Norman, D. A. The measurement of interference in primary memory. *Journal of Verbal Learning and Verbal Behavior*, 1968, *7*, 617–626.

Weber, D. J., and Castleman, J. The time it takes to imagine. *Perception & Psychophysics*, 1970, *8*, 165–168.

Wheeler, D. D. Processes in word recognition. *Cognitive Psychology*, 1970, *1*, 59–85.

Wickelgren, W. A. Acoustic similarity and retroactive interference in short-term memory. *Journal of Verbal Learning and Verbal Behavior*, 1965, *4*, 53–61.

Wickelgren, W. A. Distinctive features and errors in short-term memory for English consonants. *Journal of the Acoustical Society of America*, 1966, *39*, 388–398.

Wickelgren, W. A. The long and the short of memory. *Psychological Bulletin*, 1973, *80*, 425–438.

Wickens, D. D. Characteristics of word encoding. In A. W. Melton and E. Martin (Eds.), *Coding Processes in Human Memory*. New York: V. H. Winston & Sons, 1972.

Wickens, D. D., Born, D. G., and Allen, C. K. Proactive inhibition and item similarity in short-term memory. *Journal of Verbal Learning and Verbal Behavior*, 1963, *2*, 440–445.

Wilkins, A. Conjoint frequency, category size, and categorization time. *Journal of Verbal Learning and Verbal Behavior*, 1971, *10*, 382–385.

Winograd, E. List differentiation as a function of frequency and retention interval. *Journal of Experimental Psychology*, 1968, *76* (2, Pt. 2).

Wiseman, G., and Neisser, U. Perceptual organization as a determinant of visual recognition memory. Paper presented at meeting of the Eastern Psychological Assn., 1971.

Wood, G. Organizational processes and free recall. In E. Tulving and W. Donaldson (Eds.), *Organization of Memory*. New York: Academic Press, 1972.

Wood, G., and Underwood, B. J. Implicit responses and conceptual similarity. *Journal of Verbal Learning and Verbal Behavior*, 1967, *6*, 1–10.

Woodward, A. E., Jr., Bjork, R. A., and Jongeward, R. H., Jr. Recall and recognition as a function of primary rehearsal. *Journal of Verbal Learning and Verbal Behavior*, 1973, *12*, 608–617.

Zusne, L. *Visual Perception of Form.* New York: Academic Press, 1970.

INDEX OF NAMES

INDEX OF SUBJECTS